The Willis-Inman Debate

A Discussion on Congregational Cooperation
and Benevolent Organizations

Between

Cecil Willis, Marion, Indiana
and
Clifton Inman, Parkersburg, West Virginia

Held at

Franklin Junior High School
1511 Blizzard Drive
Parkersburg, West Virginia
September 19, 20, 22, 23, 1966

Both participants were invited by
The Marrtown Road Church of Christ
of Parkersburg, West Virginia

© **Guardian of Truth Foundation 1968.** All rights reserved. No part of this book may be reproduced in any form without written permission from the publisher. Printed in the United States of America.

ISBN 1-58427-039-X

Guardian of Truth Foundation
P.O. Box 9670

INTRODUCTION

Brethren Cecil Willis and Clifton Inman engaged in two four-night debates during the year 1966. The first was held in Parkersburg, West Virginia, and arranged by the Marrtown Road church. The second one was conducted in Dayton, Ohio, and was arranged by the Knollwood congregation. This printed debate consists of the speeches presented at Parkersburg. Brethren Hubert Showalter and James Prestinenzi, preachers at Parkersburg and Knollwood respectively, did much toward arranging for these discussions and making them significant occasions. It was this writer's good pleasure and privilege to serve as brother Willis' moderator upon both occasions.

DEBATING: Debating has long been recognized as a valuable tool of study, not only in matters religious, but also in the secular world. In the halls of Congress and in the court rooms of our great country, issues are debated to the end that truth and justice may emerge to illuminate the minds and temper the actions of men. While the utility of polemics is readily recognized in things civic and secular, it is sometimes the object of adverse criticism in religion. While we recognize that such aspersions are often cast by those who recognize weakness in their religious position, there are some who have honest convictions that such is wrong. There are two reasons for such a conclusion:

(1) *They have witnessed a debate which became a debacle.* It is, however, unjust as well as illogical to condemn debating as a tool of study because some have misused it. One could just as intelligently condemn soap because someone has dirty hands. Jude 3 commands the Christian to "earnestly contend for the faith . . ." The polemic platform is an excellent manner of doing this.

(2) *They honestly feel that debating is condemned in the Bible.* The word "debate" occurs five times in the King

James Version (Isa. 58:4; Rom. 1:29; 2 Cor. 12:20; Prov. 25:9; Isa. 27:8). The fact that it is sometimes commanded or endorsed (Prov. 25:9) and sometimes condemned (Rom. 1:29; 2 Cor. 12:20) will cause the honest Bible student to suspicion that the word has different meanings. This is actually the case. The word translated "debate" in Rom. 1:29 and 2 Cor. 12:20 in the KJV is rendered "strife" in the American Standard Version. This is what the word "debate" meant when the KJV was translated, but it does not mean that now. Strife is a work of the flesh which will cause one to be lost (Gal. 5:19-21), but the mere act of debating (discussing differences) is not strife. It might be, but not necessarily so. When Solomon said, "Debate thy cause with thy neighbor..." (Prov. 25:9), he was not endorsing something that is sinful strife. He had in mind the discussing of differences with a view to resolving them. This is not wrong. It is noble and scriptural.

THE DISPUTANTS: The disputants in this debate (Cecil Willis and Clifton Inman) are both men of considerable influence on today's religious scene with reference to the points at issue in this encounter. Both have become widely known as able preachers, and both are closely connected with two widely circulated religious periodicals. Brother Willis is editor of TRUTH MAGAZINE, and Brother Inman is owner of and a frequent writer in BIBLE HERALD. These brethren were well prepared for this discussion. Each understood what he believed, and made his arguments in a forthright and a courteous manner. At no time did either of them lose his composure, or speak in a disrespectful or deriding manner. Each presented thought-provoking material that challenged the hearers to think and study.

THE AUDIENCE: One could not ask for more attentive, well-demeanored audiences than those attending this study. There was not one untoward incident. People listened quietly to the presentations of the speakers without manifesting any outward demonstration of support of or disagreement with either. All who came with a proper attitude left with it.

LENGTH OF SPEECHES: The reader will notice a marked difference between the number of pages occupied by the respective speeches in the book. This is due to two factors: (1) Brother Willis is a more rapid speaker than is Brother Inman, and (2) Brother Willis used a large number of charts in the presentation of his material. These charts are inserted where they were used. In some cases the same chart was used more than once in the same speech. This adds greatly to the space occupied by Brother Willis in the printed copy.

TO THE READERS: The disputants agreed to give this debate wider circulation by means of publication in book form. The speeches were tape recorded, and exact copies produced from them. Some changes were then made in grammar and sentence structure in the interest of smoother reading. Mutual agreement prohibited any change in meaning or argumentation. You now have the finished product, the fruit of many laborious hours. We sincerely believe that you can greatly profit from a prayerful, unbiased reading of this work. That is our only justification for its publication. If by reading it, one soul is led to a better understanding of God's truth, the many hours and dollars expended in its production will have been richly repaid.

—James P. Needham
11-8-67

EXPLANATION

Because of a heavy load of work, I have been unable to read proofs of the original manuscripts. Since this was causing unnecessary delay, I have granted Brother Willis the freedom to make corrections, arrange paragraphs, etc. If there seem to be rougher passages in my speeches, it is because he felt it best to follow verbatim the tapes, whereas he has exercised freedom to make grammatical corrections in his own speeches.

One necessarily uses expressions which seem smooth in speech, but which seem rather rough, and perhaps disconnected, when committed to writing. I trust that the reader will make allowances and seek to follow the thought content.

Clifton Inman

AGREEMENT AND RULES TO GOVERN WILLIS-INMAN DEBATE

1. The debate will be held the week of September 19th, 1966, with sessions the evenings of the 19, 20, 22, and 23.
2. It is agreed that the debate shall take place in the auditorium of the Franklin Junior High School, 1511 Blizzard Drive, Parkersburg, W. Va. In the event this auditorium is not available, the debate will be conducted in a mutually agreeable substitute.
3. Each speaker will have two thirty minute speeches each evening, speaking alternately. In consideration of brother Inman having the first and last speeches of the debate, it is agreed that brother Willis shall have a ten minute rejoinder at the conclusion of the thirty minute speeches the last night of the debate.
4. Each speaker will select his personal moderator.
5. The elders of the Marrtown Roard congregation shall select someone to preside as chairman each evening.
6. Each speaker will be permitted the use of two recorders per session. Should brethren desire to copy the tapes, they will be made available each day.
It is requested by the disputants that the chairman caution the audience against all demonstrations.

ACCEPTED: Clifton Inman
Cecil Willis

PROPOSITIONS FOR DEBATE

-1-

Resolved that it is in harmony with New Testament teaching for one or more congregations to send money from their treasuries to another congregation (Highland Avenue in Abilene or any other), for the purpose of supporting a nationwide radio broadcast or telecast (Herald of Truth or other), which broadcast or telecast is supervised by the congregation receiving the funds.

AFFIRMATIVE: Clifton Inman
NEGATIVE: Cecil Willis

-2-

Resolved that it is unscriptural for one or more congregations to send money from their treasuries to another congregation (Highland Avenue in Abilene or any other), for the purpose of supporting a nationwide radio broadcast or telecast (Herald of Truth or other), which broadcast or telecast is supervised by the congregation receiving the funds.

AFFIRMATIVE: Cecil Willis
NEGATIVE: Clifton Inman

-3-

Resolved that it is in harmony with New Testament teaching for a congregation, or congregations, to take money from their treasuries and send it to a corporate home(such as Mid-western, Potter, Schults-Lewis, Maude Carpenter, Lubbock, etc.), which is organized for the purpose of providing a home for orphaned or forsaken children.

AFFIRMATIVE: Clifton Inman
NEGATIVE: Cecil Willis

-4-

Resolved that it is unscriptural for a congregation, or congregations, to take money from their treasuries and send it to a corporate home (such at Mid-western, Potter, Schults-Lewis, Maude Carpenter, Lubbock, etc.), which is organized for the purpose of providing a home for orphaned or forsaken children.

AFFIRMATIVE: Cecil Willis
NEGATIVE: Clifton Inman

NOTE: The reader will observe that the charts in this book were photographically reproduced from the cloth charts used in the debate. They therefore contain perhaps half a dozen lettering mistakes.

Cecil Willis

PROPOSITION

"RESOLVED THAT IT IS IN HARMONY WITH NEW TESTAMENT TEACHING FOR ONE OR MORE CONGREGATIONS TO SEND MONEY FROM THEIR TREASURIES TO ANOTHER CONGREGATION (HIGHLAND AVENUE IN ABILENE OR ANY OTHER), FOR THE PURPOSE OF SUPPORTING A NATIONWIDE RADIO BROADCAST OR TELECAST (HERALD OF TRUTH OR OTHER), WHICH BROADCAST OR TELECAST IS SUPERVISED BY THE CONGREGATION RECEIVING THE FUNDS."

Affirmative: Clifton Inman
Negative: Cecil Willis

INMAN'S FIRST AFFIRMATIVE

Brother Willis, brethren: As I look out over the audience this evening, I see a multitude of brethren with whom I have had close association through many years. I see also brethren who have marched hand in hand against sin and against error. And yet tonight many of us are not standing together as we should. We are divided in thought, and therefore it seems to me that I would indeed be remiss in my duty if I did not do my best to try to go to the word of God, and from the word of God find a solution to our problem that we might be brought closer together. I would feel that I would be a traitor against my God were I not to hope and to pray that when this discussion is finished, not only will Brother Willis and I be closer together, but that each of us, as brethren, will be closer together, and above all things, closer to our God.

This is the sole purpose of the discussion. If it has any other purpose, certainly we should not have it. The proposition we have is a scriptural proposition. That is, it concerns what the scriptures teach, or that which is in harmony with New Testament teaching.

First of all, this evening, we would like to look at the proposition that we might understand the terms that are used therein. "Resolved that it is in harmony", and by that we mean that there is no violation, no discord between the practice we are discussing and the word of God, the New Testament scriptures. By "with New Testament teaching" we simply mean the teaching that is set forth in the New Testament. It is in harmony therefore, and not in discord with New Testament teaching, for one or more congregations (that is one or more groups, where brethren assemble themselves together under common oversight for the purpose of worshipping and serving God) to take the money from their treasuries and send that to another congregation. And it does not make any difference whether that congregation be Highland Avenue, or Marrtown Road, or whatever congregation it may be. "Highland Avenue or any other for the purpose of supporting a nationwide broadcast or telecast"—that is a broadcast or telecast that is heard nationwide, be that called "Herald of Truth" or be it called by some other name.

Now, let me pause here to point out that it is not my purpose to defend everything that Highland Avenue or any other congregation may do. Neither is it my obligation or my purpose to try to defend anything and everything that may be done under the name of "Herald of Truth." The thing that is being set forth is that it is in harmony with scriptures for one or more congregations to send money from their treasuries to some other congregation, whether it be Highland Avenue, or as I said a moment ago, Marrtown Road. Now the congregation that receives the money may use it to broadcast the gospel where that broadcast is heard nationwide, and the work of that broadcasting (that is the preacher who does the broadcasting, and the work that is connected therewith) is under the oversight of the congregation that receives the funds.

When we talk about being in harmony with New Testament teaching, we want it understood that we mean *authorized* by the New Testament; that the New Testament gives authority. I do not believe that we should do anything in word or deed that is not authorized by the word of God. "Whatsoever ye do in word or deed, do all in the name of (that is by the authority) our Lord Jesus, giving thanks to God and the Father by him" (Col. 3:17). Thus is set forth a principle that we must always keep in mind, and I believe, brethren, that does not just mean when we come together to worship. That means when we are down on the job working or wherever it may be.

But when we come to the matter of authority or being authorized, I am persuaded that here is the biggest problem that is facing us in coming to an understanding of this matter. There are those who believe that before a thing is authorized it must be specifically mentioned. That is false. There is another extreme that is just as false, and that is that a thing must be specifically condemned before it is wrong. Neither of these propositions is right.

Let us then see what the word "authority" means. In Merriam-Webster's *New Collegiate Dictionary*, under definition number one, part a, "authority" is defined as "a right to command or to act." Now when one has a right to act, to command or to act, he has authority. Actually in the realm of authority, or in the field of authority, there are three different realms. There are some things that are demanded of all; obligation that is placed upon everyone. "He that believeth and is baptized shall be saved." If any man desires to be saved, he must be baptized.

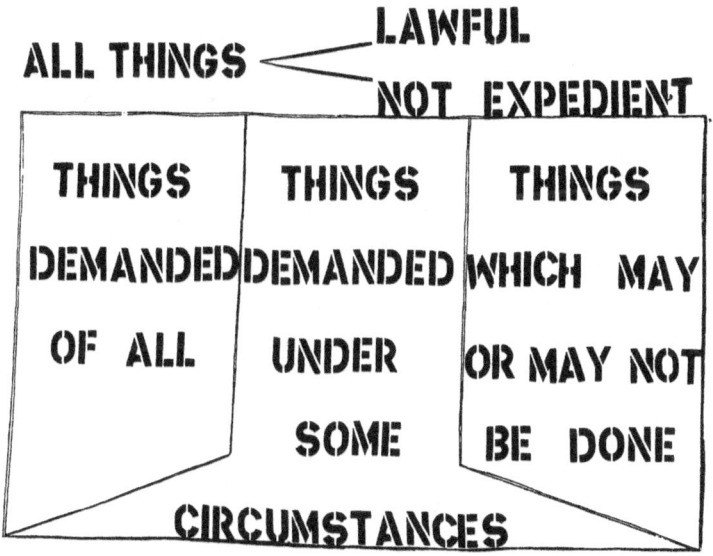

There are some other things that are demanded of some and not demanded of others. For example, the wife is told to be subject to her husband (Eph. 5:22). Now the husband does not obey that one; the wife does, or is supposed to. "Elders which are among you I exhort, who am also an elder ... feed the flock of God which is among you, taking the oversight thereof." (I Pet. 5:1,2) Now, I dare not obey that because I am not an elder.

There are some commands that we are to obey under some circumstances. If a man smite thee on the right cheek turn to him the other also. This does not mean that we go around turning our cheek all the time. But it does mean that here is behaviour we are to follow under certain circumstances.

There is another field of things over here (pointing to chart) which may or may not be done, according to the exigency of the occasion, or the expediency, if you will. (Now expediency is not something that goes on beyond authority, but is in the field of those things that are authorized.) There are some things we may leave off, and under some circumstances should leave off, though we have a perfect right to do them.

"All things are lawful unto me, but all things are not expedient," said Paul in 1 Cor. 6:12. If there is some question about the background or the context here, we would be glad to go into that. But suffice it to say that I am persuaded that Paul is talking about the matter of going to law against a brother, and he is saying that it may be lawful to do so, but it certainly is not expedient. Others, of course, think that he was saying "now you may say that all things are lawful, but let me remind you, that though that be true, all things are not expedient." In either instance, of course, we have the same idea.

There are some things which may or may not be done. Let us illustrate that from the word of God. The apostle Paul, writing in 1 Corinthians 9:1-5 said, "Am I not an apostle? am I not free? have I not seen Jesus Christ our Lord? are not ye my work in the Lord? If I be not an apostle unto others, yet doubtless I am to you: for the seal of mine apostleship are ye in the Lord. Mine answer to them that do examine me is this, have we not power (and this word here in the original language, *exousia*, is the word that is translated authority) to eat and to drink? Have we not power (that is authority, *exousia*) to lead about a sister, a wife, as well as other apostles, and as the brethren of the Lord, and Cephas?" Paul had authority or power to lead about a wife, but he did not do it. He could or he could not, depending upon that which seemed best for him to do. And it seemed best for him not to do it, while it seemed best for Peter to do it. So there is a realm of things which may or may not be done.

Now over here (pointing to chart) these things are authorized by command. And when we say this, we realize there is a difference between a grammatical command and a philosophical command. But these must be certainly commanded, or these things are commanded, or by necessary inference, are bound upon one. Over here the same thing is true. But of this field (pointing to right of chart) we have example or necessary inference. Necessary inference being that when God has not specified, man is left free. Bob, if you can help me, please. (Speaking to Bob Kessinger, his moderator asking for help in handling a chart.)

SIN IS THE TRANSGRESSION OF THE LAW

NO LAW NO TRANSGRESSION

1 JOHN 3:4

ROM. 4:15

(law not to be confused with prohibition)

Setting forth this principle, John says in 1 John 3:4, "Sin is the transgression of the law." Now before a thing is sinful it must be a transgression of the law. (Can we raise it back just a little bit farther, please?) Paul further says in Romans 4:15, "Where there is no law, there is no transgression." Now because it is possible that I am going to be misunderstood here, let us pause just a moment. Let us not confuse law with a prohibition. He did not say "Where there is no prohibition, there is no transgression." He said, "Where there is no law, there is no transgression." For example, the reason I do not believe in using instrumental music in worship is that the law specifies, the word of God specifies, to sing. There is a commandment to sing. There is a specification for vocal music. Were there not a specification, if he had left us free just to use music, then we could sing or play a fiddle or whatever we may choose.

Now to illustrate this further, let us take "baptize." If you can keep in your mind the chart, we had here at first "Baptism." "He that believeth and is baptized shall be saved." But God did not specify where to be baptized. We may be baptized in a running stream, in a baptistry, in a building or out in a pond—in the open air. But since God did not specify, we are free. Wherever God has not specified, then the necessary inference is that we are free. When it comes to singing, I do not know that anyone will demand that a man has to sing soprano or tenor or bass. God did not specify and we are free to choose. And this everyone has understood through the years.

"...NOTHING OUGHT TO BE INCULCATED UPON CHRISTIANS...NOR REQUIRED OF THEM AS TERMS OF COMMUNION: BUT WHAT IS EXPRESSLY TAUGHT AND ENJOINED UPON THEM IN THE WORD OF GOD"

Now sometimes Thomas Campbell is quoted. Campbell said, "Where the Bible speaks we speak, and where the Bible is silent we are silent." This is a wonderful principle, but let us notice that Campbell went further in this and told what he meant. "Nothing ought to be inculcated upon Christians nor required of them as terms of communion but what is expressly taught and enjoined upon them in the word of God."

Now there are those who say that when it comes to broadcasting the gospel there is a certain method enjoined upon us, by which one or more congregations may cooperate. My demand tonight is, if you say there is a certain pattern, there is a way that is enjoined, show that enjoinment from the word of God. If not, forever hold your peace.

Where God has not specified, man is not limited; where there is no law, there is no transgression. (I am giving Bob his exercise here tonight.) What is the law concerning broadcasting the gospel? Chapter and verse. What is the law concerning sending money from one congregation to another, be it support, broadcasting, or whatever it may be? What is the law? Where is it found? What is the chapter? What is the verse? If there is no law, as God has made no specification, there is no transgression—there is no violation. We want, then, chapter and verse; we want that law set forth.

(Mimeographed Sheet Distributed by Brother Inman)

What Is The Point Of Error?
1. Is it the act of broadcasting?
2. Is it the extent—nationwide or network?
3. Is it sending money from one congregation to another?
4. Is it what the money is used for?

. . . .

1. Broadcasting is teaching. Heb. 5:11 ff.
2. Teaching is unlimited.
3. Money sent from one congregation to another. Acts 11:27, 28; 1 Cor. 16:1-4.
4. No specification of limitation on money's use.

. . . .

If There Is A Pattern
1. Envoys controlled by one man. 1 Cor. 16:1-3
2. One or more volunteers. 2 Cor. 8:6
3. Several churches chose one man. 2 Cor. 8:19
4. Each church choose delegates. 1 Cor. 16:3; 2 Cor. 8:23

Now, sometimes someone says "There is a pattern—we find it in the word of God." But tonight I want to give you a pattern and see whether you are ready to accept that or not. (Let us see. You skipped one there somewhere, Bob. Did we fail to get that one up?) Oh, excuse me, we do not have a chart. Get . . . You were handed a sheet of paper when you came in. (He laughs.) I started to make a chart and I decided not to.

Look at the bottom of this (holds up paper): "If there is a pattern." When money was sent from Corinth, or from Achaia, and from Macedonia over to Jerusalem, from 1 Cor. 16:3, Paul said, "Upon the first day of the week let each one of you lay by him in store, as God hath prospered him, that there be no gatherings when I come." And then he said, "Whomsoever ye may approve by your letter, him will I send." These men were to be sent by Paul. They were under Paul's control, as it were. Later on he said, "This is administered by us." Paul said "I will send them." Then we have one or more volunteers (2 Cor. 8:6). Paul tells us about Titus, and he mentions that Titus had been forward in this. One translation says "The whole thing was his idea", suggesting that Titus was the one who had initiated the whole thing to begin with. So then we have one or more volunteers. And we will take time after a while to give more passages that talk about Titus and his work here.

But, in addition to this. several congregations went together to choose one man. We find the apostle saying, 2 Cor. 8:6, "Insomuch that we desired Titus, that as he had begun (now this is the verse I was talking about a moment ago), so he would also finish in you the same grace also." Titus started this, so we are suggesting that he finish it. Titus just started the whole matter. Now the 18th and 19th verses, "And we have sent with him (that is Titus) the brother, whose praise is in the gospel throughout all the churches; and not that only, but who was also chosen of the churches (now notice this, one man was chosen of churches) to travel with us with this grace, which is administered by us to the glory of the same Lord, and the declaration of your ready mind." So here is one man chosen by several churches. And then each church was to choose some delegates, "whomsoever ye commend by your letters" (1 Cor. 16:3).

First Night, Cooperation

(Brother Kessinger indicates he has 10 minutes.) Ten minutes. Thank you. And then here in 2 Cor. 8:23, "whether any enquire of Titus, he is my partner and fellowhelper concerning you; or our brethren be enquired of, They are the messengers of the churches, and the glory of Christ." Now, if there be a pattern, here it is. Will Brother Willis say that if a congregation sends money from its treasury to another congregation, it has to follow this pattern? I would like for you to tell us, Brother Willis, about this. Do you say this is the pattern? That when we get ready to send money, some man must volunteer and that the envoys, or those sent, must be controlled by one man? Several churches go together to choose one man to go along. And then one church, or each of the churches, choose several men and they all go together to take this money over. Is this the pattern? Is this the example? Is this the way it has to be done?

Let us come down more specifically to the matter before us, and on your sheet here let us notice some things. "What is the point of error?" When money is sent from one congregation, the treasury of one to another—is this the point of error? Is it the act of broadcasting? Well, look down in the second group. Broadcasting is teaching. "For when for the time ye ought to be teachers" (Heb. 5:12). The teaching of the word of God is authorized. There are no specifications or limitations set upon the means to teach. Teaching is unlimited, so long as it is true to the word of God.

How far man may hear it? After all, one broadcast in some nations would be nationwide. Is it the matter of money being sent from one congregation to another? If so, we find that money was sent from one congregation to another. And there is no specification, or there is no law, giving the limitation upon how this money was to be used or may be used. If there is such a law setting forth that congregations may use money for this thing or that thing, that they cannot use it for something else, let us have the law. Let us have the law that so states. How much time do I have? Seven minutes? (Brother Kessinger: Eight minutes.) Eight minutes, all right, thank you.

Now Brother Willis has given me some questions, and they have to do somewhat with the things that I have set forth, and I want to deal with them in my first speech. He says, *"Does the New Testament reveal a pattern by which churches of Christ must operate? If so, where is the pattern for 3199 (or 1999) churches working together through one eldership?"* I do not know, Brother Willis. I guess they have to stop at about two or three. But 3199 is in that same passage where you get two or three. Now, Brother Willis you are the one that claims a pattern. You give the pattern. I do not believe there is a set pattern. If there is a pattern, we have it here on the bottom of this paper. I do not believe there is one. I do not believe that this was set as a rule by which we have to operate. Brother Willis does not believe it either. If he does, he never has operated this way. Now if I am mistaken, you tell me, Brother Willis. I will get up and apologize. But I do not believe he has ever operated this way. If that is the pattern, he never has operated that way. So I want chapter and verse that gives this pattern that is binding, that gives the law which is violated.

"Whose work is the Herald of Truth? The sponsoring church's? The contributing churches'? Or both?" The work of the speaker or preacher is to preach. The work of the elders of the overseeing church is to oversee the work of this preacher. The work of the contributing churches is to have love to contribute, as the brethren in Philippi or in Macedonia. The churches in Macedonia had the love that caused them to send down and support Paul, and those with him, while they preached at Corinth. It was just their work and their act of love to send the money down. And they did it.

"If it is scriptural for some churches to send some of their money to the Highland church some of the time, would it be sinful for all of the churches to send all of their money all of the time to Highland? If your answer is "yes," please cite the scriptures the practice would violate." Was it scriptural for all the churches of Macedonia to send all of their money down to Paul? If they could send some of it part of the time, could they send all of it all the time? Now, come on, Brother Willis. (Five minutes? Thank you.) Come on, Brother Willis, let us get down to something better than this. What about Antioch and Jerusalem? If they could send their money there part of the time, some of their money part of the time, could they send all of it all the time? They sent it.

"*Where is the command, example, or necessary inference for one church sending money to another church, when the receiving church is not destitute?*" Every passage that suggests the sending. Let us understand that the rule set by the apostle Paul concerning equality in 2 Cor. 8 did not have to do with congregational treasuries, but had to do with individual needs. I do not know how many people in Jerusalem were destitute. I do not believe Brother Willis knows. I do not believe any other man does. But there evidently were many people who were. And Paul wanted an equality, not between church treasuries, but between individuals. But then, these poor churches up in Macedonia which sent over there had also, before this, been sending money down to help Paul preach at Corinth, when evidently they had money enough to support a preacher. But Paul said, "I robbed other churches taking wages from them to preach to you."

"*Does every church have a right to become a sponsoring church and to solicit money from every other church, or is this a special privilege belonging to Highland and other current sponsoring churches?*" Each has a right within the bounds of expediency and good judgment to do this (and I think we have to use a little expediency and good judgment), within the bounds of that which is authorized. Paul had the authority to lead about a wife, but he did not do it. Judgment on our part determines some things. Let us understand then, that congregations did send funds from one congregation to another to preach the gospel, to help the poor. Let us understand that the gospel is to be preached and no limitations are set upon where it is to be preached, and where there is no law there is no transgression. Brother Willis then has the obligation to stand before us this evening and give us the law that sets forth exactly how this is to be done, and if he does not have the law, there is no transgression. Thank you very much.

WILLIS' FIRST NEGATIVE

It is a pleasure for me to be here this evening and to have this opportunity to participate with Brother Inman in this discussion. I do not know anybody with whom I would rather participate in such a discussion than with Brother Inman. I think if I had been picking the man I would meet, I would have picked Brother Clifton Inman.

I wish we had a little larger speaker's stand here, so that I could keep my materials together. But we want to proceed now through the material that he presented in his first speech. I want you to understand this evening that I am in the negative on this proposition and, of course, it is just my responsibility this evening to examine the proof Brother Inman presented in the affirmation of this question. Now tomorrow evening we will just have this turned around and I will be in the affirmative, and it will be then his responsibility to examine the proof that I present. Brother Inman and I have had an agreement that actually we have two nights on one proposition. Of course we are reversing positions so far as affirming and denying are concerned on the different nights. This simply means that if there should be something this evening that he says in his speech that I do not cover in this first speech, that I will either get to it in the second, or it is permissible, according to our agreement, to cover it in the speech tomorrow evening.

Now I call your attention also, in introducing our remarks, that we are not discussing this evening the Herald of Truth only. Now we *are* discussing the Herald of Truth. You will notice that the Herald of Truth is mentioned in the proposition. (Hand me my pointer, please.) You will notice that we have mentioned specifically the Herald of Truth in the proposition, and Brother Inman made mention of the fact that he was not defending what Highland does. Well now, Brother Inman, I beg to differ with you. That is what you signed your name to do—to defend what Highland or any other church does in regard to this particular operation. And I am going to demand in this discussion that he either defend what Highland does, or that he be man enough to get up here and tell us what they do that he does not defend. Now he has insinuated that there may be something about their operation that he does not endorse. Now if that is true, I want to know what it is, and I would like for him to get up here and tell us what it is that they actually participate in *as pertains to the Herald of Truth* that he does not endorse.

Now he mentioned that he deplored the fact that we have division in the church. I deplore that just as much as he does, and insofar as this issue is concerned, I can tell you, Brother Inman, when we started having division over it. We started having division over the Herald of Truth as of February 3, 1952. That is when the thing got started and that is when we started having division over it. We started having division over mechanical instrumental music about 1860. We tried to get people to see back then that when they introduced something not sanctioned by the word of God or not authorized by the word of God, the person who introduced that for which there is no scriptural authority bore, therefore, the responsibility of any division that should result.

Now he makes some reference here to the fact that he thought I did not understand general and specific authority. I really think I do, Brother Inman. Thank you Brother Needham. (Needham supplied a larger speaker's stand.) I will have occasion to deal with that as we proceed in the course of the discussion.

Now really so far as I was able to tell this evening there was but one major argument that Brother Inman made, and that is the argument on expediency. He said that there is no law and therefore there can be no violation of the law. But if there is no order, I suggest to him there can be no disorder. Now actually, Brother Inman, that was not a brand new argument. In fact, I thought you might make that argument, so I thought I would bring along the statement of another who made this argument. When J. B. Briney was debating Brother W. W. Otey in 1908, he made the same argument. Briney said God told us to do it, but did not tell us how, and consequently man was left free to do what he wanted to do. They therefore had the permission to build a missionary society.

Here is the argument as Brother Briney made it in 1908. He said, "When a thing is commanded to be done and the method of doing it is not prescribed, those commanded are at liberty to use their best judgment (You notice Inman said "good judgment" as to which churches are to become sponsoring churches and which ones are just to be contributing churches. So they are to use their best judgment.) in devising ways and means to carry out the commandment and they are to act under the principle laid down by Paul in 1 Cor. 14:39,40." (*Otey-Briney Debate*, p. 162.) Now if I understand Inman's argument, that is his argument precisely.

Now you know it happens Brother Inman had a debate a few years ago. He published one with Brother Julian Hunt, who was a Christian Church preacher, and at that time the thing was somewhat reversed. Brother Julian Hunt was making the expediency argument; Brother Clifton Inman was answering it. And here is what Brother Inman had to say about the expediency argument when it was offered by Brother Julian Hunt, I believe in 1942. Brother Inman said, and he is really answering Brother Inman's argument, "Are we not permitted to do some things in religion because they are authorized by the law of expediency? This is claimed by many (I know a fellow that claims that—C.W.). In fact Alexander Campbell and those of his day were progressing well on the way toward a full return to New Testament principles until Campbell set forth the idea that many things are authorized by expediency. When he set forth these ideas, many of those who were working with him in the effort to return to the Bible and the Bible alone reversed their field and rather rapidly fell away from their former position." (Inman, *Bible Herald*, Dec. 15, 1954, p. 2.) Now really what Brother Inman says is that this argument on expediency, and historians will verify it, was what wrecked the Restoration movement and what brought about the division in the churches and resulted in what we know today as the Christian Church denomination.

He mentioned that the Bible specifies that we are to sing. I want to find out, and I will discuss this some more tomorrow night, if the Bible specifies how we

First Night, Cooperation

are to *work* together. I am going to argue in my affirmation tomorrow evening that there *is* a pattern. There *is* a pattern in work; there *is* a pattern in worship; there *is* a pattern in organization; there *is* a pattern in how churches may work together, and I think I will be able to show that there *is* a pattern by which churches are to discharge their obligation. I remind Brother Inman that if there is not any pattern, if there is not any order, there cannot be any disorder. You just cannot have any. If you do not have an order to violate, you cannot have any disorder. And if you do not have any order, then a missionary society is not a violation of any order. And if he wants to take that back, we will be glad to have him do so.

Now I want to come to deal with some matters this evening that I think will clarify what we are talking about. I want to suggest first of all, just by way of clarification, that we are not talking about whether the gospel should be preached. That is not what we are debating this evening. Nor are we discussing whether it is right to use radio and television in the preaching of the gospel, nor whether a local church may use or employ lawful means and methods. We are in agreement that they may. We are not discussing the range of the radio or the television stations, and we are not even discussing, at least this evening, the magnitude of the program.

But the issue we have before us tonight is whether it is scriptural for thousands of churches to *pool their resources* and then to centralize the control of these pooled resources. Centralization inevitably follows when you pool your resources; somebody has to control them. *We are talking about whether it is scriptural for churches to pool their resources and then to centralize the control of these pooled resources in the eldership of what we know today as a sponsoring church. Or, can thousands of churches work through one eldership?*

I am going to come in a few minutes, if I have time in this speech, to deal with the questions, both that I asked him and that he presented unto me. But I want to make something of an overview this evening, and to suggest to you some basic principles that are taught in the word of God that pertain to this matter of congregational cooperation.

First of all, I suggest to you that churches helped each other in time of emergency by contributing directly to the needy church (Romans 15:26; 1 Cor. 16:1-4). *Second,* that many churches contributed to one church in its time of need (2 Cor. 8,9). *Third,* that each church made up its own "bounty", as the Bible calls it, selected its own "messengers" and sent its "bounty" by its "messengers" directly to the church in need (2 Cor. 8,9; 1 Cor. 16:1-4; Romans 15:26). *Fourth,* a church with "power" or ability gave to a church in "want", or which was destitute, in order to produce mutual freedom from want, or as Paul put it, in order to produce "equality" (2 Cor. 8:13,14). The *fifth* point, I suggest (Really I think this will answer what Brother Inman has said thus far) is that individuals and not churches served as messengers in the Bible (1 Cor. 16: 1-4). *Sixth,* that these messengers served only in the capacity of delivering the contribution from the contributing church to the intended recipient (Acts 11:27-30; 1 Cor. 16:1-4; Phil. 4:10-18). *Seventh,* insofar as supporting evangelists is concerned, in Phil. 4:15,16 and 2 Cor. 11:8, we learn that several churches sometimes assisted in supporting one evangelist, but each church communicated directly with that evangelist. As far as I am able to ascertain, this is the substance of what is taught in the word on the question of congregational cooperation, and anything more than that, which one might teach, emanates from human wisdom.

(Now I would appreciate it, brethren, if you would help me on the charts. Get chart No. 3.)

Brother Inman spent a little time in defining the terms this evening. Of course it is his responsibility to define the terms, but I do not think he quite adequately defined the proposition we are talking about tonight. We are talking about sponsoring churches in general. I do not have anything in particular against the Herald of Truth operation, but it is typical of the operation of the sponsoring churches in general. So, I want to help you a little bit this evening, in case you are not already familiar with the organization of the Herald of Truth.

The Highland elders tell us that they have the oversight of the Herald of Truth. And the reason why I used the figures that I used in the questions that I gave him earlier is because 3199 churches thus far, according

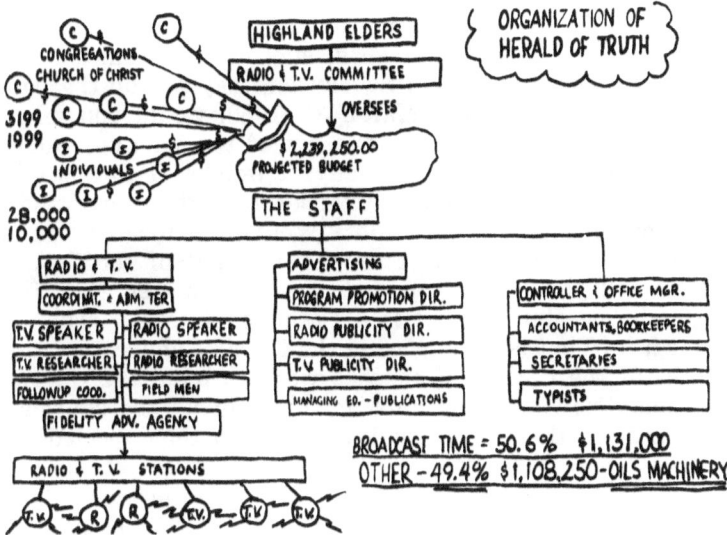

to their latest figures that I have, have made a donation to the Highland Avenue church. Presently they tell us that they have 1999 churches sending them money.

Now Brother Inman said that you would find authority for 3199 churches, or 1999 churches, to send money to a church that was not destitute, or was not in need, in the same passage where you would find authority for two or three churches to send to a church that is not in need. Well, it happens Brother Inman, I do not even know where that one is! Do you? I would be glad to have that one. Where in the Bible can I find where two or three churches sent to a *church* that was not destitute or was not in need? And I would be greatly appreciative to Brother Inman if he would cite that passage. And he tells me that when he finds it, in the same passage there will be authority for 3199 churches to send. I suppose if 1999 could send, then 19,000 could send. If 1900 could send, could not 19,000?

Now really what Highland tells us, brethren, is that they already have more than one-tenth of all the churches of Christ in the world sending them money. My Bible says that elders are to "tend the flock of God" which is among them. (1 Pet. 5:2) And if we get these men overseeing the work that is paid for by more than one-tenth of all the churches of Christ in the world, why not over ten-tenths? (And in a letter to Brown St. church, they put on the bottom of the letter, dated March 31, 1960, would you make it two out of ten? We have one out of ten sending, would you now make it two out of ten?) I wonder if that would have been the last letter? I wonder if perhaps we might have gotten another that said, "Would you make it three out of ten, or four out of ten, or five out of ten?" And let me tell you, when you get ten out of ten working through one church, that is a Catholic Church. That is what it is! That is exactly what the Catholic church is. Ten-tenths of the Catholic Churches work through the Church at Rome. Now we have only one-tenth of all the churches of Christ in the world sending money to that "pooled resources" here (pointing to "Projected Budget" on chart). It amounts to, according to their projected budget, $2,239,250.00 a year. And you know these figures get obsolete rather quickly when you are dealing with these fellows. They have already raised that to $2,330,000.00 a year; they raised that $100,000.00 since I got this chart fixed up. So I say they raise that rather fast. They are wanting presently that much money.

They have a radio and television committee that handles this money. It consists of five of their elders, two of their deacons, two others of their members, and also of three brethren who happen to be participants in the Fidelity Advertising Agency. The staff of the Herald of Truth consists of a radio and television co-ordinator and administrator, of a television speaker, of a television researcher, of a follow-up co-ordinator, of a radio speaker, a radio researcher, and of many field men. (Some of them may even be here tonight.) And they all work through the Fidelity Advertising Agency to negotiate with the various radio and television stations.

Now you remember that whatever proof Brother Inman might cite in substantiation of his proposition, that really what he is looking for is some passage in the word of God that will permit several hundred or several thousand churches to work through one eldership.

Now in addition to this staff they have over here, they have an advertising staff. This is big business, and so they have an advertising staff that consists of a program promotion director, a radio publicity director, a television publicity director, and a managing editor of publications. Furthermore they have their office staff, well ordered I suppose, in that they have a controller, and manager of the office. He controls the various accountants, the bookkeepers, the secretaries and the typists.

And here is how much of the money actually buys broadcast time. (Points to $1,131,000.00 on chart.) Now some of you people might have sacrificed a good bit to send some money to this operation. You thought you were paying for the preaching of the gospel, but 50.6%, just slightly more than 50% of that money, buys broadcast time. That is, $1,131,000.00 of the money sent out of this projected budget will go to buy broadcast time. And that just means that 49.4% of it goes for something else! It goes to oil the machinery!

Do you know Brother Inman pitched his argument on expediency! I would not have him pitch it anywhere else. He pitches it on the basis of expediency. If he wants to argue that it is expedient, I am perfectly willing to argue it out with him on expediency. They surely handle their expediencies in a rather strange way down here. You know, if you do not go along with our expedient, we will not announce your meeting! And if you do not go along with our expedient, we will not call on you for prayer when you come over. And if you do not go along with our expedient, we will cancel every meeting we can get cancelled for you. And furthermore we are going to put in our deeds that if you do not go along with our expedients, you are going to be thrown out of the property! And even they have put that in the charters of the orphan homes; that you have to go along with this expedient or you cannot have anything to do with our charter. Now I have before me the substantiation, if he wants to challenge any of that.

We have had law suits in several places over properties because some brethren objected to what he calls an expedient. Now before he calls it an expedient (I think I detected Brother Inman thought he was going to have to have some authority for it, and that is what I am asking for), where is the authority for it? Then we will start calling it an expedient. You give us a command for it, or an example for it, or a necessary inference for it. Then we will start calling it an expedient. Now you know, I wonder if they say it is like the pews in the building and light bulbs. Is that really what it is like? I wonder if they would cancel your meeting if you did not go along with light bulbs. I wonder if they are going to write a creed in their deed that you must to go along with white oak pews. And they are going to split churches over expediencies of that sort! That is really what he is insinuating; that this is like those things.

(Turn the other chart please.) Now we want to see something about the operation of the Herald of Truth. This (chart No. 3) is the *organization* of it. Here on chart No. 4 is the *operation* of it. He said it is an expedient way to preach the gospel. I am willing to argue just the opposite, that it is an *inexpedient* way, even if he could show it is scriptural. They tell us how much good it has done. I wish they would give us a list of how many churches it has split. I would like to have that. They talk about how many they baptize. I would like to have a list of divided churches in the division of which it has figured. Brother Inman has publicly said in an article that he knows of two. And if that is all he knows of, I think I could supply him with about

OPERATION OF HERALD OF TRUTH

ANALYSIS OF BUDGET:

BROADCAST TIME	50.6%	$ 1,131,000
BROADCAST PRODUCTION	21.2%	474,200
ANSWER RESPONSE	7.9%	177,500
LISTENER PROMOTION	4.7%	104,800
GEN. AND ADM.	4.5%	100,450
MISC. AND CONTINGENCY	2.4%	55,500
FUND RAISING	8.8%	196,100
	100.0%	$ 2,239,250

INCLUDES THESE ITEMS:		E.F.T.P.
PAYROLL AND SALARY COSTS	$ 219,400	(36)
RESEARCH	95,000	(14)
POSTAGE	66,500	(11)
TELEPHONE	12,000	(2)
PRINTING AND SUPPLIES	203,000	(34)
CONTINGENCY	55,500	(9)
TOTAL BUDGET	$ 2,239,250	(373)

E.F.T.P. = EQUIVALENT FULL TIME PREACHERS @ $6,000* PER YEAR

COMPARATIVE FIGURES:	UNITED APPEAL - CLEVELAND	HERALD OF TRUTH	
GEN., ADM., MISC. & FUND RAISING	5.8%	15.7%	
		TOTAL $ 351,590	(58)

* PER ERNST & ERNST AUDIT
AS OF DEC. 31, 1965

First Night, Cooperation

198 more. I know of a good many more. So this "expedient" has already divided a lot of churches—and he wants to call it expedient!

But out of this budget, $2,239,250.00 (How much time, Brother Shewmaker?), we have 50.6% of it going actually to buy broadcast time; 21% of it goes into production ($474,200.00). Answer response: It takes $177,500.00 just to answer their mail! You know how many letters they get? I have the figure right here. They say they get a thousand letters a month. (*The Herald of Truth Story*, p. 56) That means that for every letter they get requesting information, they spend $14.79 answering it. And he says that is an expedient way to spend the Lord's money! That really means that if some of you brethren here, who have local radio programs, get seven letters a week, and you are going to allocate as much money for answer response as these brethren allocate when they are spending other brethren's money, you are going to have to set aside $100.00 a week in your budget to answer those seven letters. That is what that means, if you are going to spend money at the rate that they spend it.

Furthermore, we have listener promotion: $100,500.00; general and administrative: $100,450.00. That is oiling the machinery, paying their men. That is really what it amounts to. Miscellaneous and contingency: $55,500.00. That is a rather good little sum of money just in case you get in a bind, isn't it? That is what that means: in case they get in a bind, they hold $55,500.00. And fund raising: $196,000.00. That would take ten rather good churches giving every cent they contribute just to pay for the begging of money. And actually, brethren, that is not all of it; they say 8.8%, nearly ten cents out of every dollar out of this year, is going to beg some more money. Now they have been on the air fourteen years. In fourteen years they have taken in $7,000,000.00. $7,000,000.00 in 14 years! They tell us that 11.24% of every dollar they have *ever* taken in has gone to beg more money. (*The Restoration and Unity Plea*, p. 122.)

Now you get that! Eleven and one-quarter percent out of every dollar they have ever taken in, GOES TO BEG more money. You know how much that is? That is over $770,000.00! Brother Inman, you know how many years of gospel preaching that would pay for? Just the money they spent on begging money? That would pay for 128 years of gospel preaching. And he says that is an expedient way to use the Lord's money!

Now let us notice, a little further, some of the items included in this. They have payroll and salaries of $219,400.00. Now this EFTP (pointing to chart) out there means Equivalent Full Time Preachers. If they had just used that money to pay gospel preachers out of their payroll and salaries, they could have paid 36 gospel preachers at the rate of $6,000.00 a year. For research, get this, $85,000.00 a year for research. That would pay fourteen preachers. I tell you quite frankly, I am wondering what they are researching for $85,000 a year. I would like to see them employ fourteen preachers to try to find a scripture for what they are practicing out there. I think if they would employ 14 preachers for a year to try to find scriptural authority, that might be worthwhile money spent on research. But that is what the item shows. This is out of their budget.

For postage: $66,500.00 a year postage. Postage! That will pay eleven preachers $6,000.00 a year. Their telephone bill runs $12,000.00 a year. That would pay two preachers in itself. That is a pretty good little telephone bill. Some of you fellows with teen-agers thought you had it rough, didn't you? (Laughter) But they are spending $12,000.00 a year to pay a telephone bill. I checked with a hospital in Cleveland that has a hundred and fifty beds and employs 280 people: "How much is your telephone bill?" And they said the Herald of Truth's telephone bill is three and one-half times more than theirs! I am giving some illustration of this "expediency."

Furthermore, they list printing and supplies. Now we thought we had a radio and television program, but $203,000.00 a year of this money that is sent to them is going to pay a printing bill. And that in itself would pay 34 preachers. And further their miscellaneous and contingency—that would pay 9 gospel preachers. So that you could take this sum of money that they propose to spend, $2,239,000.00, and you could pay 373 gospel preachers! Now I am willing to submit it to you,—willing to let you decide—whether or not 373 gospel preachers would convert more people than they are converting by this program.

Actually, they will not tell us how many they are baptizing. How many would 373 full-time preachers have baptized in 14 years? I asked some preachers, how many do you baptize a year? I then took a figure deliberately lower than they said. I took the figure of baptizing 20 a year. If you took 20 a year, and paid these men for fourteen years, they would have baptized 104,440 people. And yet they want to say that is an expedient way to preach the gospel!

(Turn the other chart now.) Let us notice just in closing now what we really have in this thing. We have here just a confusion in the operation of the Herald of Truth and every other sponsoring church type of arrangement. We are calling this chart the "sponsoring church pattern." He did not know there was a pattern, but there is one, the "sponsoring church pattern." And you *swap dollars*; that is what they do. We have a number of these sponsoring churches; primarily Central and Abilene and Broadway. And Central sends a dollar over here to Highland Avenue for their Herald of Truth. Highland Avenue sends a dollar back down to Central for their home for the aged. High-

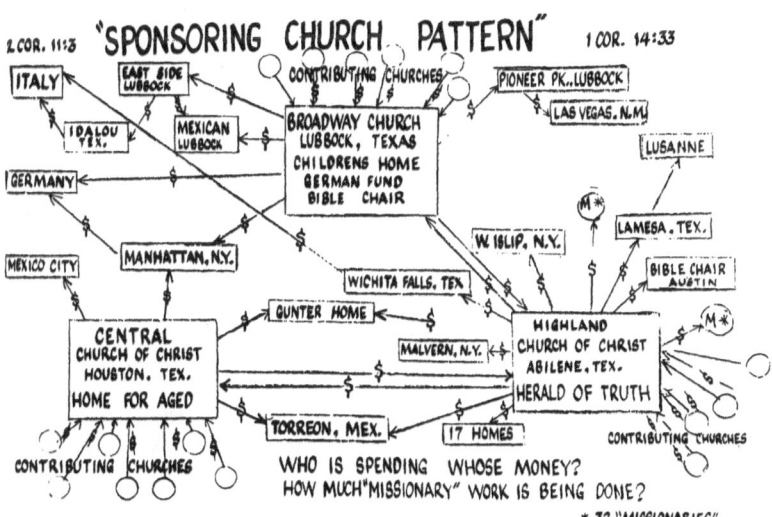

land Avenue sends a dollar to Broadway for their orphan's home, and Broadway sends a dollar back to Abilene for their radio program. Broadway sends a dollar over here to Eastside, and Eastside sends a dollar down here to another place in Texas, and then they send that money over to Italy. Now the Bible says that some have forsaken the simplicity that is in Christ, and that God is not the author of confusion. And this is taken exactly from their bulletins. That is how they practice cooperation! And they say that is an expedient way to do so.

There are several things that are missing in Brother Inman's presentation of proof thus far. He has not found a sponsoring eldership in the word of God. He has not found a transfer of funds from one church to another church in evangelism, or when the receiving church was not destitute. He has not found the doing of a work beyond the receiving church's ability; he has not found the doing of a work beyond the receiving church's membership. He has not found a separate treasury as they have here in the Herald of Truth. He has not found this band of roving promoters that go over the brotherhood. He has not found in the word of God, he will not find in the word of God, these 200, 400, or 500, or however many they have, (They want 500; I do not know just how many they have) key men that go around and try to badger and pressure churches into sending them money. He has not found, furthermore, their regional workshops. And there are a whole lot of other things that he has not found in the word of God, and I am predicting that he is not going to find in the word of God. (How much time Brother Shewmaker? One minute more?)

Let us notice now in the closing minute, he said *if* there is a pattern—*if* there is a pattern. Brother Inman is saying that there is not a pattern. And certainly, that is what the Christian Church says. There is not any pattern on worship, and there is not any pattern on work, so we can build a missionary society and we can put in an instrument. And let me tell you, brethren, what scares me is we have some other brethren still with us who are preaching the same thing Brother Inman is preaching, that there is not a pattern. But they are saying that there is not a pattern insofar as worship is concerned.

I have before me a statement by Brother Mack Langford, and he said, "there is no such thing as a final pattern for worship, polity and missions." That is what you are preaching, Brother Inman. Only he just went one step further. You are saying there is not a pattern in congregational cooperation. He is saying there is not one in worship; there is not one in evangelistic work; there is not one in organization. Just throw out this old concept you brethren have had about the New Testament being a blueprint. Brethren, I am not ready to throw it out. The word of God says in Hebrews 8:5 to "build all things according to the pattern." And until Brother Inman finds this thing he is talking about in the word of God, we are going to have to conclude that it is not authorized. There is not any pattern for it, and if it is not in the word of God, it is unauthorized and thus sinful.

INMAN'S SECOND AFFIRMATIVE

As I said in the beginning, when we are divided I would feel that I am doing you and my God a disservice, if I did not try to discuss this matter on the basis of the word of God. Again I want to set that forth and set it forth very clearly.

Brother Willis says that he is in the negative tonight, and not in the affirmative. He spent about three minutes trying to answer what was said by the affirmative, misrepresented that, and then went on to what he had already prepared in his affirmative that he might get away from the issue. I really would that he would be in the negative tonight and pay a little bit of attention to what is said in the affirmative.

He mentions that I said that I am not defending what Highland does, and then he said that suggests that they are doing something that I do not endorse. That suggests nothing of the kind. It does suggest that in our proposition we are discussing whether or not one or more congregations may take funds from their treasuries and send to another congregation, maybe Highland Avenue, or as I said a moment ago, it may be Marrtown Road. And I am quite certain that if I tried tonight to go through Marrtown Road with a fine tooth comb in all that they are doing, like he has done Abilene, or if I were to go through Brown Street like this, I would find something with which I could paint them very bad. But this is not the thing we are discussing.

And let me point out something else to you tonight, of which you may or may not be aware. And that is that all of this discussion and opposition of Brother Willis and others have not hurt Herald of Truth one particle. But I will tell you what the opposition has done. It killed the broadcast at Charleston that was being supported on the same basis. It killed the broadcast in the Huntington area, or helped to do it, that was supported on the same basis.

It has come close to killing broadcasts at Clarksburg, Fairmont, Wheeling, Steubenville, Brown Street in Akron, and a multitude of others.

Now we can get off on a tangent and talk about something besides the issue tonight. We can begin to try to pick faults with how someone operates. But our proposition has to do with whether or not it is right to take funds from the treasury of a congregation and send those funds to another congregation who uses those funds to support a broadcast, under their oversight, for the preacher who is preaching under their oversight. Now that is the question.

He says that the division over the Herald of Truth began February, 1952. I deny this. I happened to have lived through this. The *Bible Banner,* the successor of which is the *Gospel Guardian,* backed Herald of Truth, approved Herald of Truth, criticized some statements that were made in the announcements, and Abilene changed those announcements. Brother Glenn L. Wallace came out with an article questioning some things, not questioning the whole thing, but questioning some things that were done, and some of the arrangements. Brother Yater Tant said, "We have backed this program but Brother Wallace has raised some serious doubts." Then other younger men began to jump in and send articles to them criticizing, and the first thing you know, Brother Tant says "Brother Harper and I have agreed to have a debate. We are not sure about this. We want to try to find out the truth and we want you to send arguments both to me and Brother Harper." Brother Harper and Brother Tant had been bosom companions. The first time I ever met Yater Tant he was holding a series of gospel meetings at Highland Avenue in Abilene. Brother Homer Hailey was the located preacher there. But Yater, after he had this discussion, no longer was pliable in this matter. From henceforth there was open opposition.

And, Brother Willis, I want you to bring the statement where I said the Herald of Truth has divided two congregations. Now do not read a statement that says that two congregations have been divided over Herald of Truth. Read me the statement where I said Herald of Truth has divided two congregations. When we make statements, let us back them up. Let us be sure that they are there. We want that statement.

He says that I am making an argument from the law of expediency. I did not say a thing about a law of expediency. Brother Willis, listen a little closer than this. I just did not say this. I said that this matter of sending funds is authorized by the word of God. I pointed out that we must have authority; that expediency does not go beyond the law. It operates within the law. And there are some things within the law that may be done or may not be done.

Now it is true that Brother Briney, in his discussion with Brother Otey, made this argument. I have not read that debate since I was in school in Abilene. But I believe if I get the debate tonight and pick it up that I will find that, and that he will find that Brother Otey agreed that where God has not specified, then we are at liberty. But he went ahead to point out that this is not the issue.

In my discussion with Julian Hunt (Read the second proposition, and the whole proposition all the way through), I made the same arguments I am making tonight. I then argued that when God did not specify, we could preach the gospel by the use of the radio. When God does not specify, we can use the song book. That is the reason we are not to use an instrument of music. God does specify. Now, Brother Willis, read that debate and you will see where I first began to set forth this principle. It is all through the discussion, set forth very clearly. The very same reasoning I use tonight. I set it forth. Julian Hunt did not set it forth. He denied it, just as Brother Willis is denying it tonight.

He says where there is no order there is no disorder, and so they say with the Missionary Society there is no order. The reason I deny the right of the use of the Missionary Society is that I believe it is violating the order. I am not debating the missionary society tonight.

But there he tries to set forth a principle, and we want to notice that very carefully. He says that a congregation may send funds from their treasury to another congregation to teach in an emergency. Brother Willis, where was the emergency down at Corinth? He says when they are able to take care of things themselves, money should not be sent. But Paul indicates that they were capable of taking care of preachers. They were capable of supporting preachers. They did support other preachers, and yet

Paul said "I robbed other churches, taking wages of them." This is 2 Corinthians 11. "I robbed other churches," the 8th verse, "taking wages of them, to do you service. And when I was present with you, and wanted, I was chargeable to no man: for that which was lacking to me, the brethren which came from Macedonia supplied: and in all things I have kept myself from being burdensome unto you, and so will I keep myself." There was no emergency here. Corinth was able to take care of the situation. They were able to support Paul, but Paul would not let them. He received funds from up in Macedonia.

He says that the churches, all of them, here we have a pattern. They selected and sent their own messengers. Well, we have a little more than this, Brother Willis. Let us get down to this (looks for chart) . . . well it is on your paper again. (Referring to paper distributed to the audience.) Excuse me. We have it on your paper here.

(Mimeographed Sheet Distributed by Brother Inman)

What Is The Point Of Error?
1. Is it the act of broadcasting?
2. Is it the extent—nationwide or network?
3. Is it sending money from one congregation to another?
4. Is it what the money is used for?

. . . .

1. Broadcasting is teaching. Heb. 5:11 ff.
2. Teaching is unlimited.
3. Money sent from one congregation to another. Acts 11:27,28; 1 Cor. 16:1-4.
4. No specification of limitation on money's use.

. . . .

If There Is A Pattern
1. Envoys controlled by one man. 1 Cor. 16:1-3
2. One or more volunteers. 2 Cor. 8:6
3. Several churches chose one man. 2 Cor. 8:19
4. Each church chose delegates. 1 Cor. 16:3; 2 Cor. 8:23

Paul said you choose the men whom I may send. Paul sent them. You make it known in the letters, the ones you want, and I will send them. And if it is meet, I will go along too. If I decide it is a good thing for me to go, I will go; if not, I will send them.

And then there are one or more volunteers. You know, old Titus, he was one of those sponsoring fellows. He was one of these promoters. As we said, according to one translation, "he is the one who thought up the whole thing to begin with." Titus got out here raising funds from all of these churches. Paul sent him on a trip. I wonder how much of the money he spent going up there and back. We could make quite a case on that, couldn't we? But we have this volunteer.

And then several churches chose one man (2 Corinthians 8:23). If anyone inquire concerning our brother, he is the messenger chosen by the churches. Several churches chose one man. And then we do not know for sure whether each church chose separate delegates, or whether they just agreed upon some that Paul had already set forth. But either men were sent that they chose at Corinth, or men that Paul and others had already chosen, whom Corinth was to approve by their letters (1 Corinthians 16: 3; 2 Corinthians 8:23). If our brethren be inquired of, they are the messengers of the churches.

Now Brother Willis just did not pay any attention to this passage. I would like to know if it is a pattern, or if he thinks it is. If he says it is, then I want to refer him to Acts 11, and point out to him that there is another pattern. For the church at Antioch just chose Barnabas and Saul to take it up to Jerusalem. And then I want to know which of the patterns is binding upon us. I was hoping maybe he would notice and give that pattern, and since he does not, I will tell him there is another one over there in Acts 11, if he wants to get another one. Then I want to know which one is binding.

Now he suggests that Philippians 4 is the binding pattern. Paul said, after the church at Philippi sent to him at Rome, "Now ye Philippians know also, that in the beginning of the gospel, when I departed from Macedonia, no church communicated with me as concerning giving and receiving, but ye only. For even in Thessalonica . . ." (Now Paul preached at Philippi, went down to Thessalonica, was persecuted there and went from there to Berea, then down to Athens and over to Corinth). But he said, "Even in Thessalonica (the very next place he went to) ye sent once and again unto my necessity." Just a small congregation, just a few there, just come into Christ, but already, in love, sending to help in other places.

You know this reminds me of what we find in the last chapter of John. Jesus, in the last chapter of John, when Peter pointed to John and said "what shall happen to this man?" (Jesus had already pointed out to Peter how Peter was going to die) said, "If I will that he tarry until I come, what is that to thee? Follow thou me." Then went this saying abroad among the brethren that Jesus had said, "this man shall not die: nevertheless he did not say this man shall not die; but if I will that he tarry until I come again what is that to thee?"

Now over here in Philippians 4, Paul says in the beginning of the gospel you were the first to communicate with me concerning giving and receiving, for when I was at Thessalonica you sent once and again to my necessities. This is what he said, but it has gone forth from Brother Willis and others that he said, "In the beginning of the gospel you were the first to write and find out that in order to support the preaching of the gospel in another field, the money had to be sent directly to the evangelist on the field." But he said not, "ye were the first to write and find out that money was to be sent directly to the evangelist on the field." He did say ye were the first to communicate with me concerning giving and receiving. For when I was at Thessalonica, ye sent once and again to my necessity. There is no indication that he is laying down a law at all.

And again we say that when we come to the matter of authority, we must have authority. We must have it from the word of God, but when we come to the word of God and God has not specified, there is no violation. Now Brother Willis thought that the first one that made that argument was Brother Briney. Let us see who was the first one that made that argument. A fellow named Paul, Brother Willis. Romans 4:15, "Where there no law is, there is no transgression." See? The Holy Spirit beat all of us to it. He got there a long time before Brother Briney or I, or Julian Hunt or anyone else. He is the one that made the law, and I did not go to Brother Briney to get it. I read that debate a long time ago, laid it aside, and kept on reading the word of God, and I found this principle right here in Romans 4:15. Now let me point out again that he did not say "Where there is no prohibition, there is no transgression." Then someone says, "Show me where it said not to do it." We are not asking for this. We are just asking "Where did God specify exactly how it is to be done?"

He likes to make what is called an *ad Hominem* argument. He knows everybody is opposed to the Roman Catholic Church, so we will try to get this compared to the Roman Catholic Church someway. He says that all the Catholic Church operates through Rome. This is not the thing wrong with Catholicism, Brother Willis. This actually is not true anyhow. The trouble is the operation goes the other way. The Pope of Rome exercises control over and claims to be infallible in his decisions over everybody else.

He wants to know about cancelling meetings and about lights. And sometimes we hear people talking about getting emotional and saying some things at the end that appeal to peoples' emotions. Well this appeals to peoples' emotions. But, Brother Willis, if I were an elder of a congregation and I knew that you were going through the land saying that it was a sin to have electric lights in the building, and you were booked to have a meeting where I was an elder, brother, you would be cancelled. (Brother Kessinger indicates to Brother Inman that he has 10 minutes). Thank you.

When someone goes forth setting a law and saying, brethren you are going to hell, you are sinning, and they cannot point out the violation of the word of God, they cannot show where God has specified, where he has made a law, and churches are being divided over this—yes sir, elders ought to cancel some meetings. Just as if somebody started saying it is a sin to have electric lights, there ought to be some meetings cancelled.

He says that the Christian Church says there is no pattern. I have not said there is no pattern. I have said that in some things there is no pattern. That does not say there is not any general, overall pattern. I suggest that all of you go home and read that context and see how little that has to do with this. Paul was talking about how that in the tabernacle there were things that were patterns—in the earthly, there were things of a pattern to the heavenly, as God said build all things according to the pattern. And Brother Willis thinks that he said, "there is a pattern about how the broadcasting of the gospel is to be supported." That is not in that text.

That is about like the fellow who wanted to oppose wearing a topknot and got the passage that said, "let him that is upon the house top not come down and take anything out of his house." That passage is just that far from its setting. Yes sir, when God has specified, we cannot go beyond that. But let us notice again that God has enjoined the preaching of the word, but he has not enjoined how that is to be supported.

Now I am not going tonight into all the material he gives here on the budget of Highland Avenue. Maybe if I were an elder and getting ready to decide whether I would send money, I would go into whether or not I thought this was the expedient thing to do. But this is not what we are discussing tonight; whether Highland is being expedient in all that they are doing, whether they are using good judgment. We are discussing whether or not it is in harmony with the word of God to take funds from a church treasury and send to another congregation who will support a broadcast with that money. That is what we are discussing. Highland Avenue I am sure has used poor judgment. Believe it or not, I have sometimes. My wife did a lot worse than I did. (He laughs.) About everybody has used poor judgment.

But now what is the law concerning broadcasting? (Do not anyone misinterpret that either. I did not say I made a mistake when I married my wife. I said she made one when she married me. I was talking about other mistakes in life.) But what is the law concerning sending money from one congregation to another? Now Brother Willis is trying to set some bounds. We have found that these bounds do not exist; that Corinth was not a destitute place, unable to provide for themselves and to do this work. They were able to provide for preachers and to support preachers.

But we could possibly, if it were in Paul's day like it is in ours, get the budget and sit down here and say, "look how much they are spending for worshipping God." There are several thousands of dollars spent upon the building, the meeting house. There is so much money spent upon keeping the lawn. There is money spent on janitor work. (In fact, I heard someone point out how many millions it runs

—a way up into the millions of dollars that the churches of Christ spend on janitor work. Wonder how many preachers this would support?) If we would take all the money they spend upon mimeographing bulletins, what they spend upon plumbing, and all of this, we could add it up here and we could really get a jumble. But that is not what we are discussing tonight. We are discussing what the Bible has to say about supporting the preaching of the gospel at home and abroad, *and* whether or not it is in harmony with the scriptures to take funds from the church treasury of one congregation to send money over yonder.

He says, yes he agrees that you can get thousands there if you can get three; if you can find where one or two or three ever sent the money. Well I can find here in 2 Corinthians 11, "I robbed other churches, (plural), taking wages of them (plural), to do you service, and when I was present with you, and wanted, I was chargeable to no man: for that which was lacking to me the brethren which came from Macedonia . . ." Now these brethren came from Macedonia and they brought the money from churches. Did they centrally get it together somewhere, Brother Willis? When Paul took it over to Jerusalem, did they get it together in a central place, and a central group take it from many churches? He indicated that would be a violation. (Five minutes? Thank you.)

But these three churches up in Macedonia (Philippi, Berea, and Thessalonica) sent money to Paul down at Corinth, and brethren came from up there and brought it. Did they get it together centrally somehow? I am just asking. Brother Willis says he knows the answer. I would like to know the answer, and I would like to know how he found out.

Now tonight, brethren, Abilene may be doing a lot of things that are not expedient. I may be doing many things that are not expedient. You may be doing a lot of things that are not expedient. But the question is, is a thing lawful? Is it within the law? Is it authorized by the word of God? Is it a violation? Is doing this thing a violation of some principle set forth in the word of God?

Expediency puts greater limitations. It does not extend the field of operation, but it constricts the field of operation of those things that are lawful. But the very fact that it constricts those shows that there are some things which may, within the law, be done or not be done. As Paul said, we have authority to lead about a wife. They could or they could not. This was in the realm of what was authorized—what is lawful—and we will stay with what is within the word of God, and operate within that. And then if we feel that Abilene is being inexpedient in their use of funds, write and tell them so. If we happen to be the ones sending it to them, or, if we feel that we could use this money better some other way, use it better some other way. And every congregation has the right to do this.

Several years ago when I was at Beckley, West Virginia, they supported the Herald of Truth on the Beckley station. It was started when Brother Amos Orrison was there. They continued to do it until one time I was away in a series of meetings and they had a meeting of the elders and other brethren and decided to take it off. I thought they should not have, but it was done while I was gone, and when I came back home it was an accomplished fact. But you know, they sent out to Abilene and told them what they were doing, and Abilene did not jump down their throats. They did not come back and say "now you have got to put this back on the air." It was taken off and that is all there was to it.

And if some congregations feel that their funds could be used better some other way, they can use them that way. So all of this talk of coercion just does not fit what is being done. Now sometimes brethren get overly zealous for anything they are doing. They may have done this at times. The reason I am not trying to defend everything they do is that I do not want to waste my time trying to find out everything they are doing. And I do not think this audience wants to waste their time finding out everything Highland is doing.

We want to know, is this principle scriptural? Is it in harmony with the scriptures? And this is what we are discussing. Brother Willis, I would like for you to come down now. Is this principle in harmony with the scriptures? This principle of sending money to help broadcast the gospel? It is not whether Abilene has made some mistakes and misused some money. Is this principle in keeping with the scriptures? This is what you signed to discuss. Let us discuss that thing and stay with the word of God.

This is the last speech I have this evening. I hope you will go home and read the scriptures that we have discussed. I hope you will think seriously about this and your obligation before God. Then let us use the very best judgment God has given us in carrying out his laws; that we may do it for the glory of God; we may do it for the greatest good. And if you feel like supporting Abilene is one good way, and one of the fine ways that you can use the Lord's money, you use it that way. And if you do not feel that this is true, use it the way that you feel best. Every eldership has a right to do this. Thank you.

WILLIS' SECOND NEGATIVE

You have listened very patiently, and of course, we are grateful for that. Brother Inman now has presented his second speech this evening, and I was impressed by the fact that Brother Inman is considerably more charitable in defending the Herald of Truth than those brethren are in operating it. You know he indicated that you have the option as to whether you give or do not give. But he said he had not investigated it too much, and that is rather obvious. If he would just read some of the literature that they put out, particularly that which they prepare for their key workers, and some of them are here this evening, he would find out that they teach them how to pressure you. They have, each year, a summer session out there. They just completed this year's session. And I have some books over here (They are about one inch thick and are handbooks to teach the key workers how to pressure you) and I will read you just a little bit from one of them in order that you might see that you do not have the liberty to give or not to give. They are going to coerce you in nearly every way they can.

Brother Raymond Wilkerson says, "I know from experience what you (key workers) will be facing. Let me tell you in part what you can expect. Steaming hot or bitter cold telephone booths, trying to set up an appointment that no one wants to give (So they try to get you to set up an appointment but people do not want to give it). Truculent elderships that can't understand why Highland must continually have more money to carry on this program of preaching and teaching." (*The Herald of Truth Story*, p. 130.)

And I think it might be interesting if you would look up the words "truculent elderships." That is what you are if you will not let them in. You are truculent elderships, and that means, according to the dictionary: "fierce, savage, cruel, violent, rude and harsh." That is what you are if you do not let them in.

And further Wilkerson says you are going to have another problem: "The preacher with a program of his own, and he can't understand why anyone else would want to put another program in his town." (p. 130). And then in parentheses he says, "he might want to be the only preacher in the world *too*." Wonder what he meant by that *"too"*? It sounds like they have some preachers out there who want to be the *only* preacher in the world. But you might have a preacher there that wants to be the only preacher in the world. Wilkerson said he "could go on and on in this vein but not much would be accomplished."

Then in closing he said, "Don't ask if he wants to hear it." You have a fellow on the phone. Now, I want to come over and make a speech to you about the Herald of Truth. "Don't ask if he wants to hear it, or don't ask if it will be all right *if* I come to speak? Emphasize the necessity of your coming." So Brother Inman can say they do not use any pressure, but that just shows he has not read very much of what they put out.

Then he used 2 Corinthians 11:8, where Paul says, "I robbed other churches, taking wages of them, to do you service." And actually he used that to prove that it is scriptural to send to another *church*. But that is not what that says. That passage says that churches sent to *Paul*. That is what I advocate. I advocate that when we support gospel preachers, rather than sending it *through* some agency or *through* some sponsoring church, send it to the gospel preacher that we are supporting. So that scripture does not help you any, Brother Inman.

Now he wondered why I spent a good bit of time on the materials that I prepared. Well I do not deny that I spent a good bit of time in preparing. I thought I knew what Brother Inman was going to say, and it looks like I had the right material prepared. I prepared for his argument on expediency. I thought he might make that argument when he got up here, and that is about the only argument he has made: that where there is not any law, any pattern, then we can do it in any expedient way. And I am making two observations: One is he has not established that this is a scriptural way in the first place. And once he establishes that it is scriptural, then secondly, I am plenty ready to meet him on whether it is expedient or not, and that is what I had that information prepared for. I thought I knew what he was going to say.

And he said I did not spend much time answering his affirmative. I thought I spent a good bit of time in answering his affirmative, and if he had made some different affirmative argument, I would have used some different charts in answering his arguments. That is what you prepare charts for, to answer arguments. And I thought I knew some of the arguments he was going to make, and so if he had made another argument I would have used a different chart. But I prepared some answers for his arguments because I have heard the arguments made before.

Now he said he was not inferring that there is something about what they are practicing that he did not defend. Then do not complain about it. Just come on up here and say "I endorse and I defend what they are doing."

He says our opposition to the Herald of Truth has not hurt it any. Well actually there are a few Christian Churches that still have pianos in them. I have been opposing that too. And there are still some missionary societies being operated by the Christian Church, and I have been opposing that too. And he said furthermore that our opposition has killed some local programs. Now let me tell you, if maintaining that elders of the church ought to maintain the oversight of their own members, and their own resources, and their own program of work—if that kills some radio or television program, or any other kind of program that Brother Inman or somebody else has started, *then it ought to die!* It is just not scriptural. If maintaining that elders ought to tend the flock of God and exercise oversight of the church over the which they are appointed as bishops kills a program, then brother, I say it ought to be killed.

Now he said he denied that this opposition began in 1952. But what I said, Brother Inman, was that opposition to Herald of Truth began in 1952. I admit it took the brethren a little while to find out how they are running that thing. Brother Inman said he had not found out yet! (Laughter.) What I have been trying to show him in this discussion is how they are running it. But when some of the brethren found how they were running it, they began to oppose it.

Now I might make this observation: Though they did not begin opposing the Herald of Truth per se before 1952 (it had not started!), there has been opposition to sponsoring churches as long as there have been sponsoring churches. If you want to go back to a historical study of them, I think I am prepared to do that.

We could go back to 1867 when the first one started, that I can find anything about. And I find shortly afterward that the brethren were opposing it. Brother David Lipscomb and a number of other brethren around 1890, and then in 1910, began very avidly to oppose them. Brother Lipscomb said, "All meetings of churches or officers of churches to combine more power than a single church possesses are wrong. God's power is in God's churches. He is with them to bless and strengthen their work when they are faithful to him. A Christian, one or more, may visit a church with or without an invitation and seek to stir them up to a faithful discharge of their duties. (But listen now.) *But for one or more to direct what and how all the churches shall work, or to take charge of their men and money and use it, is to assume the authority God has given to each church.*" *(Gospel Advocate,* March 24, 1910.)

That is what I am charging they have done out there. They are taking the oversight of the resources of several thousand churches, and Brother Lipscomb says that is to take a prerogative that God gave to each church. He said that "Each one needs the work of distributing and using its funds, as well as giving them." And further, Brother Lipscomb said, "I have never published, or approved without publication, the assumption of elders of one church sending out a man to induce the members of other churches to direct their means from their own church treasury, and to take it from the direction of their own elders, and place it under the elders of one church. I have never approved concentrating the control of all the means and preachers of one State, under the authority of the elders of one church. . . . All such concentration of power is destructive of the activity and true liberties of the church. It tends to exalt the elders of one church and degrade and dishonor those of the other." (*Gospel Advocate*, 1890, p. 295). Now that is in 1890. So I say opposition to sponsoring churches did not begin in 1952. It started shortly after the sponsoring churches started.

And, incidentally, Brother Inman is going to have to decide whether he wants a church patterned like the church of Rome, with all the churches operating through one church, or whether he wants some sort of a mother church system like the Christian Scientists have.

And, furthermore, in 1931 Brother F. B. Srygley said, "These elders had no authority to take charge of the missionary money or any other money or means of any church except the one over which they were 'overseers'." Now that is what I am preaching; that is what I am maintaining. Srygley said further that *"Elders of one church should not try to get hold of money that has been contributed by others to direct for them in foreign fields or other places."* And then he says, "No missionary society should be started by elders of a church or by any individual." (*Gospel Advocate*, December 3, 1931). Now really what we have is a missionary society in the elders of this church out here. So I say that the opposition began as soon as the defective practice began.

He also said "I want you to cite the testimony where I said that the Herald of Truth divided two churches." Now here is Brother Clifton Inman's statement: *Bible Herald*, August 1, 1958, page 2, "In regard to the present controversies over orphan homes, Herald of Truth, sponsoring churches, etc., *there have not more than two churches divided over these matters to my knowledge."* Now I told him I could give him some more that divided, but I said

Brother Inman said that two divided over these matters, and there is the documentation.

He said the reason why he opposes the missionary society is that it violates the New Testament order. I thought we have been told for a speech or two this evening that there was not any order. But I want to know if there is not any order, if there is not any pattern, (He has answered the questions saying there is not any pattern but now says the missionary society violates the New Testament order) Brother Inman please tell me what order the missionary society violates! It violates some order, and what I want to know now is, what order does it violate. Maybe he will tell us about that tomorrow night.

He said that I said that a church could send funds to another church in evangelism *in an emergency,* and I did not say any such thing. That is not what I said. *Now there are two instances in the Bible and only two instances in the Bible, so far as I know, where a church or churches sent money to another church or churches for any purpose at all.* And if you want to read about them, they are in Acts 11:27-30, and then also Romans 15:26, 1 Corinthians 16:1-4, and 2 Corinthians 8, 9. *And in both instances it involved a benevolent work, and in both instances the churches receiving the money were destitute churches.*

The Highland church is not a destitute church, and I will substantiate that tomorrow evening, and thus it does not comport with or fit the example we have in the Bible of one church or churches sending to another church or churches.

Brother Inman had a paper here a while ago that he handed out to you in which he said *"if there is a pattern." "If there is a pattern!"* I get the idea that he does not think there is a pattern. But then he said the missionary society violates that pattern; it violates the order. But then says *if* there is an order or *"if* there is a pattern!"

He goes on to argue that these passages (1 Corinthians 16:1-3; 2 Corinthians 8:6, etc.) are not like what I am defending. Well let me show you, he says, that in this instance here the envoys were controlled by one man. He said of "the envoys", there were one or more volunteers. Several churches chose one man; each church chose delegates. But what Brother Inman needs to find, people, is

First Night, Cooperation 51

where some churches sent to another church *in an evangelistic work*. In this instance here these *men* served as "messengers", and in his arrangement he wants the sponsoring *church* to serve as your messenger, and this is not the instance that you have in the word of God, and he did not give any scripture for his practice. And there was a rather good reason why he did not!

Now let us take a look at Acts 11:27-30. (Chart No. 19, please. Hand me the pointer, please.) Brother Inman cited Acts 11: 27-30. It was in a speech in which he was giving scriptural authority, or supposedly giving scriptural authority, for the Herald of Truth. And so let us just see if Acts 11:27-30 constitutes authority for what he is endorsing here.

IS ACTS 11:27-30 AUTHORITY FOR H. of T.

THE PASSAGE	HERALD OF TRUTH
1. BENEVOLENCE	1. EVANGELISM
2. FAMINE	2. MAN MADE EMERGENCY
3. TO MEET LOCAL NEED	3. WORLD-WIDE NEED MET
4. TEMPORARY	4. PERMANENT
5. HELP SENT VOLUNTARILY	5. PRESSURE EXERTED
6. NO RECORD OF SOLICITATION	6. SOLICIT REGULARLY
7. LOCAL CHURCHES' RESPONSIBILITY	7. NOT HIGHLAND'S OBLIGATION
8. WORK NOT ASSUMED	8. WORK IS ASSUMED
9. BIBLE DESCRIBES THIS	9. BIBLE SILENT ON THIS

In this passage, first of all, we have a benevolent work under consideration, but what Brother Inman is looking for is authority for evangelistic work. Secondly, we have this precipitated by a famine; their situation down here in Abilene is a man-made emergency. In the word of God we find that they sent to the Judean churches in order to enable them to meet a local need; in this arrangement here they are sending to the Highland church in order to enable the Highland church to meet a world-wide need. The help that was sent here was temporarily sent, until their needs were supplied; this is a permanent arrangement. At least it looks rather permanent to me. It has lasted fourteen years and is getting bigger all the time they tell us, and they are wanting more and more money all the time. So I say it looks rather permanent.

The help in this instance was sent voluntarily. I have shown you before that they exert every kind of pressure they can exert to try to make churches send them money. There was no record even of solicitation in the word of God in Acts 11. But they solicit regularly and prolifically. We find that the local churches were discharging their responsibility in relieving their own needy; but preaching the gospel, in the manner that Highland is preaching the gospel, is not the responsibility of the Highland church. They do not have the obligation to spend $2,000,000.00 a year. If they do, why do not some other churches have the same responsibility? Furthermore, let us notice that the work here was not assumed; but over here the work is assumed. And further, that the Bible describes this (Acts 11), but the Bible is silent about what he is proposing to defend this evening.

Now let us notice another point or two. He says that Philippians 4:15-16 does not set a pattern. What we have in that instance is a church sending directly unto the support of a gospel preacher. Now if that were going to help Brother Inman any, he would need an instance where several hundreds or thousands of churches sent to a church in order for that church to employ a whole lot of other preachers. That is what he needs to find in the word of God.

He says where there is no law there is no transgression, and yet over in I John 3:4 the Bible tells us that "lawlessness is sin." Unless he can cite a law, either command, or example, or necessary inference, for the Herald of Truth, he is going to have to conclude that it is lawless and thus that it is sinful.

Now he said the thing wrong with the Roman Catholic Church is not that all the churches work through the church at Rome. Brother Inman, make a note and tell us if *that* would be wrong. He said that all the churches working through the church at Rome is not what is wrong with the Roman Catholic Church. What I want to know then is if that is wrong, and if that is not wrong, why did

God put overseers in each church (Acts 14:23). We have elders in every church. Wonder why God put elders in every church if they were not going to oversee anything? If they are just to turn their funds over to the supervising eldership, or the brotherhood eldership, and let them oversee in their behalf, why have elders in every church?

He said we are not discussing expediency. Well I rather thought we were! I thought about half of his speech was spent in discussing expediency, and that is why I took about half of mine in replying to his argument on expediency.

Then he tried to use the janitors as authority for what he is doing. I guess that is what he is concluding tonight. But really what he needs to find, if he wants to have a parallel, is some instance where all the churches are sending money to a sponsoring church and they are going to employ several thousand janitors for the church. That is what he ought to find. What he needs to find is where a thousand churches or three thousand churches sent $2,000,000.00 a year to some eldership, and they employed janitors for nearly all of the churches. And then he would have something to work on. He has not found that, and he will not find it in the word of God.

Now let us notice some further arguments this evening as to why we oppose the Herald of Truth (Chart No. 16, please). He talked a good bit about the subject of autonomy and I am maintaining that *the autonomy of the church is violated by these sponsoring church arrangements*, whether it be Highland's sponsoring church arrangement or any other. The word "autonomy" comes basically from a root word, "auto" which means self, and "nomos" which means law. So I cite here Philippians 1:1, Acts 14:23, and I Peter 5:2.

We are taught in the word of God that each church is to have its own government. God appointed overseers for each church. Thus we have preached throughout a good many years, and Brother Inman very likely a good many years more than I have preached, that churches are *independent*, and that they are *equal*, and that they are *sufficient*, and that they are *autonomous*. Their being autonomous simply means that they rule themselves; that they have control over their own resources; that they do not have conferences, or conventions, or synods, or councils, or

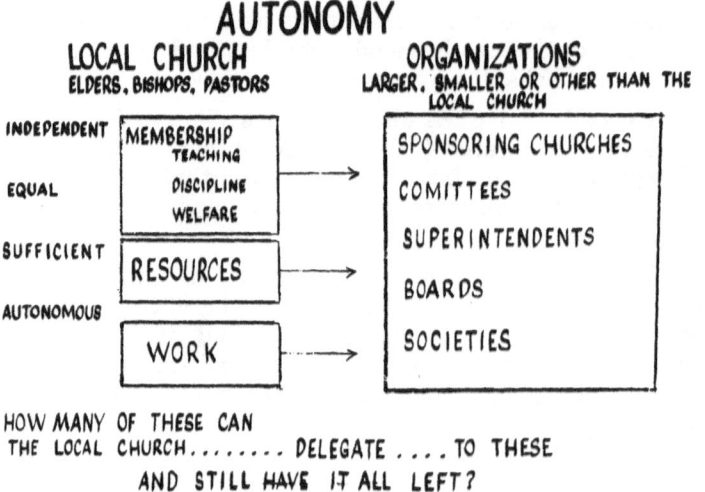

societies, or a mother church, or a sponsoring church, or earthly headquarters, or a pope. But each church has the oversight of its membership, including the teaching of its membership, the discipline of its membership, and the welfare of its membership. It has the oversight of its resources and its work, and that is what we mean by autonomy.

What I want to know is how much of these over here (i.e. control of teaching, discipline, resources, etc., of members) can a church turn over either to a sponsoring church, or to a committee system, or to the superintendents of societies that we will be talking about later, or to boards and conclaves that are unknown to the New Testament, or to societies of any sort, and still have all of its autonomy left? If it relinquishes any of its control, it violates its autonomy or it has forfeited its autonomy. If the contributing churches send earmarked money to Highland, then Highland is not free to use it as she sees fit. On the other hand, if Highland *does* have control of that money and the contributing churches have relinquished that control, then they have forfeited their autonomy. So I say either way you go, somebody in the sponsoring church arrangement has lost a part of his autonomy.

We also have a question or two that I failed to give any attention to, that Brother Inman made some remarks about. I asked him the question, "Whose work is the Herald of Truth? The sponsoring church's? The contributing churches'? Or both?" Now he might as well get set to answer that, because I am going to ask it until he does. I want to know whose work is it? Then he said it is the work of the contributing churches to contribute, and it is the work of the overseeing church to oversee. Now then what I want to know is, "How did Highland get to be the overseeing church?" What made Highland the overseeing church? What made it her work to oversee, and the work of the rest of you fellows to contribute? What I want to know is if churches are equal (and we preach they are) and independent, why is Highland an *overseeing* church and the rest of you churches around here are just *contributing* churches? I thought that they were equal.

Furthermore, I asked a question, "Where is the command, example, or necessary inference, for one church sending money to another church when the receiving church is not destitute?" His answer was "every passage that suggests the sending." What I asked for is *one* passage; just give me one. I want to know *which* passage contains the command, example, or necessary inference, where one church sent to another church when the receiving church was not destitute.

Now then, let us notice another argument and that is that *the Highland church*, in its present practice, *sets a bad example before other churches and before the world.* The Bible teaches that individual Christians are to be good examples. 1 Timothy 4:12 reads, "Be thou an ensample to them that believe, in word, in manner of life, in love, in faith, in purity." And furthermore the Bible teaches that churches are to be good examples (2 Corinthians 9:2; 2 Cor. 8:1-2; 1 Thessalonians 1:7-8). We learn that churches are to set good examples. Now really what that says is that I ought to live in such a way as an individual that you could live like I do and go to heaven when you die, and that one church ought to conduct its affairs in such a way that every other church could conduct its affairs in the same way and please the Lord. And I am saying *Highland does not do that.*

First of all, *Highland is a perpetual beggar.* If every church acted like Highland, it would be tragic; it would be chaotic; and it would be disgraceful. She is a perpetual beggar. From the day that she assumed the oversight of the Herald of Truth, she has never had enough and she will never get enough. She will keep on begging for more and more every year, as long as brethren continue to supply what she asks for.

And furthermore, Highland sets a bad example in that *she perpetually obligates herself beyond her ability to pay.* Every year the Highland elders sign a contract that is from 50 to 200 times bigger than they can pay. Suppose you elders here tonight had a member in the church that for fourteen years straight went down and signed contracts that were fifty times bigger than he intended to pay himself. And then he started taking this money and using about ten or twelve per cent of it to beg other money, and every year he just begged and begged for more and more money. I just have an idea you elders would have a talk with him, wouldn't you? And you would tell him that is not the way to conduct your affairs, and you are a perpetual beggar. And you know, we attach some stigma to a fellow that is a beggar. But you let a church become a perpetual beggar and somehow we do not attach the same kind of stigma to it. I say if every church followed the example of the Highland church, it would be tragic and disgraceful.

And further, *Highland tries to get the oversight of other churches' resources.*

Now in closing I want two other charts. (First of all, Chart No. 6.) We have tried to point out that Brother Inman has not given any authority for three thousand churches to work through one eldership. And if he has cited a passage, I want to know which one he cited. We would be glad for him to call it to our attention tomorrow night. Which command did he cite for three thousand churches working through one eldership? Or which approved example did he cite for three thousand churches working through one eldership? Or from which passage or passages did he necessarily infer that several hundred or thousand churches worked through one eldership? And,

WHERE IS THE AUTHORITY?

COMMAND _____

APPROVED EXAMPLE _____

NECESSARY INFERENCE _____
GENERAL OR SPECIFIC!

Brother Inman, I will take general or specific authority—either one you want to give. (Turn the chart over please.) I will take general authority or specific. He has not given any, and since he has not given any, it is unauthorized, and since it is unauthorized, here is the situation we have tonight.

We have Brother Inman defending something that is in the first place *presumptive*. Back in the Old Testament we read about presumptuous sins; men acting on their own. And if God did not authorize it, they did act presumptuously. It is *lawless*. There is not any command in God's word for it, and 1 John 3:4 says "Lawlessness is sin." It is *iniquitous*. That is the same word in 1 Jno. 3:4 in the original language as in Matthew 7:23. It means it is without law, and Jesus said "depart from me ye workers of *iniquity*." It is *transgressive* because it goes onward and beyond the doctrine of Christ. It is *digressive* in that they have to add to God's word to practice it. And Paul said, you remember, that we need to "learn not to go beyound the things that are written." It is *no part of apostolic doctrine*. If he denies this, I call upon him to show where it is found in apostolic doctrine.

HERALD OF TRUTH IS UNAUTHORIZED... THEREFORE IT IS...

1. PRESUMPTIVE NUM. 15:30; PSM. 19:13
2. LAWLESS I JNO. 3:4
3. INIQUITIOUS MT. 7:23
4. TRANSGRESSIVE I JNO. 3:4; 2 JNO. 9
5. DIGRESSIVE GAL. 6:1; I COR. 4:6
6. NOT APOSTOLIC DOCTRINE ACTS 2:42
7. NOT ACT OF FAITH 2 COR. 5:7
8. GOES BEYOND 2 JNO. 9; REV. 22:18,19
9. DESTROYS PERFECTION 2 TIM. 3:16,17
10. DESECRATES GOD'S SILENCE
    I PET. 4:11; I COR. 4:6
11. VIOLATES LAW OF EXCLUSION
    GEN. 6:14
12. UNHOLY HEB 9:23; LK. 22:20
13. HAUGHTY ROM. 12:3; JER 10:23
14. NOT A GOOD WORK 2 TIM. 3:16,17
15. DOES NOT PERTAIN TO LIFE
    2 PET. 1:3
16. PERVERSIVE 2 PET. 3:16
17. RENDERS WORSHIP VAIN MT. 15:9
18. DIVISIVE I COR. 1:10; I COR. 10:23

It is *not an act of faith*. The Bible says we walk by faith and we do not walk by sight. He has not found it in the pages of God's word. It *goes beyond the word of God*, and the word of God says that "whosoever goeth onward and abideth not in the teaching of Christ hath not God." It *destroys perfection*. The word of God throughly furnishes us unto every good work. But it is not to be found in God's word, and it destroys, therefore, God's divine perfection. It *desecrates God's silence*. Peter said, "if any man speak, let him speak as the oracles of God." You cannot defend this and speak as the oracles of God. It *violates God's law of exclusion*. It is contrary to the pattern of congregational cooperation taught in the word of God. It is not to be found in the New Testament, and since it is not to be found in the New Testament, it is *not sanctified by the blood of Christ*, and as such, it is an *unholy* practice. Furthermore, it is *haughty*. Like I said over here (pointing to chart), it is presumptive. It is haughty. In Jeremiah 10:23 the word of God says, "it is not in man that walketh to direct his own steps." But they are going to practice it whether they have a command, or example, or a necessary inference, either general or specific, for it.

First Night, Cooperation

Further, it *does not pertain to life or godliness*, because the things that pertain to life and godliness are to be found in God's word. It is *perversive*. You have to twist scripture in order to defend it. You cannot find it taught clearly in God's word. It *renders our worship vain*, because "in vain do they worship me teaching as their doctrine the commandments of men." And in the 18th place, it is *divisive*, and they have admitted it is. It has already divided two churches he said he knows about, and I can tell him about a whole lot more. And I have an idea that you brethren also could tell him about a whole lot more.

And it makes these brethren *pervert* some things. They would have us to believe they have a hundred million listeners—a hundred million *listeners!* (Bible Herald, August 1, 1959.) They would have us to believe that they are preaching for thirty cents per thousand listeners (Firm Foundation, March 17, 1959), and yet you write to the network and they will tell you that they are the lowest on the totem pole! The network lists eleven network programs and they are the lowest on the totem pole. The network says they have 200,000 listeners (letter from ABC, July 25, 1966). They tell us they are sending it into about 116,000,000 *homes*. There are only about 200,000,000 people in the United States, and they say they are sending it into over 100,000,000 *homes*. So, I say it makes them pervert the truth of God.

Now you might just take this into consideration: they advertise they have 100,000,000 listeners (and I have some of their advertisements). The world series will be coming up shortly. They estimate that 45,000,000 people will listen to that. And yet these brethren are saying that we are going to have twice that many listening to the Herald of Truth every Sunday. The network says they have about 200,000 listeners—one-fifth of *one* million! And if they can preach for what they tell us they can preach for (thirty cents a thousand listeners), they can conduct this program reaching 200,000 people for $60.00 a week! That is what it will cost with their 200,000 listeners. If you preach to a thousand of them for thirty cents, it will cost you about sixty dollars a week to run that program. (Time called.) I am sorry. I did not see the notice. I thought you said one minute. All right, come back tomorrow night.

PROPOSITION

"RESOLVED THAT IT IS UNSCRIPTURAL FOR ONE OR MORE CONGREGATIONS TO SEND MONEY FROM THEIR TREASURIES TO ANOTHER CONGREGATION (HIGHLAND AVENUE IN ABILENE OR ANY OTHER), FOR THE PURPOSE OF SUPPORTING A NATIONWIDE RADIO BROADCAST OR TELECAST (HERALD OF TRUTH OR OTHER), WHICH BROADCAST OR TELECAST IS SUPERVISED BY THE CONGREGATION RECEIVING THE FUNDS."

Affirmative: Cecil Willis
Negative: Clifton Inman

WILLIS' FIRST AFFIRMATIVE

It certainly is a pleasure to appear before you this evening to engage further in this discussion. We had last evening what I consider to be a very good session. I enjoyed it immensely and I trust that it was somewhat profitable unto you. I am pleased to see the number that we have present. Brother Inman had me a little fearful that we would not have many present. He said he thought there would be about 100 present, and after some attention was given to the attendance last night, I think we had about five times that many present. So that is indicative that a goodly number of you people are interested in studies of this sort. Of course, for that fact we are most appreciative.

We are engaging this evening in a continuation of the study that we began last night. In just a moment we will discuss the actual proposition that I am affirming this evening. But I want to make a few remarks concerning some questions that were handed out last evening. Brother Inman passed out some questions last evening, and I did not get the connection he made between his first list of questions and some observations that were made in connection with those. He asked the question, "What is the point of error?" I presume he meant in the Herald of Truth, in the sponsoring church arrangement. "Is it the act of broadcasting?" And then in point No. 1 below he said, "broadcasting is teaching." So I want to answer: No, the point of error is not broadcasting.

Secondly, he said, "Is it the extent that it is nationwide, or that it is a network program?" And then he says in the second place below that teaching is unlimited. Actually I might answer: No, it is not the extent. So far as the work of one congregation is concerned, the elders of a church have the perfect liberty to carry on any program of any magnitude that is within the scope of the ability of that congregation. But what we are objecting to is the *centralization of control* and the *pooling of resources* of several thousand churches under one eldership.

Thirdly, "Is it sending money from one congregation to another?" And then below, he said, "Money was sent from one congregation to another." I am not objecting to sending money from one congregation to another, *if it is done according to the passages that are cited on his sheet of paper* (Acts 11:27-28; 1 Corinthians 16:1-4). And in those instances the churches to whom money was sent were destitute churches. I do not object to money being sent to a church which is destitute, but *Highland* is not a destitute church. It is one of the richest churches in the world.

Fourthly, he said, "Is it what the money is used for?" And I answer: that partly is what is wrong with it. We showed last night that only 50% of all of the money that is sent to the Highland elders to manage the Herald of Truth radio and television program actually goes to buy broadcast time. That is partly what is wrong with it, but that is not all that is wrong with it. Brother Inman adds, in his fourth observation here, that there is no specification or that there is no limitation of the monies used. Now I beg to differ with that. I think I can show in the word of God that there *is* a specification. You know, if there is no specification, you can take the church's money and start handing out popsicles and ice cream cones on the street with it, if there is no specification.

And if there is not any limitation on what a church can do with its money, then you could take that money and send it to a missionary society, Brother Inman. Furthermore, Brother Inman says *he* makes a specification and limitation. I understand that Brother Inman thinks it is a *sin* for a church to take its money and send it to Ohio Valley College. Now if he thinks that is a sin, then that is a specification and that is a limitation on what a church can do with its money. If he limits it in any way, then this is a false statement that there is no specification or limitation on monies used.

I asked some questions last night. I did not get many answers. Maybe I asked too many questions. I asked five. And I gave them to him 20 minutes before the session started, and I still did not get any answer to most of those questions last evening. So I decided I would just ask three this evening and see if maybe I could get these three questions answered. I have given Brother Inman a copy of these questions. He said last night that the missionary society was wrong because it violated the New Testament order. You remember, he went on to say that there is not any pattern. So I am asking this question: *"What New Testament order does the missionary society violate which the Herald of Truth does not also violate?"*

Last night you twice called the messengers of 2 Corinthians 8 "delegates." That may have been inadvertently done. I do not know. But twice you called those messengers "delegates." So I want to know, Brother Inman, *"Would you please explain what you meant by delegate?"* Now I looked up the word "delegate", and here is what the dictionary says it means. It means "a person acting for another, as a representative to a convention or a conference." I want to know if he is trying to tell us that is what those messengers were. Were they representatives to a convention or to a conference? I wonder if he meant they had voting rights. Actually, I might just observe in passing, that the missionary society is at least more democratic than the Herald of Truth. In the Herald of Truth, you people who participate in it, have "taxation *without* representation." In the missionary society you have taxation *with* representation through a delegate feature.

And then thirdly, I again ask a question that I asked last night. *"Whose work is the Herald of Truth?"* And, *"How do we know which church the Lord intended to be a sponsoring church and which he intended to be merely contributing churches?"* Last night he said it was the work of the sponsoring church to *oversee,* and it is the work of the contributing church to *contribute.* I want to know, how do we find out which churches the Lord intends to be *sponsoring* churches and which ones the Lord intends to be merely *contributing* churches.

Now the proposition we are discussing this evening has already been read, and it is before you. I want to accept the definitions of terms Brother Inman gave last night, so far as he went. I do not have any objections to the definitions of terms, as far as he went. The only objection I have is that he did not go far enough, and he did not really show you what is involved in the Herald of Truth. I want to emphasize that we are not this evening just discussing the scripturalness of a radio or a television program.

Turn to chart No. 3, please. I want to use again the chart we used last night to show you what is actually involved in what Brother Inman is supposed to be defending. In this arrangement, we have presently 1999 churches sending money to the elders at Highland in order that they might put on a radio and television program. And I am not objecting to a radio and television program. There have been altogether 3199 churches that have relinquished the oversight of their funds to the elders at Highland. And

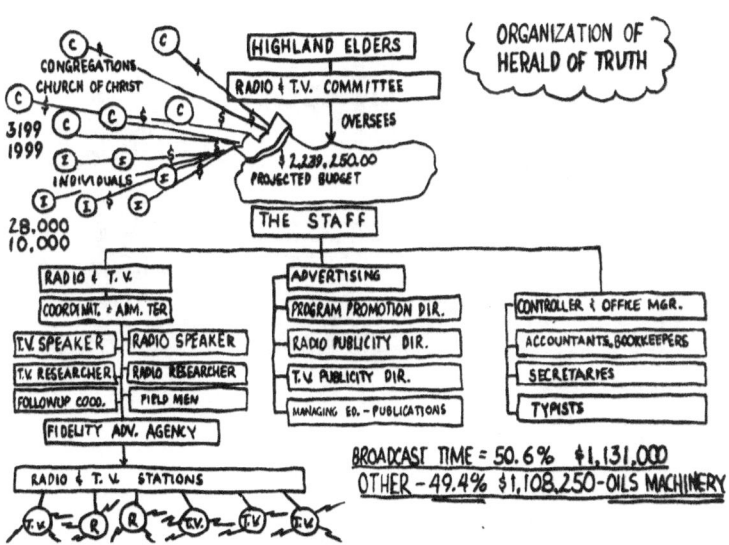

we are not just objecting to a radio program. We are objecting to 1999 churches trying to work through the eldership of one church. And when Brother Inman gets up here to present his evidence this evening to substantiate *that*, he is supposed to give us scriptural testimony. Last night he was supposed to have given us Bible authority for 1999 churches working through the eldership of one church.

Let us now turn to chart No. 4, please. Last evening I made a number of arguments in opposition to several hundred or thousand churches working through one eldership. And one argument I made last night against the Herald of Truth was that it entails a sinful waste of money. Now we are not just discussing the Herald of Truth. We are discussing sponsoring churches in general and if he wants to cite some instances *larger* than the Herald of Truth, we will talk about those. We will lump them together if they are operated like that. If he wants to talk about some sponsoring church arrangements *smaller* than the Herald of Truth, the same principles will apply.

OPERATION OF HERALD OF TRUTH

ANALYSIS OF BUDGET:

BROADCAST TIME	50.6%	$ 1,131,000
BROADCAST PRODUCTION	21.2%	474,200
ANSWER RESPONSE	7.9%	177,500
LISTENER PROMOTION	4.7%	104,500
GEN. AND ADM.	4.5%	100,450
MISC. AND CONTINGENCY	2.4%	55,500
FUND RAISING	8.8%	196,100
	100.0%	$ 2,239,250

INCLUDES THESE ITEMS:		E.F.T.P.
PAYROLL AND SALARY COSTS	$ 219,400	(36)
RESEARCH	85,000	(14)
POSTAGE	66,500	(11)
TELEPHONE	12,000	(2)
PRINTING AND SUPPLIES	203,000	(54)
CONTINGENCY	55,500	(9)
TOTAL BUDGET	$ 2,239,250	(373)

E.F.T.P. = EQUIVALENT FULL TIME PREACHERS @ $6,000* PER YEAR

COMPARATIVE FIGURES:	UNITED APPEAL - CLEVELAND	HERALD OF TRUTH	
GEN., ADM., MISC. & FUND RAISING	3.8%	15.7%	
		TOTAL $ 351,590	(58)

* PER ERNST & ERNST AUDIT AS OF DEC. 31, 1965

We are talking, first of all, about the sinful waste of money. They intend to take in $2,239,250.00 a year for this program. And last night it was pointed out what they were going to be spending that money for. They are going to spend $85,000.00 of it in some kind of research. And we suggested last night it might be good to use that money that would pay 14 gospel preachers $6,000.00 a year each, that it might be well to employ those men, to try to find some Bible authority for a practice like this.

And also we pointed out that $66,500.00 of the money that brethren are sending down there is being used to buy postage; $12,000,00 of it each year is spent on telephone bills; $203,000.00 of it each year is being used to pay printing and supply costs. We simply were answering his expediency argument last night. Even if he could prove that this is scriptural, it is not expedient. It entails a sinful waste of money.

Secondly, we pointed out that the Highland church sets a bad example before the church and the world in that it does three things. Highland, first of all, is a *perpetual beggar.* They have been beggars ever since they started this program. Secondly, Highland continually *obligates herself beyond her ability to pay. Thirdly,* Highland *seeks to get control* of other churches' resources. We argued last night, that if that is a good example, then all of the other churches ought to be doing the same thing.

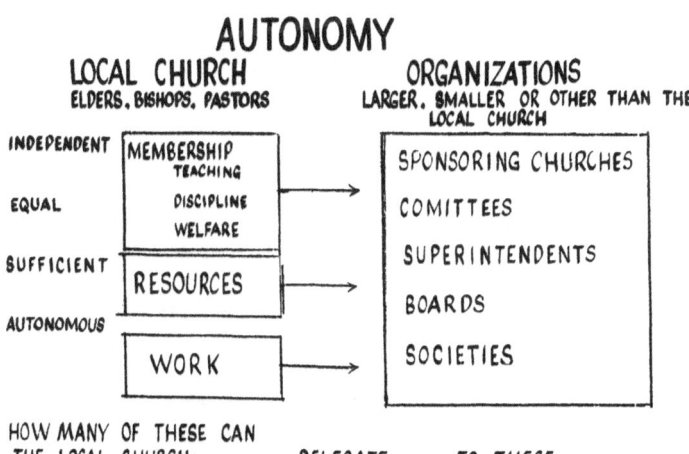

We further showed that in the operation of the Herald of Truth the autonomy of either the *contributing* or the *sponsoring* church is violated and we used chart No. 16 on that.

Further we argued that since there is neither command, example, nor necessary inference for the sponsoring church arrangement, then there is not any such arrangement authorized in the New Testament. I remind you again, Brother Inman, that I will take either generic or specific authority for that; generic or specific command, example, or necessary inference.

WHERE IS THE AUTHORITY?

COMMAND _____

APPROVED EXAMPLE _____

NECESSARY INFERENCE _____
GENERAL OR SPECIFIC!

Give me chart No. 7, please. We argued last night that it is, therefore, unauthorized and since it is *unauthorized* it is something that is *lawless, presumptuous, transgressive, digressive.* It is *not apostolic doctrine.* It is *not an act of faith.* It *goes beyond.* It *destroys perfection.* It *desecrates God's silence.* It *violates the law of exclusion.* It is *unholy.* It is *haughty.* It is *not a good work.* It *does not pertain to life and godliness.* It is *perversive.* It *renders worship vain* and it is *divisive.* Those were the points that we made last night.

HERALD OF TRUTH IS UNAUTHORIZED... THEREFORE IT IS...

1. PRESUMPTIVE NUM. 15:30; PSM. 19:13
2. LAWLESS 1 JNO. 3:4
3. INIQUITIOUS MT. 7:23
4. TRANSGRESSIVE 1 JNO. 3:4; 2 JNO. 9
5. DIGRESSIVE GAL. 6:1; 1 COR. 4:6
6. NOT APOSTOLIC DOCTRINE ACTS 2:42
7. NOT ACT OF FAITH 2 COR. 5:7
8. GOES BEYOND 2 JNO. 9; REV. 22:18,19
9. DESTROYS PERFECTION 2 TIM. 3:16,17
10. DESECRATES GOD'S SILENCE 1 PET. 4:11; 1 COR. 4:6
11. VIOLATES LAW OF EXCLUSION GEN. 6:14
12. UNHOLY HEB 9:23; LK. 22:20
13. HAUGHTY ROM. 12:3; JER 10:23
14. NOT A GOOD WORK 2 TIM. 3:16,17
15. DOES NOT PERTAIN TO LIFE 2 PET. 1:3
16. PERVERSIVE 2 PET. 3:16
17. RENDERS WORSHIP VAIN MT. 15:9
18. DIVISIVE 1 COR. 1:10; 1 COR. 10:23

Now then, let us proceed a little further and observe that this sponsoring church concept began *this side of* the New Testament, and not only this side of the New Testament but *outside of* the New Testament. And I am simply citing here some historical references to substantiate this, and every man that I am quoting from tonight agreed with Brother Inman on this point.

G. C. Brewer told us *when* the sponsoring church concept began. He said in sponsoring a missionary, a church simply underwrites his support. "It is, therefore, responsible to the missionary for the amount that it takes for his maintenance and is also responsible to any brethren who may be willing to help in his support for the missionary's soundness, for his Christian character, and for his qualifications as a missionary." Now get it, *when* did it start? "This whole idea was born because of a very sad condition which existed in the brotherhood *forty or fifty years ago.*" (*Gospel Advocate*, August 27, 1953, p. 544.) He said that in the *Gospel Advocate* in 1953. That is why Brother Inman has not found it in the New Testament. It only started forty or fifty years ago, about 1900.

Furthermore, Brother William Banowsky, in a recently published book, not only tells us *when* it started, but he tells us *where* it came from. Here is what he has to say about it. He says, "The absence of an organized missionary society among churches of Christ created several unique handicaps . . ." (That is an indictment of what God gave to us.) . . ."in selection and preparation of qualified missionary workers. Since no official board existed, congregations were free to select and send." But the lecturers at Abilene Christian College, he said, "came to desire a missionary procedure which would more effectively involve the hundreds of small congregations. But they also sought a program whose scope would be more far reaching than even the best, but isolated efforts of any one large congregation." Where did it come from? Listen. *"They could not resist the temptation to shop about and contrast their plight with the obvious strong points in denominational machinery."* (William Banowsky, The Mirror of a Movement, p. 273, 274, 313.) There is where it came from. They started "shopping about" and they saw that the "denominational machinery" used this type thing, so he said. What did they come up with? The sponsoring church.

Banowsky further said, "At the Abilene lectureship, a momentous Biblical principle governing missionary methods was articulated and recommended as a remedy for this brotherhood predicament. The principle was described as inter-congregational cooperation without ecclesiastical organization. It greatly expanded the scope of the church's evangelistic opportunities and led logically to the recognition of the special role of sponsoring churches, or the sponsoring congregation as compared with the part to be played by the smaller participating churches." (*The Mirror of a Movement*, p. 313.) So we looked around and saw sectarianism with the sponsoring church and we borrowed that from them, and the result was we *denominationalized the church*.

Brother G. C. Brewer said this about the Herald of Truth: "When the Herald of Truth broadcast of Abilene, Texas, was proposed, I told the brethren who were soliciting help for the venture that it would put the Lord's church before the world as a denomination. . ." (Well, it ought to. This idea came from denominationalism.) ". . . and this program would be the *Church of Christ Hour* just as distinctly

SECOND NIGHT, COOPERATION 69

as we have a *Catholic Hour* and *Lutheran Hour*. The brethren said they would avoid this by calling it the Herald of Truth. This they have done, but they have not avoided the error that I feared." (G. C. Brewer, *Autobiography*, p. 139.) And then he adds, "The greatest grief of my soul as I face eternity (This is written just before his death) is the fact that brethren have seemingly almost universally denominationalized the church." (page 119.) So we see *when* it began—about 40 or 50 years ago. *Where* did it come from? It came from denominationalism, and the *result* was that it denominationalized the church.

Now let us notice another argument, and that is that *the Herald of Truth radio and television program exists as a type of congregational cooperation that is without scriptural precedent*. More specifically, it is contrary to, or it violates, the New Testament pattern of congregational cooperation. Now then let us notice this chart here right behind me. In Hebrews 8:5 we are given the admonition to

ACCORDING TO THE PATTERN - HEB. 8:5
SCRIPTURES COMPLETELY FURNISH US - 2 TIM. 3:16-17, 2 PET. 1:3

THE PATTERN:

WORSHIP	VIOLATIONS
LORD'S SUPPER (ACTS 20:7)	BACON AND EGGS
SINGING (1 COR. 14:15)	THURSDAY NIGHT OBSERVANCE
PRAYER (ACTS 2:42)	INSTRUMENTAL MUSIC
GIVING (1 COR. 16:1-2)	COUNTING BEADS
TEACHING (1 THES. 5:27)	CAKE SALES---- RUMMAGES
WORK	
EDIFICATION - (EPH. 4:16)	ENTERTAINMENT PARTIES ETC.
EVANGELISM -(1 TIM. 3:15)	COMMERCIAL BUSINESS
BENEVOLENCE -(ACTS 6:1-4)	BALL TEAMS, BOY SCOUTS
ORGANIZATION	SUBSIDIZE HUMAN INST.
PLURALITY OF ELDERS-(ACTS 14:23, PHIL. 1:1)	ONE PASTOR- BOARD OF DIRECTORS
DEACONS - (1 TIM. 3:8 FF)	STEWARDS,
EVANGELISTS -(2 TIM. 4:5)	BOARDS, SYNODS, ETC.
SAINTS - (EPH. 1:1-2)	
COOPERATION	
INDEPENDENT ACTION OF CHURCHES-(PHIL. 4:14-16) (1 THES. 1:7-8)	JOINT ACTION OF CONGR.
NO OTHER ORGANIZATION THAN THE CHURCH. (PHIL. 1:1)	HUMAN ORGANIZATIONS
ELDERS OVERSEEING WORK - ONE CONGREGATION (1 PET. 5:2-3)	CATHOLIC POPE
AUTONOMY OF EACH CHURCH. (SELF-GOVERNING) (ACTS 20:28)	CENTRALIZATION OF FUNDS & WORK

OPPONENT JOINS THE SECTARIANS AND MODERNISTS WHO SAY THERE IS NO PATTERN !

"build all things according to the pattern." We find, further, that the scriptures thoroughly furnish us unto every good work. Consequently, we have argued for a good many years that there is a pattern in the New Testament as to how we are to worship, and that there are certain things that are violations of that pattern. When you deviate from the pattern, you violate the pattern. Thus, we have a pattern in worship.

We also have specifications as to what the church is to do, a pattern in work. We have also stated in the Word of God the organization of the church; thus a pattern in organization, and these over here (pointing to "violations" on chart) constitute violations of that pattern. And in a like manner, we have a pattern in congregational cooperation. The pattern is, according to Philippians 4:14-16 and 1 Thessalonians 1:7-8, *independent* action of churches. Now you violate that when you have *joint* action of churches.

We might also note that the pattern in the New Testament was that there was no other organization than the church (Philippians 1:1). Now Brother Inman said we do not have any other organization than the church, but you listen to him Thursday and Friday and he will be defending another organization. In the New Testament (1 Peter 5:1-5), the elders were overseeing the work of one church. It said, "tend the flock of God which is among you." And any time we turn the oversight of the work of the church over to anybody else, whether it be a pope, or sponsoring elders, or a conference, or a convention, we have violated the pattern. Each church was autonomous, that is, it was self-governing. But in this arrangement we have the centralization of the control of the pooled funds.

Turn the chart, please, brethren. We now want chart No. 2. I want to notice with you further what the Bible says concerning how churches cooperated in the New Testament. This chart is entitled, "How Churches May Cooperate: Answers Given." There are just two answers that can be given. One is from divine wisdom, and one is from human wisdom. Divine wisdom said that they were to act *independently*, even though on some occasions they might act concurrently, or at the same time. Human wisdom said they could act *jointly*. They could pool their resources and they could centralize their control.

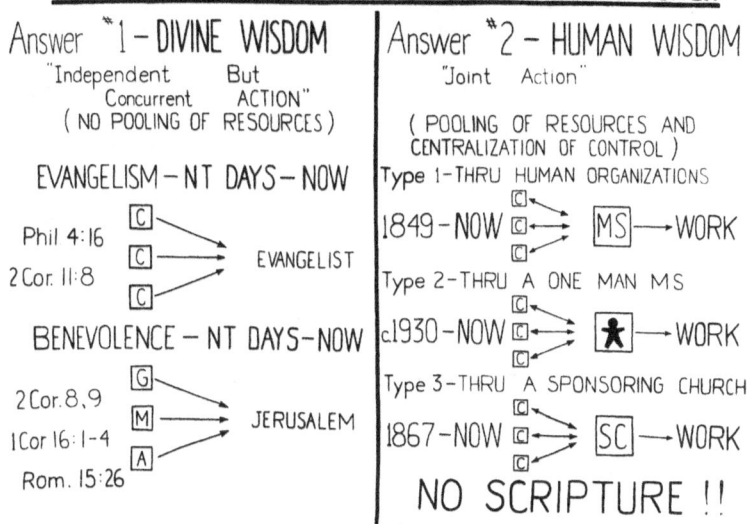

In the New Testament, in evangelism in every instance that Brother Inman can cite, when a gospel preacher was being supported, the wages for his support went directly unto the evangelist. The Bible tells us that Paul said, "when I departed from Macedonia, no church had fellowship with me in the matter of giving and receiving but ye only; for even in Thessalonica ye sent once and again unto my need." (Phil. 4:16). And then further he said in 2 Corinthians 11: 8, "I robbed other churches", a plurality of churches. He even names the brother that brought the money over there (Philippians 4:10-18). So this money was not sent to a sponsoring church who in turn then sent it to the evangelist.

Now then, in benevolent work in New Testament days, and unto the present, faithful churches of the Lord Jesus Christ have practiced this (pointing to "Benevolence" on chart). On some occasions, when there were destitute churches, the other churches sent to their relief. In 2 Corinthians 8 and 9, 1 Corinthians 16:1-4 and Romans 15:26, we find that Galatia, Macedonia, and Achaia sent to relieve the poor saints that were in Jerusalem. They selected their messengers and they sent the funds.

Now over here (under "Human Wisdom" on the chart) brethren said that churches could *pool their resources* and *centralize the control* of them through missionary societies. More recently, men have said churches can pool their resources and centralize the control of them through a one-man missionary society. And now, Brother Inman tonight is saying that churches can pool their resources, act jointly, and centralize the control of these resources through what he calls a sponsoring church. And there is not any scripture for that.

Turn the chart please. Now there is one other instance of where a church sent to another church or churches in the Bible. We gave you one (2 Corinthians 8 and 9; 1 Corinthians 16:1-4), where Galatia, Macedonia, and Achaia sent to Jerusalem. The other instance is Acts 11:27-30, where we find the brethren at Antioch sent relief unto the brethren that dwelt in Judea and they sent this money, the Bible says, by the hands of Paul and Barnabas unto the elders that were in Judea.

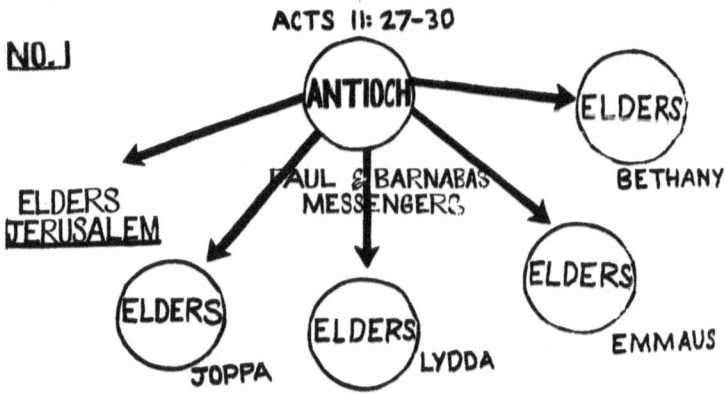

SECOND NIGHT, COOPERATION 73

Brother Inman tried rather hard last night to make a sponsoring church out of Jerusalem. He tried to say that they sent that money over to Jerusalem and then they distributed it throughout Judea. Now he would like to prove that, wouldn't he? But what he has so far is merely his assumption, his statement. He cannot prove that to save his life. But, my friend, that is what he *must* prove. In order to substantiate his proposition, he must prove that money came to Jerusalem, and then they violated the autonomy of these other Judean churches, and went out here and distributed that money among the members of the other churches. Now he must prove that, and he cannot prove it. The Bible says the scope of the authority of elders is *limited*. We have now before us two instances in the Bible where a church sent to another church. In both instances, the receiving church was destitute.

Now brethren, *Highland is not a destitute church.* I have before me some of their bulletins. On April 19, 1964, their contribution at Highland totaled $10,182.57. Does that sound like a needy church? Further another bulletin dated September 4, 1965, their contribution is said to total $16,325.99. Does that sound like a needy church? Now if it does not, Highland does not fit the pattern. On December 13, 1964, their contributions totaled $37,150.19. That is not talking about the Herald of Truth contribution. That is talking about their local contributions. In 1964 their local contributions totaled $375,000.00 and yet they are perpetual beggars of other people's money. This year their budget is over $400,000.00 and on September 1, 1966, their bulletin reported that so far they are averaging about $7,500.00 a week in contributions. Yet they would have you believe that they are a needy church and are, therefore, appealing to brethren that they might send them money.

Now let us notice chart No. 15. This is a brotherhood work; it is not their work. It is a brotherhood work. In the work that Brother Inman is to defend this evening, we have a *brotherhood eldership* to oversee a *brotherhood treasury* that is carrying on a *brotherhood work*. We have a lot of churches out here that are sending to various sponsoring churches, such as Broadway in Lubbock, Highland, and Central. They in turn send their money to the Herald of Truth that has its own *treasury*. The Herald of Truth's money is not even kept in the same bank where Highland's money is

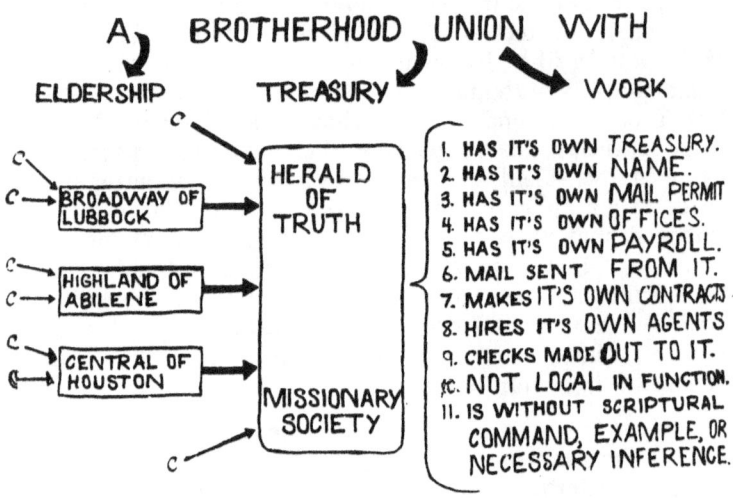

kept. It has its own *name*, its own *mailing permit*, its own *offices*, its own *payroll*. They send out their own *mail*. Herald of Truth makes its own *contracts*. You are to write out your checks to "Herald of Truth." They have their own *agents*. It is not local in function, and it is without scriptural precedent, either by command, example, or by necessary inference.

Chart No. 18 please. Now they do not know whose work it is. Brother Inman was honest with you last night when he did not tell you whose work it is. I wanted to know, "Was it the sponsoring church's or was it the contributing churches'?" He does not know whose it is, and I put some blanks on the chart so he can tell us tonight. Now sometimes they have said this is the work of the Highland congregation. The elders out there at Highland said it was their work for awhile, but later on they said, we want to give you some information about "this *your* national broadcast." (*Looking Ahead*, 1952, p. 2.) It is not Highland's; now, it is *yours*.

If it is a brotherhood work, I want to know what business Highland elders have overseeing it, *unless they are brotherhood elders*. Furthermore, Brother John Reese, one

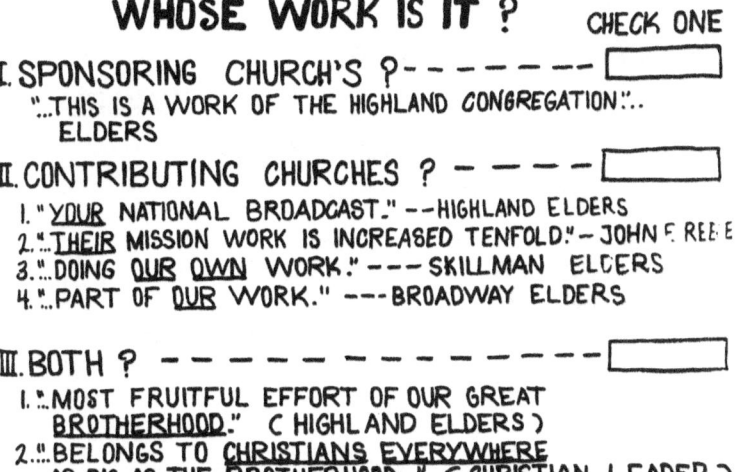

of the elders out there until his death, said that' when churches send the money, they are increasing *"their* mission work" ten fold. (Letter to N. Military St. Church in Lawrenceburg, Tenn.) Now if it is *"their* mission work", what are the Highland elders doing overseeing it? The Skillman Avenue elders in Dallas said that they were doing their *"own* work" when they sent to Highland. (Quoted in *Cogdill—Woods Debate,* p. 199) The Broadway elders in Lubbock said, "it is part of *our* work." *(Cogdill— Woods Debate,* p. 199.) Now then, I want Brother Inman to get up and tell *whose* work it is.

Now sometimes they say it belongs to both contributing and sponsoring churches. They say, "it is the most fruitful effort of our great *brotherhood"* (Brochure), and it " 'belongs' to Christians" everywhere. *(Christian Leader,* April 14, 1953.) The only pretense under which Highland elders can oversee it is to argue that it is the work of the Highland Church.

And I would like another chart now, chart No. 17. If it is not the work of the Highland church, I want him to tell us what business they have overseeing it. If he is going to argue that it is the work of the Highland church, I want

WHAT MAKES IT HIGHLAND'S WORK?

1. HIGHLAND DID NOT START IT.
2. HIGHLAND DID NOT SELECT THE SPEAKERS.
3. HIGHLAND DOES NOT PAY FOR IT.
   - LESS THAN 1% (.83) IN 1952
   - LESS THAN 1% (.51) IN 1954
   - 2.3% IN 1965
   - 3.1% IN 1966
   - 2.4.% OF THE NEW PROPOSED BUDGET.
4. HIGHLAND COULD NOT STOP IT.

to know *what makes it Highland's work? First, Highland did not start it.* It was first in Madison, Wisconsin and in Cedar Rapids, Iowa. They had the Herald of Truth up there and some fellows decided that if they were ever going to make much of this thing, we had better get it down where the big churches are, where a lot of money is. Thus, they moved it down to Texas, and put it first under the elders of the College church in Abilene. And soon the College church elders decided they did not have any business trying to oversee something like that. So they moved it over yet to a third church (Highland). I say, then, they did not start it.

Secondly, it is not Highland's work because *Highland did not select the preachers.* Let me tell you what the Highland elders said. Some asked, why did Highland pick James Walter Nichols and James Willeford, two young preachers, instead of older preachers to do the speaking. Highland replied, "The elders were on the wrong side of the table to pick." (*Firm Foundation,* July 14, 1953.) I wonder if that is the way you elders deal with your preachers. I tell you, that is not the way the elders where I preach deal with this preacher. Highland elders said, "we" were on the wrong side of the table to pick. "The whole idea was a 'brainchild' born out of the mind of Nichols and Willeford," the Highland elders said.

SECOND NIGHT, COOPERATION 77

And so I say, Highland did not start it. They did not select the preachers. Furthermore, *they do not pay for it.* They paid less than 1% of the money that was spent in 1952, less than 1% in 1954, and in 1965 they paid 2%. This year they are proposing to pay 3%. Really what that means, brethren, is that every time they put down $2.00, somebody else plunks in a hundred dollar bill! Now you know, I could settle my financial problems rather quickly if somebody would do that for me. If every time I put two pennies down you plunk down a dollar by it and say, now you can have that. And every time I put down $2.00, somebody else puts in $100.00. That is what is being done in the Herald of Truth. So I want to know precisely, *"what makes it Highland's work?",* if it is Highland's work. Highland did not start it; they did not select the preachers; they do not pay for it.

Furthermore, *they could not stop it.* The fellows who have moved it twice all ready could just move it again. If the elders said "we do not want to oversee it," the preachers who have moved it twice could just move it again. Hence, I want to know *what makes it their work?* If it is not their work, then I want to know what business they have overseeing a work that belongs to the brotherhood.

Now brethren, these are precisely the issues that are involved in this present discussion. I do not believe I will have time to make the other argument that I had intended to make. (A brother gives him a two-minute signal.) Two minutes. I will take that other argument up in the next speech. I might have time briefly to introduce it.

I would like to go on to chart No. 14. I am charging further, that not only are we making brotherhood elders out of the elders at the Highland church, but that *this is an effort on the part of the Highland church to activate the church universal through the elders of the Highland church.* Now as we study in the New Testament, we find the word church occurs about 110 times. Eighteen times it refers to the church universal, but we do not have any earthly *organization* for the church universal, no headquarters. We do not have any earthly *officers.* We do not have any earthly *mission* for the church universal.

But on the other hand, the church local does have an *organization,* the congregation (Philippians 1:1). It does have *officers,* elders and deacons (Acts 14:23 and 1 Timothy 3:1-13), and it does have a *mission* (Ephesians 4:12).

THE CHURCH

UNIVERSAL (18 TIMES)	LOCAL (92 TIMES)
1. NO EARTHLY ORGANIZATION	1. HAS AN ORGANIZATION — PHIL. 1:1
2. NO EARTHLY OFFICERS	2. HAS OFFICERS — ACTS 14:23; 1 TIM. 3:1-13
3. NO EARTHLY MISSION	3. HAS MISSION — EPH. 4:11-12,16; ACTS 6:1-6; PHIL. 4:15,16
	<u>ONLY FUNCTIONAL UNIT IN N.T.</u>

The congregation is the *only* functional unit that God put here to do the work that He assigned His church to do. But the Highland brethren are trying to activate the church universal through a sponsoring church, just as brethren in the past have tried to activate it through a one-man missionary society. Our brethren before that tried to activate it through the missionary society, and this is an unscriptural activation of the church universal. But we will speak further concerning this point in the speech that we will make in closing on this proposition. We will move the chart now for Brother Inman and I have some questions of his that I will deal with in just a few minutes.

INMAN'S FIRST NEGATIVE

Again this evening I want to express my appreciation also for the presence of each one, and again to say that the situation that faces us today is too serious for me to approach it and try to find an answer for it in any way except to turn to the Word of our God. We want a scriptural answer to the questions we have before us. I would like again to point out what that question is. Do we have the chart with the proposition on it? "Resolved that it is unscriptural (That is contrary to the scriptures) for one or more congregations to send money from their treasuries to another congregation, Highland Avenue or any other (That may be Marrtown Road), for the purpose of supporting a nation-wide radio broadcast or telecast, whether it be named the Herald of Truth or have some other name, which broadcast or telecast is supervised by the congregation receiving the funds."

Now this is the proposition we are supposed to discuss. Our question is not whether Highland Avenue, in operating a broadcast, has used poor judgment. The question is not whether they have sinned. But the question is, is it unscriptural, is it contrary to the scripture and a violation of the scriptures, for one or more congregations to send money from their treasuries to another congregation for them to use this money to put on a broadcast or a telecast? That is the question that he signed to affirm this evening. That this is unscriptural, contrary to the scriptures. Not that Highland Avenue, in operating a broadcast, may have violated the scriptures somewhere along the line, but whether or not this principle violates the scriptures.

We will try to notice his charts. They get rather lengthy. I told someone last evening they reminded me, Cecil, of the drunk over at Washington, D. C., who went there when they have leaves in the fall of the year around the Washington monument, and they were burning them and he said, "five will get you ten they will not get it off the ground." And I have come to wonder if some of these are going to get off the ground.

Let us notice, first of all, that he said that I failed to answer his questions last evening. Let us go over them again. I went over them; he replied to what I had to say about them. But came back this evening and said I did not say anything about them, that I did not answer them. Well, he spent quite a bit of time trying to reply to my answers last evening, a little too much to come back this evening and say that I did not answer them. Let us get them again.

"Does the New Testament reveal a pattern by which the Churches of Christ must operate? If so, where is the pattern for 3199 or 1999 churches working together through one eldership?" My answer to that was, Brother Willis, you claim there is a pattern. Give it, chapter and verse, please! He has not given it yet. I want to see that New Testament pattern. Now listen, if a woman here had a book of patterns for dresses and someone would say, now the pattern for this particular dress is not in that book, would someone get up and say, "they said there are no patterns in that book"? I am not saying there are not any patterns in the Bible. What I am saying is, give us the pattern from the Bible that tells us how money may be sent from the treasury of one congregation to another. Now let us have it or let us just back up and say, "brethren there just is not any such. I have been contending for something that is not there. I cannot show it." And he has not shown it yet. I want to see it.

Now last evening on the sheet of paper that I gave you, and on the back of the one I gave you this evening, we have 1 Corinthians 16:1-3 listed where Paul says "whomsoever ye shall approve by your letters, them will I send." Centralized control and oversight? Paul is sending them, Brother Willis. They had one or more volunteers: Titus (2 Corinthians 8:6). Then several churches went together and chose one man (2 Corinthians 8:19). "If anyone inquire concerning our brother, he is chosen of the churches."

And then each church chose delegates. What do I mean by delegates? All right, Brother Willis, one definition of a delegate is someone sent to the House of Representatives of the United States. That is not the one I meant. I meant exactly what the dictionary says here: "One sent and empowered to act for another." They were sent. The church could not take the money. Therefore, they empowered someone else to take it for them. That is what I meant. They delegated these men to carry it. The church, all of them together, could not take it, and they delegated, that is they sent someone else to do what they could not do. And I did not mean anything about sending for a conference. There happens to be a semi-colon here, and if you find the other definition about going to conference, I will give you one about going to the United States Congress. Then you can say that I was talking about sending to the United States Congress. That is exactly what I meant by delegate. Each church then chose delegates (1 Corinthians 16:3; 2 Corinthians 8:23). Is this the pattern? Is this the way, Brother Willis, that you think a congregation today must take money or send money, if they send it, from one congregation over to another?

"Whose work is the Herald of Truth, the sponsoring church's, the contributing churches' or both?" I said last evening the work of the speaker is to speak. The work of the elders of the sponsoring church, or the ones that are immediately putting on the broadcast, is to oversee the speaker and the operation of this, and the work of the contributing churches is to contribute. Now he has been trying to leave the impression that when several congregations send money to another congregation, they give up their oversight.

Brother Willis, these congregations sent their money to the church at Jerusalem, and by the way, you never heard me say that last night at all. I just did not say it. I never said that they sent money to Jerusalem and Jerusalem sent it out. I did not say it. That is a question that has been argued, and I think there may be some worthwhile arguments here. But I did not make that argument because, personally, I think it is a little obscure. I did not make it, and I am not going to make it. You can get up and argue about it if you want to, but I did not make it. I do not know what was done there. Maybe you do. Some brethren think that they are very certain of this, but I just did not say it.

But money was sent from these congregations to Jerusalem and the Jerusalem elders then evidently saw after the dispensing of it. At least, in Acts 11 they sent it to the elders. Money was sent to elders and elders then, receiving this money from contributing churches, evidently used it. Now when they sent this money from Corinth and other places from which the money was sent, whose work was it when it was given to the poor saints in Jerusalem? Whose work was it? Was it Corinth's? Was it Philippi's? Whose work was it? Could it just possibly be that they were working jointly? That would be a terrible sin, wouldn't it?

"If it is scriptural for some of the churches to send some of their money to Highland church some of the time, would it be sinful for all of the churches to send all of their money all of the time to Highland? If your answer is yes, please cite the scriptures that the practice would violate."
Well, would it have been right for Corinth, Philippi and the other congregations to send all of their money all of the time up to Jerusalem?

You see we need to stay in the Bible. You know someone asked me sometime ago, are you getting boned up for this discussion? I said, well, I have an advantage over Brother Willis. I just have one book that I am going to be studying for this discussion and that is the Bible. He is going to be reading all of the old papers he can find. He is going to be going back and digging up all the books. He is going to try to get financial statements and dig all the scandal and slander and everything else he can. He is going to offer that, but I just have one book that I need to study, and that is the Bible. I have an advantage; I do not have to spend as much time as he does. And so I want to stay in the Bible. It is much easier when you do it that way.

He implies here that if it is all right to send any of the money, it is all right to send all of the money; if it is all right to send some of the money some of the time, it is all right to send all of the money all of the time. Then if they sent some of the money down to Paul some of the time, it is all right to send all of it all of the time. So they should have sent it all to Paul. Yes, I answered that one, Brother Willis, last night and again tonight.

"Where is a command, example, or necessary inference for one church sending money to another when the receiving church is not destitute?" Look at the paper that I gave you this evening at point No. 3 on "points to note." Money was sent to Paul while he was at Corinth. There is no indication that Corinth was suffering any financial distress or need. And yet this money that was sent to Paul

brought relief to them, so that they had funds to use for other things. In fact, in 2 Corinthians 8:14 Paul said that their abundance might be a supply to the need over at Jerusalem. They had an abundance down at Corinth, Brother Willis. They had an abundance there, a wealthy congregation, and yet money was sent to Paul to preach there. Does this give the passage?

"Does every church have a right to become a sponsoring church and solicit money from every other church? Or is this a special privilege belonging to Highland and other current sponsoring churches?" Each has a right within the bounds of expediency and good judgment, Brother Willis. Just to be sure that you do not forget that I have answered them, there are my notes (He hands them to Brother Willis) written out on it. I would like to have another blank copy when you get through.

Now, this evening's questions: *"You said last night the missionary society was wrong because it violated the New Testament order. What New Testament order does the missionary society violate which the Herald of Truth does not also violate?"* I do not have time tonight, and neither am I going to take time, to try to delineate all of the differences between a missionary society and the Herald of Truth because this is not my obligation; this is not the discussion. I am not here to debate the missionary society. Now if Brother Willis thinks that the scriptural principles set forth by me in this discussion also authorize the missionary society, if he will sign a proposition to debate that these principles authorize a missionary society, I will deny it, and I will be glad to have a debate with him on that any time he wants it. But we are talking about the scriptures as related to this thing, to this matter here(points to chart giving proposition).

"Last night you twice called the messengers of 2 Corinthians 8 delegates. Would you please explain what you meant by delegates?" One sent and empowered to act for another. They were sent to take the money when the men themselves could not go.

"Whose work is the Herald of Truth? And how do we know which church the Lord intended to be a sponsoring church and which he intended to be mere contributing churches?" Well, which church does God want to publish a

bulletin and which one does he not want to publish a bulletin? How do you determine which church the Lord wants to publish a bulletin and which one he does not want to publish a bulletin? We could run into this kind of quibble all night long. When an opportunity presents itself to do a good work, a congregation takes advantage of that and other congregations decide to help in this. This is within the authority of the New Testament and this is all that we need.

(Mimeographed sheet distributed by Brother Inman)

POINTS TO NOTE

1. What is authority?
2. Benevolence was always to relieve financial stress, so of necessity was given in time of stress.
3. Money was sent to Paul while he was at Corinth. No indication that Corinth was suffering financial stress.
4. Whether money was sent directly to Paul or to Paul through the church, the church was the beneficiary.

    Question: Would it be all right to have a nationwide broadcast or telecast if money were sent directly to preacher?

5. Money was not for Paul alone. He worked with his own hands, making tents. Acts 18:3. He used proceeds of his work for others. Acts 20:33, 34.
6. Paul and others went out from center of operation. (The church in Cenchrea; Titus left at Crete, etc.)
7. Willis says that helping Herald of Truth is not an expediency. Would it be all right if it were expedient?
8. A representative of Herald of Truth is reported to have said that some elders are truculent. He at least showed courtesy to elders of having representatives to call upon them. What courtesy is shown elders when lists of members are obtained and printed matter sent them without consent of elders and even over pleas of elders?
9. If elders lose oversight when money is sent from their treasury to that of another, then Macedonian and Achaian elders gave it over to Jerusalem.
10. Oversight of elders is primarily over people and not over things. Their oversight is over things only as these things relate to persons.

SECOND NIGHT, COOPERATION 85

WHAT IS THE POINT OF ERROR?

1. Is it the act of broadcasting?
2. Is it the extent—nationwide or network?
3. Is it sending money from one congregation to another?
4. Is it what the money is used for?

....

1. Broadcasting is teaching. Heb. 5:11
2. Teaching is unlimited.
3. Money sent from one congregation to another. Acts 11:27,28; I Cor. 16:1-4.
4. No specification of limitation on money's use.

IF THERE'S A PATTERN

1. Envoys controlled by one man. I Cor. 16:1-3
2. One or more volunteers. 2 Cor. 8:6
3. Several churches chose one man. 2 Cor. 8:19
4. Each church chose delegates. I Cor. 16:3; 2 Cor. 8:23

Now, could we have your chart No. 6 please. "Where is the authority, command, approved example or necessary inference?" I pointed that out several times last evening; let

WHERE IS THE AUTHORITY?

COMMAND _____

APPROVED EXAMPLE _____

NECESSARY INFERENCE _____
GENERAL OR SPECIFIC!

us do it again. Over here are some things that are demanded of all. "He that believeth and is baptized shall be saved, he that believeth not shall be damned." But over here there

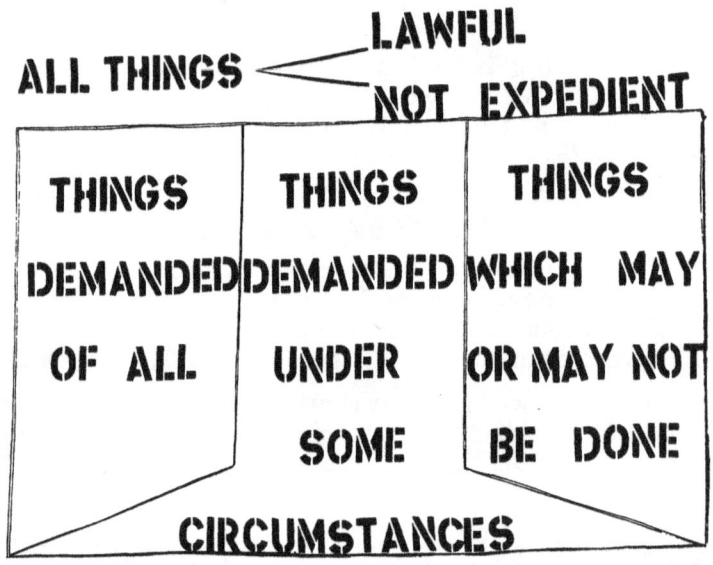

is another category within the things that are authorized. Baptism may be done in an open stream, in an open pool or enclosed baptistry, because the Lord did not specify where.

Teaching is commanded, but where do we teach? In a building, beside the road, in a chariot? Where do we teach? God did not specify. We can teach anywhere, if it does not violate some other teaching of the Lord. And we can go on and on. We are commanded to sing. What voice? Tenor? Soprano? Alto? We are free here to choose. God says to teach.

Let us notice, then, some things that Brother Willis has to say along this line in answer to my questions. He said he is not opposed to the act of broadcasting. It is not the extent, whether it be nationwide or not. He said it is partly what the money is used for; 50% he says buys their broadcast time out there. Well, I imagine about 60% or 70%

at Brown Street probably buys the place in which Brother Willis preaches, and then the other percent goes to his salary. I suppose that the men who preach out there have to have some salary. They have to have something to live on. Would you call that going to preach? And the letters that are sent out to further teach and the correspondence courses, would that not be part of the teaching? I do not know whether good judgment is always used or not, but I do know that there is a violation of some things.

And, Brother Willis, while I am on that, I just want to stress one point. That statement that you had last night where I spoke about the two churches being divided, do you have that? (Hold my time.) Last evening Brother Willis said that I said that the Herald of Truth had divided two congregations. I said I never said this. (Brother Willis tells him the quotation is at the bottom of the sheet he handed him.) I said I never said any such thing. I did not even know what statement he was going to refer to, but I just knew I had not made that statement. I said, now Brother Willis, do not come back and read a statement where I may have said that two congregations had been divided *over these* issues. Read where I said that the Herald of Truth *has divided* two. Well, he came back and he read that "In regard to the present controversies over orphan homes, the Herald of Truth, sponsoring churches, etc., there have not been more than two churches *divided over* these matters to my knowledge." (*Bible Herald*, August 1, 1958, p. 2). Now does that say that the Herald of Truth split two churches? Did I say it? I did not say any such thing. I did say that I do not know more than two that have divided *over these matters*. Now I will tell you, a man that cannot read any straighter than that, I do not know what he is going to do when he gets into some of these financial statements. I can see how he can easily get lost.

Could we have your next chart please? We can say something about a multitude of things. Lawless. Let us notice that we have been going to the Law, and when we have come to the Law we find that God has not made or set any particular pattern. He has not set forth in particular the way that money is to be sent from one congregation to another, or how money is to be sent to support someone who preaches the gospel. When a man then comes along and acts as if his word is the Law and begins to give a Law of his own, I think that is getting a little lawless. Don't you?

Iniquitous? Transgressive? When God has not set the pattern? Let us notice here (points to Chart on authority). What about singing tenor? What about the baptistry? I could go down through and with the same kind of reasoning argue these things. You could put any one of them there. Digressive, going aside? Well, is it going aside to sing tenor? Is it going aside to have a baptistry?

I know what he is going to say. He is going to say that is a Christian church argument. It is no such thing, because the Bible specifies vocal music and singing. Now if he can find a specific pattern, we will take it. Just the moment he finds a specific pattern, we will take it. There is no specific pattern on this thing. Now do not tell us that I said there is no pattern on anything. I said no such thing. I said there is no specific pattern telling us how this was done. If there is, trot it out and let us look at it.

It is not an act of faith. It *is* an act of faith. Eating meat is an act of faith and not eating meat is an act of faith. Whatsoever is not of faith is sin. He that doubteth is damned if he eats. By going to the Word of God and finding that there is no prohibition against it, then I walk by faith knowing that since God has not set.....That was an inadvertent statement there. But when there is no law specifying what we are to do, then we are free and when we act within that freedom, we are acting within the Word of God; we are walking by faith. We are not going beyond. We are not destroying any of the perfection. We are going to the Word of God and walking within it. We are not desecrating his silence. I have said before, you can take any of a multitude of things. His idea really comes down to this. He may not state it, but this is actually the whole argument: If a thing is not specifically mentioned, we cannot do it. And this idea is as false as it can be. How much time now? (Brother Kessinger: Seven minutes.) Seven minutes? We hope to get to some of the other charts. I cannot remember all of the charts and where they are. But we will try to get to some of those after awhile. (Brother Willis: I will give you the chart numbers when you get ready for them.) Brother Inman: All right.

But I want us to notice some of the things we have on the paper under "points to note." He talks about relieving a destitute situation. Now, first of all, we have the matter, what is authority? Last evening we pointed out that authority means a command or freedom to act. We act by authority when we act within that which is permitted.

Now he talks about these passages on benevolence as referring to destitute situations, but benevolence by its very nature is always to relieve financial or physical stress. So of necessity it has to be given in time of stress. That is what it is for. Now if that time of stress lasts ten years, fifty years, or one hundred years, it still needs to be taken care of. But according to the idea we got last night, it can only be done momentarily, during an emergency, and then it is over. Money was sent to Paul while he was at Corinth, and we have already noted that whether the money was sent directly to Paul or to Paul through the church, the church was the beneficiary.

Now this is something I would like to know. Would it be all right to have a nationwide broadcast or telecast if money were sent directly to the preacher? I would like to have an answer on that one. If the money were sent directly to the preacher instead of to some church, would it be all right? This money that was sent to Paul was not all for Paul alone. He worked with his own hands making tents (Acts 18:3). He used the proceeds of his work to help others (Acts 20:33-34). Now unless he kept a separate treasury and separate banking (Brother Kessinger indicates he has five more minutes), then what he made and what he received from other churches were put together.

Now we got the idea a moment ago that if it were put separately, there would be some sin about this. If it were kept separate so he would not get his own funds mixed up with someone else's, this would make it kind of sinful you know. Paul and others, when they received funds, went out from the center of the operation. The church in Cenchrea is an example of this. Here is Corinth over on the Western side of the Isthmus, and here is Cenchrea on the other side. I think the evidence is that Cenchrea was established while Paul was at Corinth spending this time there. And we find also that Paul left Titus at Crete. There were indications that Paul sent men who were with him to other places. Now he worked with his own hands to help those men.

Willis says that helping the Herald of Truth is not an expediency. He said it is not expedient. Would it be all right, if it were expedient? If it were expedient, would it be all right? A representative of the Herald of Truth is reported to have said that some elders are truculent. He at least showed the courtesy of having these representatives to call upon the elders of the church to get their consent. He at least did this. But what courtesy is shown elders when lists of members are obtained and printed matter sent to these members without any consent of the elders and oftentimes in violation of their wishes? Nearly every congregation here in Parkersburg receives bulletins from Moundsville, Akron and all over. Lists of members were obtained and no one ever went to an elder. He did not call him a truculent elder. He just did not go to him, and sometimes when elders have asked that it not be sent, they send it anyhow. I think I would rather be called truculent, don't you?

If elders lose oversight when money is sent from their treasury to that of another, then the Macedonia and Achaia elders turned their oversight over to Jerusalem. The oversight of elders is primarily over people. How much time? (Brother Kessinger: Three minutes.) Three minutes? Primarily over people and not over things. Their oversight is over things only as these things relate to persons. When does the oversight of money given into the treasury cease anyhow? If the church buys some chairs from a man down at the hardware store and they give the money to him, how much oversight do they have over the money? None. When the elders over here at Corinth and Philippi sent money to Jerusalem, how long did they have oversight over it? Did they lose oversight of the people in their congregation? Certainly not.

Has any congregation lost oversight of any single member of that congregation because they have sent funds to Highland Avenue? Now you just think about that a moment and it gets a little far out, doesn't it? They have not lost oversight of one single member. They are still controlling their own work. The oversight is primarily over people and not over money or other things. Elders are not primarily over money or other things. Their oversight over these things is only as they relate. After all, the elders have oversight of all the money that I have in my pocket to some extent. If I use that to gamble, to drink, to destroy my fellow-being, they have a right to come in and tell me I am mishandling that money.

WILLIS' SECOND AFFIRMATIVE

We have come now to the last speech that I will have an opportunity to make in this particular session, and on this proposition. In the beginning, I want to cover a number of things that Brother Inman just recently said. He made the statement that I misunderstood what he said last night about Acts 11:27-30, and I may have done that. If I did so, I did it unintentionally. I thought you said last night that the elders at Jerusalem distributed that money throughout Judea. Actually, whether he said that or not, that is what he must prove. He has to find a sponsoring church somewhere in the word of God. He is defending one and if he cannot find one in Acts 11:27-30, I wish he would tell us where it is. That is the argument that the brethren generally make on it, and that is the nearest thing they think they can find to a sponsoring church. But he says he is not going to make that argument because it is obscure. Well, we have known that all along. It is very obscure! But his obligation is to unobscure it. He has to find one somewhere and until he has done so, he has not done his duty.

He made also a statement about the fact that I had dug around in a lot of books trying to find some scandals and these sorts of things. All he had read was the Bible. That was the only thing he read in order to prepare. But if he had prepared adequately in the Bible, in his first speech the first night he would have gotten right up here and said, now here is the passage where you can find either general or specific authority for a sponsoring church. He has not done that yet. He did not prepare very well in his Bible. If Brother Inman has only used a Bible in his preparation, Brother Inman, would you tell what is under your table over there? (Pointing to a stack of books under Brother Inman's table.) It looks like books to me. That is what I thought they were. I thought they were some other kind of books than a Bible. (Laughter.)

He said also that his statement about two churches being divided was misunderstood by me. I do not claim to be any genius, but it still sounds like it said what I said it said. "In regard to the present controversies over orphan homes, Herald of Truth and sponsoring churches, etc., there have not more than two churches divided over these matters to my knowledge." (*Bible Herald*, August 1, 1958, p. 2) That sounds like the Herald of Truth and orphan homes and sponsoring churches had something to do with dividing at least two churches he knew about, and if that is all that he knows about, then I will tell you he has not kept up very well. Now he may be saying that the Herald of Truth did not divide the church; that the people divided it over the Herald of Truth. That might be what he said.

But, you know, I do not know of any church that a piano divided, do you? I know of some churches that have divided over pianos, but I do not know of any that a piano divided. And I do not know of any instance where a missionary society divided any church, but I know of some churches that have had a lot of contention over them, and a lot of debate over them, and have divided over them. But the missionary society itself perhaps did not divide the church. Perhaps that is the differentiation he is making, and if so, that is a rather close one. Perhaps he lost me there.

Now he said something about Brown Street. I would like to have your chart No. 2 please. He wanted to know how much overhead does Brown Street have. Perhaps you could check about that and see how much overhead Brown Street has. I tell you, we do not have $100,450.00 for general and administrative costs, but that is what they have out at Highland. Over $100,000.00 for general and administrative costs. I just thought Brother Inman might ask about that, so before I left, I asked the Treasurer to give his statement about our financial report last year. He said our contributions last year were about $700.00 a week, a total of $38,794.98. He said that $22,485.45 of that money went directly to the support of gospel preachers.

Now, he said, "we like the way we are doing it better than the way you are not doing it." I did not know you had that chart up last night, Brother Inman. I did not see it, just to tell you the truth. You did not make any argument on it, and I did not really see that. I hoped that you would make an argument on it. In fact, I saw him put it up before the

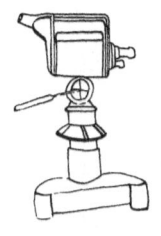

WHICH IS BETTER

OUR WAY OF DOING IT

OR

YOUR WAY OF NOT DOING IT?

debate began, and I hoped that he would make an argument on it last night.

When you sit down and figure out how much money they are getting at the Herald of Truth, you find their budget this year is $1,932,000.00. Now the projected budget is $2,239,000.00. He made the big play about the fact we are not hurting it any. Their budget is $1,932,000.00. That is what it was last year, too. Do you know how much they collected? They collected $922,000.00. (W. F. Cawyer in letter August 9, 1966.) They lacked more than a million dollars getting what they had to have in order to operate this thing. It looks like somebody might be hurting it a little bit.

Now when you take the $922,000.00 they did get and divide that by the 2,000 churches that sent, that means that each one of them sent $500.00 a year. That is how you fellows *are* doing it. He likes the way they are doing it: $500.00 a year! Now last year Brown Street spent $22,485.00 supporting gospel preachers. That is the way we are *not* doing it! That is his argument on that.

The Moundsville church (He made, I believe, some reference to them) has a radio program. They spend about $20,000.00 a year supporting gospel preaching, and not only that, but they support a daily program that costs $2,400.00 a year. That is the way they are *not* doing it, according to Brother Inman.

Just before I left the Treasurer posted a financial report for last month at Brown Street. You wanted to know what we are doing and how we are *not* doing it. I took a look just before I left, and it showed that last month, to 11 different gospel preachers we sent $2800.00. That is the way we are *not* doing it. But he likes the way they are doing it; $500.00 a year a church. And I wish they would make us a list of how many churches that contributed to splitting.

Now further, he said he was not making Christian church arguments. Now you would never have known that if he had not told you, would you? It sounded like Christian church arguments he was making. I read his speech last night from J. B. Briney. And I have marked over here in the *Otey—Briney Debate* his speech about how much good we are doing. J. B. Briney argued we have 700 missionaries sent out by this missionary society. We have built 1109 church buildings, and we have 108 living link churches that are supplying support for preachers. Look how much good we are doing. What does that do? That is supposed to take the place of Bible authority for the missionary society. That is what that is supposed to do. What Brother Inman is trying to tell us with this chart is that he does not have any Bible authority for 2000 churches working through one eldership. But he thought he would tell you about how much good they are doing, and he thought that would suffice for Bible authority.

Now I have heard today (I do not know whether this is true, but I got it from five different people) that a Christian church preacher was here last night and that he went to Brother Inman today and told him that he made Christian church arguments last night. That is what he said. The very arguments you made last night, Brother Inman, to defend the sponsoring church are the same ones I have been trying to use to defend instrumental music, he said. That sounds like he might be using some Christian church arguments. Not only that, if we have some other debates (And we are supposed to. We have one scheduled over at Dayton and I hope to schedule some others with him.), I would like to take one of them and just document out of one book, the *Hunt—Inman Debate*, nearly every argument he will make. Then I can take the *Hunt—Inman Debate* and document my answer from Clifton Inman, when he was speaking against Julian Hunt, on every argument he will

Second Night, Cooperation 95

make. Then he wants to say he is not making Christian church arguments.

Now then, let us notice some of the points that he observed here on the "points to note" from the sheet he handed out tonight. He said now, "the money was sent to Paul while he was in Corinth." That does not help you any, Brother Inman. You need to find where it was sent to a sponsoring church. That is what you are looking for. I have on my chart where they sent money to Paul. That is what I have been advocating; that in the support of gospel preaching, the Bible pattern is: the money was sent to Paul. He said you do not have to follow that pattern. You can send it to the sponsoring church. You have not cited any passage for it yet, Brother Inman.

He wants to know in the fourth place, would it be all right to have a nationwide broadcast or telecast if the money were sent directly to the preacher. No, Brother Inman. It would not. It surely would not be! There is no Bible authity to activate the church universal through any kind of single agency, period! There just is not any Bible authority for it, and if you tried to activate the church universal and put on the Herald of Truth through sending· it to a preacher, you would have the one-man missionary society. That is what you would have then. Now you have just the sponsoring church missionary society, but if you were to send it to a preacher and make him the agency through whom 2000 churches were going to act, then you would have a one-man missionary society. So that would not be all right. In 2 Corinthians 11:8 the apostle Paul said, "I robbed other churches taking wages of them that I might do you service." The only thing I know of in the Bible that is scriptural to send to a preacher is "wages." You cannot make him a brotherhood agency.

And then in number seven he said, "Willis said that helping the Herald of Truth is not an expediency. Would it be all right if it *were* expedient?" You sound rather uncertain about that tonight. Last night you said it was expedient, and tonight you want to know would it be all right *if* it were expedient. Now what I argued last night was, first of all, it is not lawful. There is not anything expedient that is not lawful. The Herald of Truth is *neither lawful nor expedient*. If he could prove it were lawful, I would still be willing to meet him on whether or not it is expedient. But he has to prove that it is lawful first.

And then he wanted to know in number eight, What about sending out church bulletins? I suppose that is what he is getting at. I want to know, Brother Inman, if when the Highland church sends out stuff like this (holding up some Highland booklets), and we did not ask for all this stuff, to our members and to all the churches in the brotherhood, are they violating the autonomy of all those churches? They are mailing to 10,312 churches and they say there are only 12,000 churches. I wonder if they are violating the autonomy of all those churches. Now, what he really needs to learn, if he has not learned it, is that God did not make elders *brotherhood censors*. I do not have to ask elders if I can subscribe to TIME MAGAZINE, and if you want to send me TIME MAGAZINE, you do not have to write to the Brown Street elders and find out if it would be all right if I send a subscription to Brother Willis for TIME MAGAZINE. Now, if there is something immoral or unscriptural about it, then just attack what is unscriptural or immoral about it. There is no violation of autonomy in mailing a paper.

And he said the elders are overseers of people, and not of "things." His inference is that it is all right to let just anybody oversee the "things", just as long as the elders keep the oversight of the people. Now, Brother Inman, the missionary society never did seek to control and oversee anything except "things." They wanted to oversee the same "things" that Highland wants to oversee, and that is dollars. That is what they want to oversee. Those are the "things" that they want to oversee.

And then on the paper he handed out last night (He went through that again tonight) he said, "If there is a pattern." He made a number of observations about that. But everything about that is answered by one statement, and that is: this money was delivered by *MEN* and not *BY CHURCHES*. Brother Inman needs to find some place where some churches were the messengers; where they sent THROUGH A CHURCH. He cannot find that. He has not found it so far.

And now to the questions I gave him tonight. He said last night that the missionary society was wrong because it violated the New Testament order. *"What New Testament order does the missionary society violate which the Herald of Truth does not also violate?"* And he said, "I do not have the time to show the difference." Well, that is right. It would take a whole lot of time to show the difference, if there is any. He would have a good bit of work to do to show the differences, if there are any. Really, the trouble is, they are both (the missionary society and the Herald of Truth) simply unauthorized in the word of God, and that is what is wrong with them.

And then, I asked in the third question *"Whose work is the Herald of Truth?"* And *"How do we know which church the Lord intended to be a sponsoring church and which he intended to be a mere contributing church?"* Brother Inman said, "you just use good judgment and know." Well, I wonder if we are not all perhaps to be sponsoring churches. And how do we know that God obligates Highland to oversee a work that costs one hundred or two hundred times more than they can pay, but he did not expect you other brethren in Parkersburg to do that? What good judgment and what expediency, Brother Inman, taught you that?

I want to notice now all of the passages Brother Inman has used in this debate so far. He has used Colossians 3:17. Now remember he is trying to prove it is scriptural for 2,000 churches to work through one church. He used Colossians 3:17, "Whatsoever you do in word or deed, do all in the name of the Lord Jesus Christ." That did not help him any. I believe that. His trouble is, he cannot find anything in the word of God to authorize what he is advocating.

He has used 1 Corinthians 6:12 and 1 Corinthians 9:1-5, and he made an argument there on expediency. I will attend to that in just a minute.

In the third place he has used 1 Corinthians 16:1-3; 2 Corinthians 8:6, 14, 18-19; 2 Corinthians 8:23, and his argument was on the messengers. Of course, he said, they used some messengers to take that money from Galatia, Macedonia and Achaia over to Jerusalem and those messengers are his authority for a sponsoring church. Now, he needs to keep two things in mind. One is: the church they were sending to was a destitute church and Highland is not. That is one thing he needs to keep in mind. Another thing he needs to keep in mind is that they did not send that money THROUGH A CHURCH. They sent it by some messengers. They did not send it through a sponsoring church eldership, or through a one-man missionary society, or through a missionary society either.

In Philippians 4:15-16 and 2 Corinthians 11:8, 10, he used passages where wages were sent to Paul. But that is not what he needs to find. He needs to find, to justify the sponsoring church, where funds were sent *to a church* not in need *through a church*. He has not shown that yet and I will still be glad to have it.

He used Romans 4:15-16, where there is no law, there is no sin. I suggested that if there is no order, then there cannot be any disorder, and just anything will be all right. If there is no pattern, then there is no violation of the pattern. Brother Inman, if there is no pattern, and there is no order, and there is no law, then a church could send its money to a missionary society *or to Ohio Valley College!* Couldn't it? If there is no order, there could not be any disorder and Brother Inman's argument is that it would be all right. That is what the implication of it is. If there is not any order to violate, you could not violate that order. And he has argued all the way through, *there is no order!*

SIN IS THE
TRANSGRESSION
OF THE LAW
NO LAW
1 JOHN 3:4
NO TRANSGRESSION
ROM. 4:15

(law not to be confused with prohibition)

Titus 2:11-12, he said, "Where is the law that regulates radio preaching?" And he argued that teaching is authorized. Well, of course, it is. But what he needs to find is the passage that authorizes, in teaching, several hundred churches to work through *one* eldership.

Then, he used Acts 11:27-30, and we made our reply to that.

Now, the main argument last night was on expediency. He said it was expedient and now tonight, he said, *"If* it is expedient." But he said last night it was an expediency, and let us talk a little about what the Bible says about expediency. *First,* in order for a thing to be called Biblically an expedient, it must be lawful (1 Corinthians 6:12; 1 Corinthians 10:23). Brother Inman so far has not given general or specific authority for that which he wants to call an expedient. He said I was demanding specific authority. That is just not so. I am perfectly willing to take either a general command, example, or necessary inference. General or specific would be all right, Brother Inman. Just either one of hem, general or specific. But until you get that, do not call it an expedient, because an expedient has to be lawful.

Secondly, it must edify (1 Corinthians 10:23). To edify means to build up. I want to know if the churches throughout the Ohio Valley are being built up by the Herald of Truth, or if it is tearing them down. They are being torn down by what Brother Inman wants to call an expedient.

And *thirdly,* an expedient, in order to be called such, must be in the realm of personal judgment or private privilege. But the Herald of Truth is contrary to the faith once delivered. It just is not in God's word. It is unauthorized.

Further, in the *fourth* place, it must not lead another to violate his conscience, if you are going to call it an expedient (1 Corinthians 8:12-13; Romans 14:21). And they say they will not make you violate your conscience. They give you an option. You do not have to give. You can either give *or get out!* You can take your choice. That is the way they handle their expedient. You can either give or go along with it, or get out, or get your meetings cancelled or they will not announce your meetings, or they will lock you out of the building, or they will sue you for the property. That is the way they handle their expediency.

And *fifth*, one using an expedient must not condemn a brother who differs with him (Romans 14:3). Brother Inman is trying to condemn me because I differ with him. But Romans 14:3 says (speaking of an expedient), you must not do that sort of thing.

Now then I want to notice a summary of the arguments that I have made thus far in opposition to this arrangement by which several hundreds and even thousands of churches are operating *through* one eldership.

I noticed in the first place that *the Herald of Truth is a sinful waste of the Lord's money*. Brother Inman said he had not investigated that very much. I suggest that before he gets up to defend something like that, that he do a little investigating of it. Before he gets up and pitches a whole speech on the fact that it is expedient, he should investigate it. Every fact that I presented (I believe this to be correct) is in these two books (Holding up two highland booklets).

Now you brethren are paying for stuff like this. This is what they printed up *(THE HERALD OF TRUTH STORY)* and handed out that to their key workers when they called them all down to the convention in Abilene in 1964. Then last year they called them all back again and they printed this up, *THE RESTORATION AND UNITY PLEA*. This is their sales package. You go out and get the money out of the brethren. They are paying for that. And so I went through those books, and that is where those figures came from. I suggest, Brother Inman, before you defend this either as scriptural or as expedient, you get some of their literature and find out what you are supposed to be defending.

Secondly, we pointed out that *Highland sets a bad example before the church and the world*. She is a perpetual beggar. She never gets enough. She has been a constant beggar for 14 years! They all ready have their plans to beg for a good many years in the future. She continually obligates herself beyond her ability to pay. Highland sets a bad example in that she seeks to get the control of other churches' resources. He has not said a word about this so far, that I know about.

If he wants to get up and say that Highland is a good example, that this is the way a church ought to conduct its business, then let us all get busy and do like they do. Let us all start begging one another. Let us all start trying to get control of the other's money. That is what they are doing out there. They are trying to get control of everybody's money they can. They have even said they would like to have every church in the world sending them money. And Brother Guy Woods said that if two could do it, four could do it. And if four can do it, eight can do it. (Guy N. Woods, *Cooperation in the Field of Benevolence and Evangelism,* p. 9)

And also he said something about Acts 11. Would it be all right for all of the churches to have sent to Judea, or for all of the churches to have sent to Jerusalem? Certainly so. It would have been all right for all of the churches to send all of their money *until their need was met,* and that is all. That was a temporary matter. We have a permanent thing on our hands, and that is not a destitute church out there. They have a contribution of $7500.00 a week, and they are still begging money. Thus they are not like Jerusalem or the Judean churches.

And then we noticed that *the Herald of Truth violates the autonomy, either of the contributing churches or the receiving churches,* the sponsoring churches. Somebody has to give up control.

And *the Herald of Truth is unauthorized.* We are going to notice this in just a minute.

We studied about the origin of the sponsoring church. It started about 50 years ago. It came from sectarianism, and we showed also that it has made of the church virtually a denomination in the eyes of the world. Brother G. C. Brewer said as much.

And then we noticed that *the Herald of Truth violates the pattern of congregational cooperation.* Now, what is that pattern? The pattern was that the only time in the word of God (Get it clearly; it is simple) any church sent to another church *for any reason,* the church receiving the money was destitute. Now write that down. He said, "What about their sending wages to Paul?" They did not send to a church. They sent *to Paul.* They supported a gospel preacher. But I want to know where in the word of God did any church ever send to another church when the church receiving the money was not destitute? And until he finds that, he has not found what he signed his name to prove to be in the word of God.

We showed further that *the sponsoring church type of congregational cooperation seeks to activate the church universal.* On one of our big charts, we showed that such has

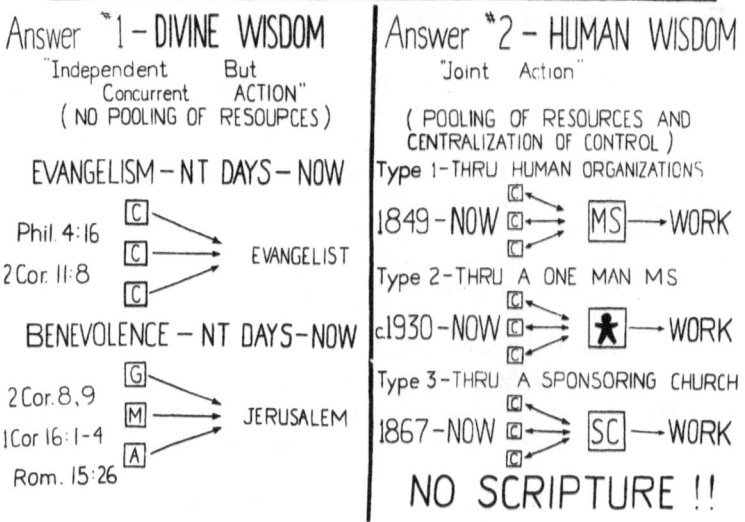

been done in three different ways by the brethren. One time they tried to do it through the missionary society. They finally decided that would not be so good. The Christian Church has that. So they said, "Well, we will all put it through the one-man missionary society." That is what he tried to lead me into tonight, and I did not take the bait, because that is unscriptural. You just cannot activate the church universal. There is not any agency in God's word that God assigned to oversee the work of more than one congregation. We have a congregation. I would just like the name of an officer (Give me the name of the officer, Brother Inman) in the word of God that can oversee the work of two churches—not 2000 churches. I will just take two, because if you can get two, then you can get 200, and then you can get 20,000, and that is all of them. You have a Catholic Church then. I would like to know what is the name of an officer in the word of God that God said was to oversee the work of two churches.

Now, to the elders in the word of God, the Bible says, "Tend the flock of God which is among you." The oversight of elders, brethren, is limited, and it is limited to "a flock." We showed that the work these brethren are overseeing is a brotherhood work. They said it "belongs to the brotherhood." It is as "big as the brotherhood." This is "*your* program." You have increased *your* mission work tenfold when you send your money to us. This is a brotherhood work. Brotherhood elders and a brotherhood treasury. There just is not anything in the word of God to sanction that. If there is, I would like to know where it is. I do not know what those fellows are called in the word of God that God assigned to oversee the work of the brotherhood. If Brother Inman knows, he will do us a big favor if he would tell us. And so we also observe that *the Herald of Truth unscripturally makes the Highland elders overseers of a brotherhood work.*

Give me chart No. 6, please. (How much time, Brother Needham?) Four minutes? All right, chart No. 6 please. I want this thing to stand out in your mind; that I have asked him over and over and over to give us the authority for the sponsoring church. Now that is what he is defending. Not just the Herald of Truth, but he *is* defending the Herald of Truth. That is in it, but I am asking for the authority for the sponsoring church. So I said, "Where is the authority?" Suppose I had gotten up here and asked him tonight, "Where is the authority for immersion?" Do you think he would have put anything up on the chart? I think he would have. Suppose I would have said, "Where is the authority to take the Lord's supper on the first day of the week?" Do you think he would have cited any passage? I think he would have. But now, what passage (And if he wants to tell us again now, I would be glad to have him do it) has he given us where there is a command or approved example, or necessary inference (That is the only way you get authority in the word of God), either general authority or specific authority, where 2,000 churches ever tried to work through one eldership? Now I want to know where that is, and if he has given it to us, I want him to come up

WHERE IS THE AUTHORITY?

COMMAND _____

APPROVED EXAMPLE _____

NECESSARY INFERENCE _____
GENERAL OR SPECIFIC!

here and tell us: "Now, here is the command that I cited where 2,000 churches worked through one eldership," or "Here is the example that I cited where 2,000 churches worked through one eldership," or "Here is the necessary inference from which we conclude that 2,000 churches can work through one eldership." Until he has done that, his proposition falls without authority and thus we come to the next chart.

And since it is without authority, it is therefore the different things that we mentioned here on the chart. He went through this and tried to answer this chart by saying that we can say a lot of things are presumptuous. Let me tell you, Brother Inman, until you give us authority, command, example or necessary inference, general or specific, for what you are defending, you are being presumptuous. And the same thing is wrong with the Herald of Truth, brethren, that is wrong with sprinkling. It is just not in God's word. The same thing is wrong with the Herald of Truth that is wrong with mechanical instrumental music; it just is not authorized in the word of God. That is what is wrong with it. And until he finds it authorized in the

HERALD OF TRUTH IS UNAUTHORIZED... THEREFORE IT IS...

1. PRESUMPTIVE NUM. 15:30; PSM. 19:13
2. LAWLESS 1 JNO. 3:4
3. INIQUITIOUS MT. 7:23
4. TRANSGRESSIVE 1 JNO. 3:4; 2 JNO. 9
5. DIGRESSIVE GAL. 6:1; 1 COR. 4:6
6. NOT APOSTOLIC DOCTRINE ACTS 2:42
7. NOT ACT OF FAITH 2COR. 5:7
8. GOES BEYOND 2 JNO. 9; REV. 22:18,19
9. DESTROYS PERFECTION 2 TIM. 3:16,17
10. DESECRATES GOD'S SILENCE 1 PET. 4:11; 1COR. 4:6
11. VIOLATES LAW OF EXCLUSION GEN. 6:14
12. UNHOLY HEB 9:23; LK. 22:20
13. HAUGHTY ROM. 12:3; JER 10:23
14. NOT A GOOD WORK 2 TIM. 3:16,17
15. DOES NOT PERTAIN TO LIFE 2 PET. 1:3
16. PERVERSIVE 2 PET. 3:16
17. RENDERS WORSHIP VAIN MT. 15:9
18. DIVISIVE 1COR. 1:10; 1 COR. 10:23

word of God, it is therefore presumptive. It is lawless, iniquitous, transgressive, digressive. It is no part of apostolic doctrine; it is not an act of faith; it goes beyond; it destroys perfection; it desecrates God's silence; it violates God's law of exclusion, it is not sanctified by the blood of Christ in his testament. And thus, it is unholy; it is haughty; it is not a good work; it does not pertain to life and godliness; it is perversive; it renders worship vain; and it is divisive. I tell you I would not want to be standing up here trying to defend something that is all that! He wanted to know, well, now where is the point of sin? Right there is where it is. It is just not in the word of God.

Now, we come to the close of the debate tonight, and I want you to understand the point upon which I have pitched the battle. *Where is the authority?* He has not given it so far. I have enjoyed this discussion. Brother Inman and I have another session assigned now. We are to begin October 31 in Dayton, Ohio, and I am looking forward to that. Of course, we have Thursday and Friday night to discuss the institutional orphan home question, and I am looking forward to that also. It has been a pleasure speaking to you. You have listened attentively, and for that I am most appreciative.

INMAN'S SECOND NEGATIVE

This is a dictionary (holding up the book) that gives the meaning of words. This is a concordance that tells you where to find passages in the Bible and, over in the back, gives you the meaning of the Greek and Hebrew words in the Bible. This is Thayer's Greek Lexicon that gives you the meaning of the Greek words used in the Bible. And this is the Bible that has the words that those books give the meaning of. That is what those books are, Brother Willis. (He laughs.)

First of all, in my last speech, I want again to point out that authority is of various kinds. There is that which is demanded of all. This we have in commands. There is that

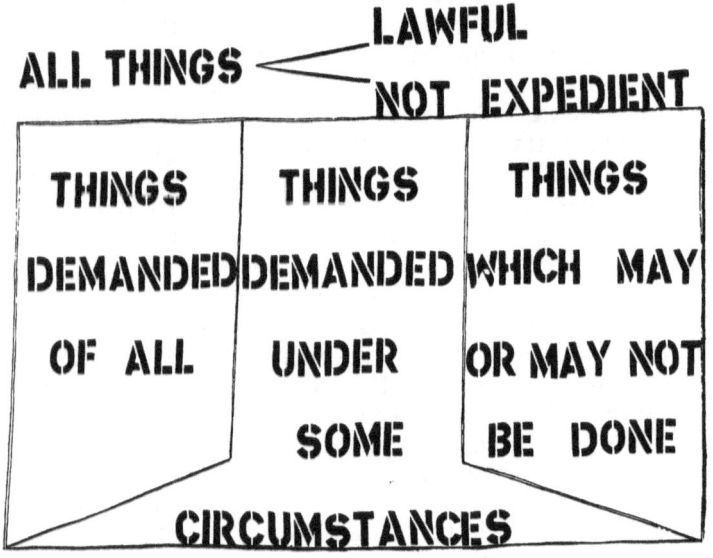

which is demanded of some, as wives are to be subject unto their husbands. Husbands are not to obey that. There are some things that are commanded under certain circumstances: "Whosoever shall smite thee on thy right cheek, turn to him the other also." Then there are other things that are authorized either by example or necessary inference, which may or may not be done, according to the circumstances.

And someone got on to me for using some big words last night, but exigencies is about the best word I know. I just cannot think of another one to take its place right now. It means considering all circumstances surrounding it that advise the use or the leaving off the use of. There are some things that may or may not be done. Now, everything that we have an example of is not necessarily binding upon us. On the other hand, when God said to be baptized and then he does not specify where, then it may be done in an open pond, an open stream, or enclosed baptistry.

Now, he said that if I am called upon to offer authority for the Lord's supper, I will give it. Yes, I would. But you know, if I were called upon to give authority for the use of a cloth on the table when we serve the Lord's supper, I would give that too. But it is a different kind of authority. It is arrived at in different ways, and we understand this. I hope so. We have authority, but it is a different kind of authority. God has told us to teach. He has not said to teach by radio. He just said teach. And when God has said teach and then he has not specified the means or the methods, we may use any method that does not violate some other passage of scripture. When God has shown us that money may be sent from one congregation to another, and has set no limitations upon that, we may use that in any way that does not violate some other principle of scripture. Now, of course, this is a limitation we gave last evening and have pointed out all the time: it must not violate some other principle of scripture.

We, then, have given the authority. We have cited the passages of scripture that showed that money was sent from one church to another. But he says that we have to find something else. You know we keep hearing that term, "sponsoring church arrangement." He says that I have to find this: where money was sent out from Jerusalem to all these other places. I have to find that. Well, the proposition says that "it is unscriptural for one or more congregations to send money from their treasuries to another congregation." What for? So they can send it out to other congregations? No. So that they can put on a broadcast or a telecast. Now, if there is anything in that proposition that says money is to be sent out yonder somewhere else, you find it. Brother, it takes a lot of loose reading to get that one. There is nothing said in this proposition about sending money from a receiving congregation out to others. That is one reason that there is no need for me to deal with whether they did or whether they did not. That is not in this proposition.

We come now to this matter of the sponsoring church. We are talking about a specific sponsoring, and that is sponsoring a broadcast or telecast. There are a lot of things that the church should not be sponsoring, but we are talking about sponsoring a specific thing.

Then this matter about whether the Herald of Truth has divided churches. Last night he said the Herald of Truth has divided churches. He said tonight that the piano has not divided any churches. But last night he said the Herald of Truth has, and said I had said the Herald of Truth has. I said no such thing. I know of instances when churches have been divided over whether a man stood to lead a prayer or not, but I do not know where a man standing to lead a prayer has divided a church. I know where some people divided it *over* this.

Now he talks about the overhead expense. Well, I have learned a little something from being in business, and that is when we had a little store our overhead was not as much as when we got a larger one. I am quite sure that the more the church is doing, the more overhead it has. And I have learned something else too, and that is that there are very few people who can read a financial statement. In my business I do not depend upon my ability to read a financial statement. I have a man like Brother Lyle Knapp that knows what he is doing to tell me what that financial statement means, because I can get all mixed up in it. And I think Brother Willis has too. (He laughs.)

He talks about Briney's speech and the *Hunt—Inman Debate*. Brother Willis, I made the same argument for radio broadcasts with Julian Hunt in the *Hunt—Inman Debate* that I have made here. Now that Christian Church preacher who was in town today and in the store has had some discussions with me and some of the other brethren. One of the main things he wanted to point out was how disgraceful it was that we disagreed, that we have divisions in the Church of Christ. He said they did not have any, and I just did not have presence enough of mind to ask him how he is getting along now with Beechwood Avenue after he split it and took some people with him over yonder. And maybe I should not say that tonight, because he is not here. But you know, he suggested an affinity for Brother Willis and his position. Now I can say, "Well now, that puts Brother Willis way over yonder with the liberals. He has the Christian Church backing him now. They like his arguments better than they like mine."

He mentions this again about no pattern. I have asked him from the time we started, "Brother Willis, show us the pattern." I have even outlined here how money was sent from one congregation to another and I said, "Brother Wil-

What Is Law Concerning — Broadcasting?

Money From one Congregation To Another? ⟷

lis, is that the pattern? If it is not, give us a pattern. Where is the pattern? Where has God specified?" And until this moment he has not told us where God has specified. "Where there is no law, there is no transgression." He has not found it. Therefore, there is no transgression.

Now, he has said we would give up oversight. Now if sending money to put on a broadcast gives up oversight, then sending money to help the poor gives up oversight. Whether it is sent to preach or whether it is given to help the poor, if turning that money over to the control of another eldership is giving up oversight, then oversight is given up in either case. And if that is the sin, it is committed. The Corinthian church committed it. The Philippian church committed it. The Berean church committed it, and the Thessalonian church committed it, because they sent funds to another church for that church to use those funds. Now, he says the giving up of the oversight is here.

Someone is afraid that they will activate the church universal. To activate is to put into action. I think the universal church ought to get into action. I do not think they need a head over it to do it, but I think it ought to get busy. Don't you? The busier we get the better; universally busy.

He says that the Herald of Truth tears down congregations. He gives me an argument here that, if I answer, I am condemned if I do, and condemned if I do not. If I point out to you tonight the truth that many congregations, because they have supported Herald of Truth and have had that in their community (as Tenth Avenue and Twenty-first Street church in Huntington), have reaped benefits and that the congregation has been built up, he says, "Now then, he is saying that if it is successful, it is not wrong." You see, either way I go, I am condemned if I do, and condemned if I do not, with this kind of reasoning. But the fact is that multitudes of congregations have been built up. There has been something that has been tearing down, and that is people in a lawless way ignoring the law of God and going in and becoming a law unto themselves.

He says that I condemn him because I disagree. Brother Willis, I have never said you were presumptive, iniquitous, transgressive, digressive, and all these things. I wrote articles in *Bible Herald* pleading with brethren not to cause all the division over these things, and for men to be fair with one another and not make false accusations and harsh accusations that were not true. I have suggested, and I believe today, that if there is within a congregation someone who believes what Brother Willis does, and he does not begin to make wild accusations and to go out and undermine the elders and the other brethren and tear the church down, that that man ought to be received with all kindness. But, as I said last evening about the lights (He wanted to know about the lights), if a man comes into the church and begins to teach that we are sinning if we have electric lights in the building and he begins to go out from house to house and sow the seeds of discord over this, then the brethren need to take some action. If he will not cease this, then we need to take some more action.

I have had some meetings cancelled, and I have never yet had a part in getting someone else's cancelled because of what was taught on these matters. I have had some cancelled. Brother Tom Butterfield had some cancelled and some other brethren I know.

Let us note again, in the matter of authority, that we do not need the same kind of authorization for being baptized as for using a baptistry. Yet they both are authorized. "Where there is no law, there is no transgression." Paul made this statement; G. C. Brewer did not. Paul made this statement and this is his argument. This is the one we have stayed with. We have asked him to show us specifications. None has been shown us. Since no specification has been shown, we are acting within the authority given us in the word of God, just as when he did not specify whether we must use a baptistry, open stream, or what else. We are certainly not presumptive when we baptize in an open stream, or when we baptize in an enclosed baptistry. We are not presumptive, because God has not specified. We are not presuming to go beyond the limit of what God has taught. We are not presuming to act beyond his authority. We are not lawless, because we have gone to the law and have found from the law that God has made no specification.

Now, let us notice again that there is an assumption made when Paul said, "in the beginning of the gospel, . . . no church had fellowship in the matter of giving and receiving but ye only; for even when I was at Thessalonica, you sent once and again to my need." It is assumed and presumed (He gets quite presumptive) that he said, "You were the first to write and to learn that when money is sent to preach the gospel from some church treasury, it must be sent directly to the preacher."

When I was at Oak Hill, West Virginia, brethren sent time and again. The congregation at Wheeling sent time and again to my necessity. The congregation at Tenth Avenue and Twenty-first Street in Huntington sent time and again to my necessity. The congregation at Bolivar, Texas, sent time and again; and Justin, Texas, sent time and again to my necessity. They sent it to Brother Riley, the Treasurer of the congregation there. So then, it is presumed that Paul said, as we pointed out last evening, that you were the first to communicate with me concerning the pattern by which money is to be sent from one congregation to another. But he said not that you were the first to learn the pattern by which money is to be sent from one congregation to another, but you were the first that communicated with me concerning giving and receiving.

Now, anything beyond this is assumption. It is presumptuous; it is going beyond the word of God and saying something that he did not say. We need to say what the word

HERALD OF TRUTH IS UNAUTHORIZED... THEREFORE IT IS...

1. PRESUMPTIVE NUM. 15:30; PSM. 19:13
2. LAWLESS 1 JNO. 3:4
3. INIQUITIOUS MT. 7:23
4. TRANSGRESSIVE 1 JNO. 3:4; 2 JNO. 9
5. DIGRESSIVE GAL. 6:1; 1 COR. 4:6
6. NOT APOSTOLIC DOCTRINE ACTS 2:42
7. NOT ACT OF FAITH 2 COR. 5:7
8. GOES BEYOND 2 JNO. 9; REV. 22:18,19
9. DESTROYS PERFECTION 2 TIM. 3:16,17
10. DESECRATES GOD'S SILENCE 1 PET. 4:11; 1 COR. 4:6
11. VIOLATES LAW OF EXCLUSION GEN. 6:14
12. UNHOLY HEB 9:23; LK. 22:20
13. HAUGHTY ROM. 12:3; JER 10:25
14. NOT A GOOD WORK 2 TIM. 3:16,17
15. DOES NOT PERTAIN TO LIFE 2 PET. 1:3
16. PERVERSIVE 2 PET. 3:16
17. RENDERS WORSHIP VAIN MT. 15:9
18. DIVISIVE 1 COR. 1:10; 1 COR. 10:23

of God says, and then we will not transgress it; we will not go beyond. We will not digress from it. We will stay with apostolic doctrine. We will act within the faith, and we will act in faith. We will not destroy the perfection of the word by adding our fallible opinions.

We desecrate God's silence by presuming we can make a law where God does not make one. When God is silent about where we are to be baptized, someone then violates God's silence and desecrates it by telling us we have to be baptized in an open stream. When God does not specify concerning this matter, God did not set forth a law concerning this matter, someone desecrates his silence when he makes a law where He has not made one.

I meant to ask him about the law of exclusion, but that is too late. I would like to have that described and printed out for us sometime, but all this other, we can go right down the same way with everything that is here. (Speaking of chart.)

Brethren, tonight you and I can go to the word of God and understand that the word of God was given to suit all men for all times, and we can see the great beauty of the word of God, and that it is timeless. God knew that man was going to make progress in the world. He did not set man up here at the pinnacle of his progress, but he knew that man would make progress. He gave a word that is flexible enough that we can use it and abide by it as man does progress. He could have had man on a radio broadcast when he was here on earth, but he left man to progress and to learn how to broadcast and to send out his voice. He could have set up a telecasting station in Jerusalem when he was here, but he left man free to progress and learn how to do this. He did not set up any laws that would bind us and so hamper us that we could not use this medium to its fullest.

I used to have professors and fellow-students in college who would say to me, "Why you have a book that is 2,000 years old", and recently someone put out a book that is called *Voices of Concern*. They keep talking about this doctrine that is 2,000 years old. But the great beauty of the word of God is that, though it is 2,000 years old, it is timeless. There is not one single thing in it that you and I cannot do today. We can find water in which to be baptized. Water today, in being baptized, has the same symbol that it has always had. We can sing God's praises today. And singing is not out of date. It still thrills the human heart; it stirs to action. We still can pray unto God because God is in heaven and God will hear. There is not a thing that is dated in the word of God, except the Old Testament. The Jewish religion was dated, and our religion today is not dated.

But when we come to try to make restrictions where God has not made restrictions, we try to set up patterns where God has not set up one. And let us point out again, that when man says that in this pattern book here there is not a pattern for a certain dress, that does not mean that he is saying that that book does not have any patterns. And when I say tonight that there is not a pattern in the word of God that tells us exactly how congregations are to send money to another congregation to put on a telecast or broadcast, this does not mean that the word of God does not have patterns for anything else. It does mean that it does not have a pattern for this, and Brother Willis has not shown one.

He has brought a lot of charges, rather wild charges. Yet he has not shown this pattern that is violated. Tonight then, the word of God is timeless and you and I can take advantage of it. We can send out the human voice today to thousands of souls, not only through one nation, but through many. We can support this and see that it is done in any way that does not violate any other principle of scripture. Certainly the elders of Highland and those who have to do with this broadcast need to receive criticism. They need to re-examine themselves and re-examine what they are doing. Every congregation needs to examine what they are doing and see if it is more profitably done this way or more profitably done some other way. But neither I nor you, after they have made this decision, and they have made their search and they have come to their conclusion, should come along and try to read a law into the Bible that condemns their choice. Neither should we try to send that into their midst that undermines what they are doing.

Now, Brother Willis spoke of these books here. (Referring to two books published by Highland.) Where are those books that you had there? How many thousands did you say these are being sent out to? (Willis: I do not know. I do not have any idea. I said they had 10,312 on their mailing list.) Didn't you folks get the impression that he said these were being sent out to that mailing list? (Willis: Those were the key workers' books, Brother Inman.) All right, these were just for the key workers. There is some material sent out to 10,000 people. Let us just get what is being sent out and make that clear. This is just sent out to some key workers. Let us not make charges that do not fit the truth. They may be making errors. I am sure they are. If they are not, then they are the only people I know that are not. Let us in grace and in love help one another to overcome our errors. Let us do all we can for the glory of God.

I say unto you again tonight, when I look into the faces of these people and I see you out there, those who have had me in your homes, those whose hospitality I have partaken of, I see those whom I love dearly (And I believe that you love me), even as I love Brother Willis and I think he loves me. When I see those of you who have worked closely together in times past who today are not working closely and when I see that there is the kind of suspicion that is harming the church; when I see on the other hand, neo-orthodoxy, false ideas about the Holy Spirit and other things becoming rampant, and that we cannot get the atmosphere cleared where we can really make an attack upon these things that are destructive to the soul because we become so confused with some of these things, I believe it is time for us to go to the word of God and stay with the word of God and find an answer from the word of God.

It is not a time to make laws of our own. It is not a time to make restrictions where God has not made any. But it is time for each of us to go to the word of God and search it diligently, walk in it, and to reach out yonder to those thousands of souls that are lost in sin and help to bring them in whether by the use of radio, by the use of papers, or any other means that we possibly can. May God help us to do that. May God help each of us to come to an understanding of his truth and to a closer working relationship with one another. I thank you.

PROPOSITION

"RESOLVED THAT IT IS IN HARMONY WITH NEW TESTAMENT TEACHING FOR A CONGREGATION, OR CONGREGATIONS, TO TAKE MONEY FROM THEIR TREASURIES AND SEND IT TO A CORPORATE HOME (SUCH AS MID-WESTERN, POTTER, SCHULTS-LEWIS, MAUDE CARPENTER, LUBBOCK, ETC.), WHICH IS ORGANIZED FOR THE PURPOSE OF PROVIDING A HOME FOR ORPHANED OR FORSAKEN CHILDREN."

Affirmative: Clifton Inman
Negative: Cecil Willis

INMAN'S FIRST AFFIRMATIVE

Brother Willis and brethren: I, too, am thankful for another opportunity to be here that we may search the word of God and try to find the answer to those things that trouble souls and trouble God's people. I want again to say that when I see before me those who have worked closely together in times past, both with me and also one another, and yet today I see that there is division, there is aloofness and coolness, where there should be the warmest of feeling and the greatest of understanding, I dare not try to find an answer to our problem from any other source than from the word of our God. And so, I want to do my best in this discussion with Brother Willis to seek out the word of God, to understand it, and to abide by it.

Let us turn our attention now to the proposition: "Resolved that it is in harmony with." Let me again say that by "in harmony with", I mean that it is not contrary to, or we could just put in there, it is authorized by "New Testament teaching for a congregation, or congregations, to take the money from their treasuries", that into which the brethren have contributed their funds, and "send it to a corporate home." By a "corporate home", I simply mean not that home where man and woman have come together in the contract of matrimony to form a home, but one that has been formed through the means of incorporation. Now, the proposition I submitted originally went from there to here (pointing to chart): "which was organized for the purpose of providing a home for orphaned and forsaken children." Brother Willis wanted to put in "such as Mid-Western, Potter, Schults-Lewis, Maude Carpenter, Lubbock, etc." I think he wanted it worded a little differently but he agreed to including it like this. Now by "such as Mid-Western, Potter, Schults-Lewis, Maude Carpenter, etc.", we simply mean that these are corporate homes.

And let me say again that this does not mean that I am obligated to try to defend everything that is done by these homes. Let me illustrate what I mean here. Let us suppose tonight that there were a man present who does not believe that a church, from its treasury, should support a located preacher. And so I say, "Well, I will affirm that the scriptures, the New Testament, authorize a church, from its treasury, to support a preacher while he works with them in the capacity of a located preacher." But he would say, "Now, listen, I have to have it a little more definite than this." Let us have it worded like this: "that a congregation may, from its treasury, support a located preacher such as Clifton Inman, Bob Kessinger, Cecil Willis and James Needham." I say, "Well, all right, I will sign that."

But then we come to discuss it, and he goes and gets the financial statement of Clifton Inman. He looks around with a fine tooth comb. He begins to look into the life of Clifton Inman and some things that Clifton has done here and there. Then when he gets up, he spends all of his time trying to find where Clifton Inman has made a mistake somewhere and says, "Now, do you really believe that it is right to take money and spend it on a man who is engaging in such foolish things?" And we all say, "Man, that is beside the point. That is not what you are discussing." Get the point? I think you do. The point is, does the scripture authorize, or do the scriptures authorize, a contribution from the treasury of a congregation to be sent to a home which is organized for the purpose of providing a home for orphaned and forsaken children?

(Mimeographed sheet distributed by Brother Inman)
POINTS TO NOTE
1. Things authorized may be placed in 3 categories. See chart.

2. To be authorized a thing must not necessarily be bound.
3. Where there is no law, there is no transgression. Romans 4:15.
4. Paul had authority to lead about a wife, but he did not lead about a wife. 1 Corinthians 9.
5. We are enjoined to care for orphans. James 1:27.
6. We are not told to do this separately or conjointly.
7. Where there is no law there is no transgression.
8. Jesus said that people will be judged individually by whether they visit the hungry. Matthew 25:31-46.
9. The apostles activated this command by forming a common treasury. Acts 2:44,45.
10. A principle is set forth in 1 Timothy 5:16 that when one member has prime responsibility he should not permit this responsibility to be shifted to all, but that when there is no prime responsibility, the whole church is to be responsible.
11. Who must have legal custody of the one who is helped?
    A. Three agencies who may have legal custody.
        1. Husband and wife
        2. Church
        3. Corporate home
    B. Does the Bible set forth a pattern for helping in different ways if different agencies have custody? If so, where?
12. The act of helping is not that of helping an institution but of helping a needy child.
13. Concerning those who are not members of the church. Luke 10:25-27; Luke 4:25-27.

CARE OF ORPHANED OR FORSAKEN CHILDREN

1. Is any specific manner of caring for these set forth in the New Testament?
2. Are we enjoined to care for them? See James 1:27.
3. If care is enjoined and specific manner is not, then any manner may be used which does not violate some other New Testament principle. Romans 4:15
4. Some questions to elicit exact point of difference:
    A. Is it wrong for a group of brethren to form a corporation for the purpose of maintaining a home for orphaned or forsaken children?

B. Is it right to take funds from a church's treasury to help orphans or forsaken children at all?
C. If right to help orphaned or forsaken children at all, is it possible to help them in any way way if they happen to be in a corporate home?
D. Is it possible to help an orphaned or forsaken child who has been adopted by a man and his wife?
E. Is it possible for the church, from its treasury, to give money directly to the man and wife, or must it be given to the child directly?
F. Is it right or wrong to take funds from the treasury of the church to help one who is not a member of the church?

Let us notice again that things are authorized in different ways. As we noted the other evening, they may be placed in three categories. There are some things demanded of all. These are authorized either by direct command (and by that we are talking about a grammatical command or couched in that language—imperative language),

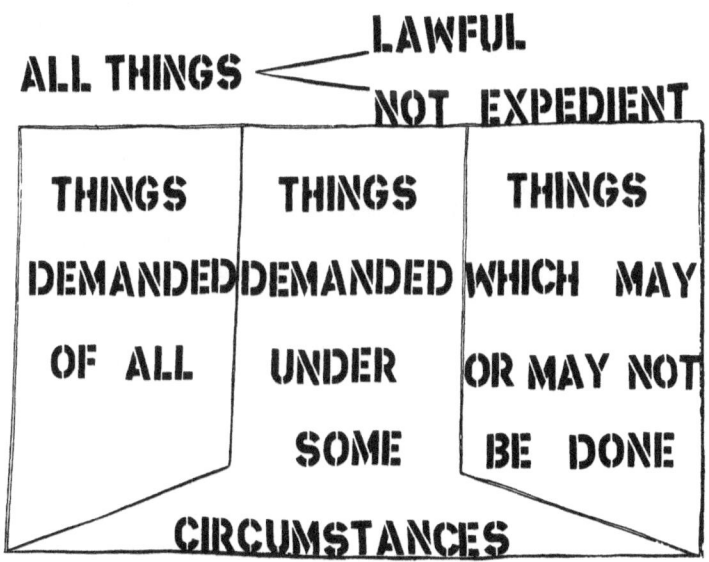

or there is a necessary inference, drawn from all that is said in relationship to this, to cause us to understand that God meant for all to do this.

There are some things that are commanded of some, such as we illustrated, that the wife is to be subject to her husband. Husbands do not obey that. Here is something that is demanded of some. There are those things that are demanded under certain circumstances. If a man smite thee on one cheek, turn the other also. Now there is another category of things that we may do or we may not do, and I want again to point out the fact that neither in this discussion, nor at any other time, have I said that anything is authorized by expediency. Anybody that says that I have said that has not listened very well.

I have pointed out that expediency restricts and does not expand. A thing must be authorized, but sometimes a thing that is authorized may not be expedient to use, even though it is authorized. We pointed out from 1 Corinthians 9 that Paul said, "Do I not have a right to lead about a wife, a sister, as the other apostles and Cephas?" The word translated "right" here is "exousia" which is also translated "authority." "Do I not have authority to lead about a wife?" And yet, he did not lead her about. He thought that in his case it was not expedient for him to do it. Yet, Peter, in his case, thought it was expedient for him to do it. Neither one of them sinned. But they were acting within the authority of Jesus Christ.

Again Colossians 3:17, "Whatsoever ye do in word or deed, do all in the name of our Lord Jesus, giving thanks to God and the Father by Him." We must have authority. But let us notice that those things that are demanded are authorized by a direct command. We have things that are authorized by necessary inference. The necessary inference may be that a thing is demanded. Again the necessary inference may be that God has set no bounds, and so we have in Romans 4:15, "Where there is no law, there is no transgression." Where God, in any field, has not made specifications, man does not violate them.

For example, baptism is demanded of all. Yet we have baptism authorized by command, but we have a baptistry authorized by necessary inference. It may not be expedient always to use a baptistry enclosed in a building, and if it is not expedient, of course, it should not be used. But it

Third Night, Benevolent Institutions 121

is authorized. The use of one is authorized. How? By necessary inference. God did not say where to be baptized.

Now with these principles set before us, let us proceed to notice then, that a thing in order to be authorized does not necessarily have to be mentioned. There does not have to be a specific mention. There is no mention of a baptistry. Paul had authority to lead about a wife. And I hope that you have one of the slips that I passed out here and have followed me with this.

Coming now to orphans. We are enjoined to care for orphans, just as men are enjoined to be baptized. Christians are enjoined to visit the fatherless. "Pure religion and undefiled before God and the Father is this, To visit the fatherless and widows in their affliction, and to keep himself unspotted from the world." We are not told whether this is to be done separately, individually, or conjointly. Now, the word "visit" here, I think all will agree, means more than just to go see. Therefore, since we are not told whether we are to do this individually, or whether we can all pool our resources in the common treasury and do it, it is assumption upon my part, or of any other man, to come along and say that it has to be done in a certain way. It is assumption to say that when I help or visit an orphan, I have to do it by myself, and if all of us put our money together in the common treasury and from that take the money and give it to them, that is a sin. God has made no such law. But sometimes someone gets the idea that this is true from James 1:27. Someone gets the idea that this is individual action, and that means that we act individually, and that when we all put our resources together in the common treasury, and from that visit the fatherless, there is some kind of sin.

Well, let us notice the principle. Point No. 8 here. Jesus said that in the judgment people will be judged. He is talking about individuals here, being judged by whether they visit the hungry. "I was hungry and ye visited me. I was naked and ye clothed me." Here, then, he is talking on an individual basis. Now later, when the church was set up, the apostles activated Jesus' teaching. That is, they carried out what he had taught here. How did they interpret what Jesus had said? Did they interpret this to mean that they would sin if they did it from a common treasury? In Acts 4:34 and 35, we are told that they had all things common, that men who had possessions sold them and "brought the prices of the things that were sold, and laid them down at the apostles' feet: and distribution was made to every man according as he had need." When the apostles interpreted Jesus' commandment which was given on an individual basis, they then fulfilled what he had taught by doing it collectively from the common treasury of the church. I think they set a pretty good example of how to interpret such language.

Then, there is a principle set forth in 1 Timothy 5:16, that when one member has prime responsibility, he should not permit this responsibility to be shifted to all. But, when there is no prime responsibility, the whole church is to be responsible. He says that if any brother has widows, he then is to provide for them and to requite them at a home, and let not the church be charged. Now let us take this to illustrate this and I hope you can see it. (He holds up a chart drawn on a large cardboard.)

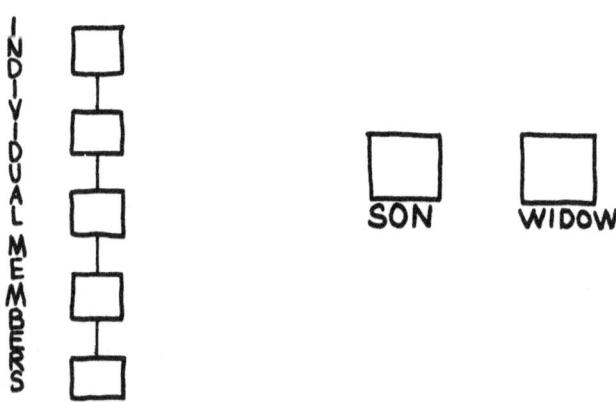

Third Night, Benevolent Institutions 123

Here is a son. He has a widowed mother. He has prime responsibility to that mother, to take care of that mother. But now, if there were no son, if there were no one in the congregation who had prime responsibility, who would be charged? Who would have the responsibility? The whole church. Let the church be charged. This man is to assume his family responsibility so they will not be charged. If he fails to fulfill that prime responsibility, then the church will be charged. The church does not sin by accepting this. He sins by not accepting his prime responsibility.

Now, this is an application of James 1:27, "Visit the widows." But this same passage says to "visit the fatherless." Now, when there is a fatherless child, he, like the widow, bears the same responsibility to every member. Let these blocks here represent members. We put orphan in here (points to word "widow"). When this orphan bears the same responsibility to every member of the church, then the church should be charged.

Somebody says, "You ought to take them into your home." Well, **you** ought to take them into yours. Why should I do it? You do it. So we can just kick it around all night. It is no more my responsibility than it is yours. It is no more yours than it is mine. No more ours than it is the next fellow's. It is a responsibility that is equal to everyone of us. And this is the principle. The interpretation is set forth by the Holy Spirit Himself in 1 Timothy 5:16, of what is taught in James 1:27.

Now, there comes another question though. A child who becomes homeless must have a legal custodian. Who must have legal custody of this child when we visit it? Now, someone, when we visit the fatherless child, must have legal custody of that child. There are three agencies at least (Maybe someone can find another one, we will not argue about this) that may have legal custody. This was point "A" under point 11 on the mimeographed sheet.

A man and his wife may adopt the child. Some say that the church itself may adopt the child. I think that there are some legal procedures here that we might find a little difficult. But then there may be a corporate home. Four or five or six or a hundred of us may go together and form a corporation, get a charter, become chartered in the state, build some buildings and take into these buildings orphaned or destitute children, forsaken children, and there care for them. Does the Bible (and here is a question I would like to ask) set forth a pattern for helping in different ways, if different agencies have custody?

Now, by that I simply mean this: We find various ideas concerning this among different people. We have noted ideas changing radically in the last few years. There were those who used to say that if a man and his wife had legal custody of a child, the church, through its treasury, could visit or help that child by giving money directly to the child or food directly to the child, by sending money to the father and mother to use for that particular child (We will say little Johnny to be specific here). Or they could just send money to this man and his wife and say, "We know that you will have extra expenses because little Johnny is in your home. You have adopted him, and so you take this money and use it the best way you see fit to help you with the livelihood and the care of little Johnny."

Then they said if the church had legal custody, again visitation could be made in the same ways. To the child directly, to the church specified for the child, or just given to the church that had charge of a home that has several orphan children in it, and say, "Now, you give it to them." But it is all right to have a corporate home, too. We could all go together and form a corporate home, and I would like now, Brother Willis, when you get up, for you to tell us whether or not there is anything sinful about a group of men forming a corporate home to take orphans into it. Is the very act alone of incorporating a home and taking children into it sinful? They say, "No, this is not sinful." And the church still can visit the fatherless here by giving directly to the child, by sending to the home and specifying for the child, but you cannot give it to this home and say, "You use it to the best of your wisdom in caring for the children." Now, where in all of God's word did they read all of these distinctions? That it is to be done this way if this one has legal custody? I would like to know where is the verse of scripture that makes all of this distinction.

There is much made of the idea of giving and building a human institution, and building up a human institution in rivalry to the church. Let us notice point No. 12: the act of helping, the act of sending this money, is not to build the corporation. The corporation is all ready built. The purpose of sending the money is to visit orphaned or forsaken children. (Moderator tells Brother Inman he has 10 minutes.)

Now, there is another thing. Someone says, "Well now, the church from its treasury just cannot help any orphan child unless it is old enough to be a member of the church, because it is a sin. It is wrong to take the money from the church treasury and give it to someone who is not a member of the church." And yet, in Galations 6:10, we are told, "Let us do good unto all men, especially unto them who are of the household of faith."

Now, Brother Inman, you know that that is talking about the individual. Do you? Yes, sir, that is the individual. All right, whatever this individual is to do to all men, and whatever is required concerning all men, is specially and specifically required, in a special way it is required, if it happens to be of the household of faith. "Especially unto them who are of the household of faith." Now, if this is saying that the individual alone, separate and apart from the common treasury, has to provide or to give to the one who is not a member of the church, to "all men" here, then it means in particular and especially when it comes to the ones of the household of faith, he has to do it. And so, brother, you have eliminated the saints. "Especially unto them who are of the household of faith."

Well, let us notice the attitude of Jesus. When Jesus said the greatest commandment is to love God and the second like it was to love your neighbor, that old lawyer, "willing to justify himself, said, 'who is my neighbor?'" And Jesus then told the story of the good Samaritan. The Samaritan was a man who looked upon the Jew as having a false religion. But Jesus said that that Samaritan helped this man who had fallen among thieves. And then he said to this lawyer: "Now who was neighbor of him that fell among thieves?" He said, "I suppose he that showed mercy." He said, "Go thou and do likewise." You go to help those who are not of your religion too. You go help those that you think have a false religion. Do not try to exclude them.

Then in Luke 4:25-27, Jesus said, In the days of Elijah there were many widows in Israel amongst God's people. But in this particular instance God, for some reason, did not send Elijah to a one of them, but sent him only to the widow of Zarephath, a Phoenician woman up there on the coast. And he said there were many lepers in the days of Elisha, but not one of them (there were many lepers in Israel) was healed or cleansed, but only Naaman the Syrian. Here, for some reason, God chose one that was not even among his people. Jesus said, "If a man smite thee on one cheek, turn to him the other also." He said, "pray for them that despitefully use and persecute you." This is individual, isn't it? Yet, when the apostles carried this out, and interpreted this, they came together when Peter and John had been persecuted, and all together as the common body prayed.

We see then, from the word of God, that God has specified that we visit the fatherless. We have seen that God has not specified who is to have legal custody of the child that is being visited. When any man comes along then, and begins to tell us who must have legal custody, and that we can visit one way if this one has legal custody, and another way if another has custody, then we know that individual is saying something that the word of God does not say. On the back of your paper there: "Is any specific manner of caring for orphaned or forsaken children set forth in the New Testament? Are we enjoined to care for them? See James 1:27. If care is enjoined and the specific manner is not, then any manner may be used which does not violate some other New Testament principle. Romans 4:15, 'Where there is no law there is no transgression.'"

Some more questions: Is it wrong for a group of brethren to form a corporation for the purpose of maintaining a home for orphaned and forsaken children? Is just the act of incorporating wrong if it is done for this purpose? Is it right to take funds from the church's treasury to help orphans or forsaken children at all? If it is right, is it possible to help them in any way if they happen to be in a corporate home? Can we take it to them directly? Can the church, from its treasury, take something to them directly, from the common treasury? Is it possible, number "d", to help from the church treasury, an orphan or forsaken child who has been adopted by a man and his

THIRD NIGHT, BENEVOLENT INSTITUTIONS 127

wife? Is it possible for the church from its treasury to give money directly to the man and wife, or must it be given directly to the child? Is it right or wrong to take funds from the treasury of the church to help one who is not a member of the church? Now, we need to have some answers to these to narrow the issue. How much time? (Brother Kessinger: three minutes.) Three minutes.

(QUESTIONS ASKED BY BROTHER WILLIS)

1. *During the first two nights you contended that though there are SOME patterns in the New Testament, that there is no pattern as to how churches may cooperate. Is there a New Testament pattern showing how an institutional Orphan Home should be operated? If so, what is that pattern?*
2. *Would it be scriptural to incorporate the Herald of Truth or the Bible Classes in the same way that the Mid-Western Children's Home is incorporated to do benevolent work?*
3. *If the board of directors of Mid-Western Children's Home were to alter or to expand its program of work so as to include evangelistic work, would you object to it? If so, why would you object?*
4. *In the Hunt Debate you told Brother Hunt: "I know nothing of a Nashville Orphans Home. I will not defend it unless I find that its function is not contrary to New Testament principles." (page 23). Since Brother Inman would not defend Nashville Orphan Home unless it was operated according to "New Testament principles", would you please tell us what these "New Testament principles" are that regulate the operation of Orphan Homes?*
5. *Please tell us how the Nashville Orphan Home could have been operated so as to be "contrary to New Testament principles", and therefore to have elicited your opposition. What kind of an orphan home would you not endorse?*
6. *Are there any of the institutional orphan homes among us that you know about that are not operated according to "New Testament principles"? If so, which ones are they?*
7. *Inman, Bible Herald, April 1, 1954, page 2. "Brother Inman, what about orphan homes and old folks'*

homes. *I HAVE NOT REACHED ANY DEFINITE CONCLUSIONS ON THESE except that I am persuaded men may have such homes IF THEY ARE PRIVATELY OWNED AND OPERATED. I believe also that a local congregation may own and operate such homes locally to care for orphans and aged in the locality. I have not fully decided about homes operated otherwise. Let us study the question carefully."*
Name some of there "homes operated otherwise."
8. Please tell us when you decided the homes were scriptural about which you earlier had not reached "any definite conclusions."
9. What features about these "otherwise operated" homes caused you then to be undecided and to have reservations concerning them?
10. What scriptural arguments convinced you these "otherwise operated" homes (like the ones in your proposition) are right?
11. Is it possible (or probable) that twelve years from now you may be defending the church support of colleges which you now contend must be "privately owned and operated"?
12. Are the Orphan Homes mentioned in your proposition human institutions or divine institutions?

I have some questions now that have been handed me. We have covered the proposition. We shall wait for an examination of it. I have been given some questions: "During the first two nights you contended that though there are some patterns in the New Testament, that there is no pattern as to how churches may cooperate." I never contended any such thing. I did say that there is no set pattern as to how money may be sent from the treasury of one congregation to the treasury of another congregation. I set forth what was done, how they did do it when they sent it from over at Macedonia and Achaia to Jerusalem, and I asked if that were a pattern. I never did get an answer. I pointed out that it was done in another way in Acts 11, and I asked if this was a pattern. I never did get an answer. And when we see it done two ways, I said for this particular thing, there is no pattern. I did not say for any kind of cooperation.

"Is there a New Testament pattern showing how an institutional orphan home should be operated?" No, sir. "Would it be scriptural to incorporate the Herald of Truth or the Bible classes in the same way that the Mid-Western Children's Home is incorporated to do benevolent work?" No. No more than it might be right to incorporate them the way you might incorporate TRUTH MAGAZINE.

"In the *Hunt—Inman Debate* you told Brother Hunt: 'I know nothing of the Nashville Orphan Home. I will not defend it unless I find that its function is not contrary to New Testament principles.' " Now, he has another one over here and I think I need to read it. He has a quotation from *Bible Herald* of April 1, 1954, page 2: "Brother Inman, what about orphan homes and old folks homes?" Now, I am giving that question there that may be asked by someone else and then I answer it. "I have not reached any definite conclusions on these except that I am persuaded men may have such homes if they are privately owned and operated. I believe also that a local congregation may own and operate such homes locally to care for orphans or aged in the locality. I have not fully decided about a home operated otherwise. Let us study the question carefully." Now, this was several years after I made the statement to Hunt. (Brother Kessinger: Time.) Thank you. We will deal with that later.

WILLIS' FIRST NEGATIVE

I see Brother Inman has hung out his chart again. He likes the way that they are doing it better than the way we are not doing it. Each night, I think, he has hung that up, and so I thought it might be in order if I just tell you, to start off this evening, how they are doing it. I have

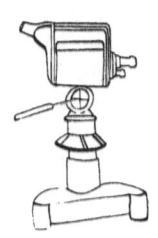

WHICH IS BETTER

OUR WAY OF DOING IT

OR

YOUR WAY OF NOT DOING IT?

a quotation here from *Boles Home News,* February 25, 1966. Here is what it says: "There are two million members of the churches of Christ," and then the article states that *"this means that we are spending the stupendous sum of fifty cents per member per year for benevolence."* Now, that is the way they are doing it. Fifty cents per member per year for benevolence! If that is the way you are doing it, Brother Inman, I do not believe I would be boasting about it.

This evening my duty is that of being a respondent; replying to what Brother Inman has had to say this evening. He now has had two speeches since I have had one. Before I reply to his speech just made I want to go back to just a thing or two that he said the other night. He has referred to our earlier speeches also this evening. I do not intend to rehash the Herald of Truth discussion. We are not here to do that. But there are two or three things I want to call to your attention.

Brother Inman made a big point the other night of the fact that he is a man of just one book. Then I pointed to a whole stack of books underneath his table that were not Bibles. But also, as I look through the *Hunt-Inman Debate,* I find repeatedly that Brother Inman quoted from historians to show when mechanical instrumental music began. That is all I did, Brother Inman. I just quoted from historians to show when this concept of a sponsoring church began. And that is the same practice that he employed a good many years ago. And, by the way, Brother Inman, in 1942 when you debated with Brother Hunt, were you a man of one book then? He somehow quoted from some history books back then. And also, you know, you are a rather poor fellow to be talking about being a man of one book, when you have a whole bookstore full of books! Maybe he is advertising that he should *not* sell them! Perhaps that is what he is doing.

Brother Inman also charged, night before last, that a Christian Church preacher, who was here on Monday evening, had said he "had an affinity for my position." Now, I just could not believe that. I have not run into any Christian Church preachers who have an affinity for my position. I thought, well, that man might be a fellow we are about to convert. So, I called him up today to see what actually he did say. And here is what he said. He said that he had an affinity for my position; *that I was consistent and Brother Inman was inconsistent!* You cannot blame a man for preferring consistency over inconsistency.

And he was rather emphatic in saying that he did not agree with my **position**! And I knew that. I knew that was not what Brother Inman should have said about it. Inman said that he had an "affinity for my position." And the Christian Church preacher said, "Oh, no I don't!" And further, he said, "The way Inman is arguing to defend the Herald of Truth, he could not now say a word about a piano." That is what I said the other night. I charged Brother Inman with making Christian Church arguments. And further, the Christian Church preacher said, "Inman is using the same arguments in his efforts to defend the

Herald of Truth that I have always used to defend instrumental music." I said that too.

And he went on to say, "Even if the Herald of Truth were scriptural, even if somebody proved the Herald of Truth were scriptural," (And he said there was not any question about it; Brother Inman did not prove it.) "I would not support it because it showed a lack of stewardship, a misuse of funds, a misappropriating of funds."

And then he went on to say, "If the figures on your chart about the Herald of Truth budget were correct, I would not support it for the simple reason that it showed a lack of stewardship." And then he said further, *"In substance the Herald of Truth is the same as the Missionary Society."* So, I want to set before you correctly what the Christian Church preacher *actually* said. Brother Inman has said he was not making Christian Church arguments. This Christian Church preacher said he was. And if anybody ought to know a Christian Church argument, I would think a Christian Church preacher would be the fellow that would know it.

In the last speech night before last, Brother Inman inadvertently made a Christian Church argument. He said, "by going to the word of God and finding *there is no prohibition against it*, then I walk by faith, knowing that since God has not said . . . uh . . .", and then he saw where he was going. He said, "uh . . ." (Laughter.) And he stopped and said, "That was an inadvertent statement." Now, Brother Inman, that was not only inadvertent; that was an unfortunate statement, because I have heard for years that the justification of a piano is "there is no prohibition in the Bible of it." And so, he inadvertently made a Christian Church argument the other night.

Brother Inman also inferred, on the chart I had the other night on the Herald of Truth budget, that I might have gotten my figures mixed up. He said, "You know, it is pretty hard to read one of their financial reports." And he said he could not read one. And his inference was perhaps I could not either. Now, Brother Inman, just because you cannot read one, do not infer I cannot. He also said, perhaps you ought to have had an accountant check that. And so I did go to an accountant after I got all done, and I said, "Would you run through all of these figures of this very complicated financial report, and would

THIRD NIGHT, BENEVOLENT INSTITUTIONS 133

you tell me if my figures are correct?" And he said, "Yes, sir, they are correct."

And we had another accountant go over another one of their reports, and you know what he found? He found a $21,088.66 error in the Herald of Truth financial report (1960 Report). Now, it looks like, even if I could not read a financial report, that I could *read* one as well as they can *write* one. And so, I just call that to your attention. They said it was typographical error. They have explained that, after a lot of prodding! They said it was a typographical error! But I just got a copy of their explanation this week, and they made *more than twenty changes* in their financial report to correct a *typographical* error. Now that is some typist, isn't it? I tell you, I would like to know if they still have that typist out there. And they were trying to explain a $21,000.00 error, and when they got done, they had $27,000.00 more than they had before. So, actually, they over-juggled their books $6,123.67!

Now, one other thing, and we will pass to the discussion of this evening. Brother Inman made quite a point last night of the fact that I had misrepresented him on what he said on Acts 11:27-30. The brethren who share the position that Brother Inman holds generally argue on Acts 11: 27-30 that the money was sent over to Jerusalem, and Jerusalem then scattered the money throughout the churches of Judea, and that we have a sponsoring church in the Jerusalem church. He said, "I did not say that, Brother Willis. You misrepresented me."

I was taking some notes at the time and I was not sure but what I did misunderstand him. But actually, Brother Inman, that was another of your inadvertent statements. I went back and checked the tape, and if you want to jot down where it is, it is seventy-five feet from the beginning of the tape. Brother Inman said, "Now, Brother Willis just did not pay any attention to this pattern. I would like to know if it is a pattern, or if he thinks it is. If he says it is, then I want to take him back to Acts the 11th chapter and point out to him there is another pattern. For the church at Antioch just chose Barnabas and Saul to take it *to Jerusalem*." I thought that was what he said. He said, "That is an obscure argument," night before last, and that was why he did not make it. But that is what he said. He said they took it *"to Jerusalem"*, and the money was for the brethren in Judea.

Now, it is my duty this evening to be in the negative, and I am supposed to reply to what he has had to say and so I want to give some attention to that. First I want to go through my questions to which Brother Inman has given some attention. I said, "During the first two nights you contended that though there are some patterns in the New Testament, there is no pattern as to how churches may cooperate." Now, Brother Inman, if that is not what you said, I misunderstood you for two nights. I thought that was what you said. Then I asked, *"Is there a New Testament pattern showing how the institutional orphan home should be operated? If so, what is that pattern?"* And he said "No." Now, I knew that all ready. There was not any Bible instance about operating an institutional orphan home. Old Brother F. B. Srygley said many years ago: there is no scriptural way to organize a thing that is not in the scriptures. That is what Inman's trouble is. He is trying to organize something that is not in the scriptures.

He said, "Well, it is just like *Truth Magazine.*" Oh, no it is not, Brother Inman. *Truth Magazine* is not a church-sponsored organization, and churches are not contributing money from their treasuries to *Truth Magazine.* And if they were to start doing so, I would oppose it. And I think perhaps Brother Inman might, too.

I asked, *"Would it be scriptural to incorporate the Herald of Truth or the Bible classes in the same way that the Mid-Western Children's Home is incorporated to do benevolent work?"* And he answered very plainly, "No." Now, the first two nights he was maintaining that the Herald of Truth is not a separate organization and he is scared to death of that separate organization. Do you know what he is doing tonight? *He is defending one*! First two nights—"Do not call it a separate organization. It is not a separate organization." Tonight he is defending one.

Further, I asked, *"If the board of directors* (He has not replied to all of the questions. He will get to the remainder of them in his next speech.) *of Mid-Western Children's Home were to alter or to expand its program of work so as to include evangelistic work, would you object* to it? If so, why would you object?" Jot it down, Brother Inman, please.

And then in the *Hunt—Inman Debate*, Hunt asked a question about the Nashville Orphan's Home. Brother Inman said: "I know nothing about the Nashville Orphans' Home. I will not defend it unless I find that its function is not contrary to New Testament principles" (page 23). Now Brother Inman, look back at question number one. I asked you, "Is there a New Testament pattern showing how an institutional Orphan Home should be operated?" He said "No." But then he said, I will not endorse that one down at Nashville unless it is "not contrary to New Testament principles."

And so, I have some questions about that, Brother Inman. Since Brother Inman will not defend Nashville Orphan Home unless it is operated according to "New Testament principles," *"Would you please tell us what these 'New Testament principles' are that regulate the operation of Orphan Homes?"* You will not endorse one unless it is consistent with "New Testament principles." Now, what are these "New Testament principles"? *"Please tell us how the Nashville Orphan Home could have been operated so as to be contrary to these New Testament principles and therefore to have elicited your opposition. What kind of orphan home would you not endorse?"* There is some kind you will not endorse. So what kind is it? *"Are there any of the institutional orphan homes today among us that you know about that are not operated according to 'New Testament principles'? If so, which ones are they?"* Then also, we have some other questions if I can find my other sheet of questions. I do not believe I got here with all the questions. Let me borrow your copy, Brother Inman, please. Thank you, sir.

Somebody asked him, "Brother Inman, what about orphan homes and old folks' homes?" He said, "I have not reached any definite conclusions on these . . ." Now let me tell you, he has reached some conclusions now. This was written in 1954. He said "I have not reached any definite conclusions on these except that I am persuaded that men may have such homes *if they are privately owned and operated.*" Now, Brother Inman, that is what I believe tonight. I wonder if you were getting your meetings cut off back in 1954 about that. And I wonder if brethren were writing in deeds about you back in 1954 because you believed that. The only thing I believe, he says, is that they "may have such homes if they are privately owned and operated."

"I believe also", he said, "that a local congregation may own and operate such homes locally to care for orphans and aged in the locality. I have not fully decided about homes operated otherwise." Now he has tonight! We have Mid-Western Children's Home. That is one that is operated differently from the ones you talked about there. And we have also the Schults-Lewis Orphan Home that is under a board of directors. And he said he had not decided about that in 1954. Now I want you, Brother Inman, if you will please, to *"Name some of these 'homes operated otherwise.'"* I want to know which ones you had in mind in 1954, that you had not decided about. Please tell us *when* you decided these homes were scriptural, about which you earlier had not reached any definite conclusions. And *what features* about these "otherwise operated homes" caused you then to be undecided and to have reservations concerning them?

And tenth, and this one I want answered particularly: *"What scriptural arguments convinced you that these 'otherwise operated homes' (like the ones now in your proposition) are scriptural and right?"* Then I want to know this. He has done some changing since 1954. Tonight he says it is wrong for a church to support a college. I am just wondering if perhaps in twelve years he might be saying it is all right for a church to support a college. So I have this question: *"Is it possible (or probable) that 12 years from now you may be defending the church support of colleges which you now contend must be privately owned and operated?"* That is what he said about institutional orphan homes in 1954. I wonder if twelve years from now he will be defending church support of these institutional educational societies. *"Are the orphan homes mentioned in your proposition human institutions, or are they divine institutions?"*

Now let us come to what he had to say tonight. He wanted to know, first of all, concerning his chart. Now I would like to have his chart. Will you flip it back, Brother Inman? I hate for you people not to get to see that (referring to "We like the way we are doing it" chart)

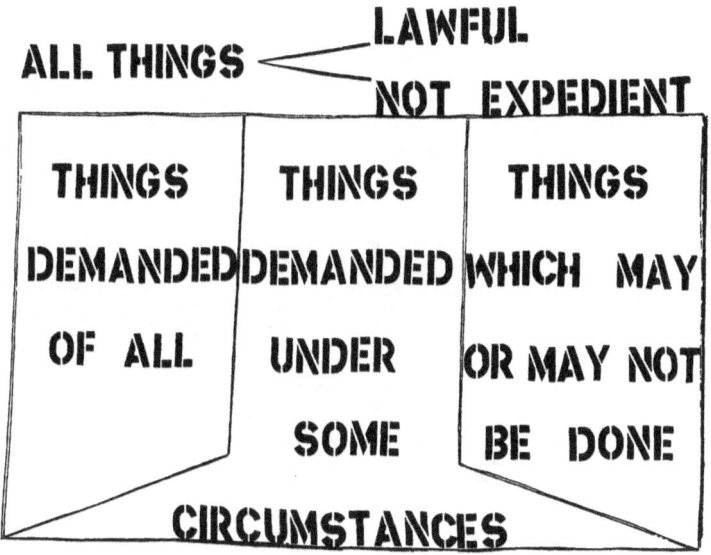

through another speech or two, but I want to look at another one.

Now Brother Inman has argued that there are some things that are demanded of all. Some things are demanded under some circumstances. And orphan homes do not fit under either one of those, do they, Brother Inman? They are not *demanded* of all, or *demanded* of some under some circumstances. So they do not fit there.

He says there are things which may or may not be done. That is the only place he can put them on his chart. Now what I want to know, Brother Inman, is by what scriptural right do you put them over there under the category of things which may or may not be done. He said you can do your benevolent work through this corporation here, and I want him to tell us now, how you put institutional orphan homes under things which may or may not be done, but you cannot put a missionary society over there and do your evangelistic work through one of those corporative boards. I want to know why he can put one in there, but cannot the other. And the thing he really needs to do is to prove that a human institution is an indifferent thing.

Let us notice also, in this connection, my chart No. 8. Really his argument is the same one he has made the first two nights on general and specific authority. Let us talk about it a little bit. There are some commands that are general, and some that are specific. And I have told Brother Inman all the way through that I will take

GENERAL AND SPECIFIC AUTHORITY

COMMANDS	INCLUSIONS	PERVERSIONS	INCIDENTALS	ADDITIONS
BUILD AN ARK GEN. 6	GOPHER WOOD 3 STORIES	OAK, CEDAR, PINE TEN STORIES	TOOLS, SIZE OF TREES TRANSPORTATION	ANOTHER BUILDING
TEACH MT. 28:19	WHOLE COUNSEL THE TRUTH	HUMAN TRADITIONS DOCTRINES OF MEN	BLACKBOARD, T.V. CHARTS, RADIO	CHRISTIAN MISSIONARY SOC.
BAPTIZE MT. 28:19	WATER-BELIEVER BURIAL	WINE, INFANTS SPRINKLING	OCEAN, RIVER POOL, BAPISTRY	CHRISTIAN BAPTIZING ASSOCIATION
SING EPH. 5:19	SPIRITUAL SONGS MELODY IN HEARTS	WORLDLY SONGS MELODY ON HARPS	BOOKS, FORK VOICE PARTS	SINGING SAINTS SOCIETY
LORD'S SUPPER MT. 26	1ST. DAY, BREAD FRUIT OF VINE	MIDWEEK BEEF & MILK	PLATES, CUPS PLACE	CHRISTIAN COMMUNION CONFEDERATION
PRAY PHIL. 4:6	TO GOD IN FAITH	TO MARY IN PRETENSE	LENGTH OF PRAYER, POSTURE	CHRISTIAN PRAYING LEAGUE
GIVE I COR. 16	AS PROSPERED CHEERFULLY	SPARINGLY GRUDINGLY	COLLECTION PLATES, LAY ON TABLE	CHRISTIAN FELLOWSHIP FEDERATION
RELIEVE I TIM. 5:16	FOOD, CLOTHING SHELTER	OPPRESS VEX NEGLECT	HOUSE, TENT, CITY, COUNTRY	CHRISTIAN BENEVOLENT COOPERATION

either one, general or specific authority. We have commands and we have some things that are *included* in those commands, some things that are *perversions* of those commands, some things that are *incidentals* to those commands, and then some things that are *additions* to those commands.

Now God told Noah to build the ark. Included was wood. A certain kind of wood was specified and how big it was to be—three stories high. Now he could have perverted God's order by using oak, cedar or pine, or by building it ten stories high. Now there were some incidentals, like the tools and the size of the trees and how to transport the materials, but there also could have been an addition, such as another institution.

God told us to teach. He told us to teach the whole counsel. We pervert that order when we have human traditions or the doctrines of men. We may use incidentals like blackboards, television, charts, and radio. But an addition is a Christian Missionary Society. God says we cannot have that.

Now we are commanded to baptize. God told us we are to bury a believer in water. We can pervert that command by using wine or sprinkling infants. And incidentally, it can be done in a river, an ocean, a pool or a baptistry. But an addition would be to found a Christian Baptizing Association or society. That is what Brother Inman is defending here this evening in substance.

God told us to sing spiritual songs and make melody in our hearts. Perversions are worldly songs or melody on a harp. Incidentals are books, forks, and voice parts. Now he has tried to say these institutions are authorized like song books. But actually Brother Inman, if we had a Singing Saint Society, we would have the parallel to what you are defending.

And the Lord told us to take the Supper. On the first day of the week we are to break bread and drink the fruit of the vine. We pervert that when we do it in the middle of the week and use beef and milk. Incidental to that command we use plates and cups, and a place to take of it would be incidental. But if we had a Christian Communion Confederation, then we would have what Brother Inman is defending. And this is an addition.

And God told us to pray in faith. We might pray to Mary in pretense and have a perversion. The length of the prayer and the posture we take while we pray would be incidentals. But we might form a Christian Praying League and try to turn our praying over to it.

God told us to give as we have been prospered and to give cheerfully. A perversion would be to do so sparingly and grudgingly. We use collection plates incidentally, or we could lay it on the table, or we might add a Christian Fellowship Federation.

Now, God also told us to "relieve." In the passage (1 Timothy 5:16), he said, "relieve them that are widows indeed." Included are food, clothing and shelter. We might pervert that command by oppressing or vexing or neglecting. We may use a house or a tent. It might be in the city or it might be in the country. But when we form a Christian Benevolent Cooperation we have an addition. Or you could just call it a "corporate home", Brother Inman, and you have an addition.

Now, let us notice also another argument he made in this connection. On 1 Timothy 5:16 he argued that this is

I TIMOTHY 5:16

INDIVIDUAL MEMBERS

SON   WIDOW

talking about individual responsibility. Then he used Matthew 25:31-36, and he said there also is individual responsibility, and there were some other passages that he cited. I have a notation of the different passages that he cited. Under individual benevolence, he used James 1:27, Matthew 25:31-46; 1 Timothy 5:16; Luke 10:25-37; and Luke 4:25-27. Everyone of those, Brother Inman, are instances of *individual action* in benevolence. And he wants to make those authority for *church* action.

Now, I happened to get a paper today, and it is called *Bible Herald*. It is put out by a fellow that is a man of one book. But he has the *Bible Herald*. Where is the paper?

Third Night, Benevolent Institutions 141

Somebody see it here? (The paper had been mislaid.) Well I do not see it just now. Yes, here it is. He made the statement today in his paper that when you make this argument, "what the individual can do, the church can do", you are in error. Tonight he says we can transmit this individual responsibility unto the church. Here is what he said in the paper: Some people are making the argument that "whatever the individual does, that is the church doing it." Brother Inman said, that is not so. He says, "This is an often made statement that has no basis in fact. A few quotations from scriptures will suffice to show the fallacy." (*Bible Herald*, September 1, 1966, page 5.) And let me tell you something else that will show its fallacy just as quickly. Can an individual send money to Ohio Valley College? Can you transfer *that* individual responsibility to the congregation? Can *congregations* then send money to Ohio Valley College? Or can we *not* transfer individual responsibility to a congregation?

Then he was talking about their having a hard time getting somebody taken care of. He said it would cause a big fuss. One would fuss, "he is not my responsibility", and another would say, "he is not my responsibility", but *"we like the way we are doing it, better than the way you are not doing it!"* Looks like to me they need a little conversion. They are having a rather hard time getting anybody to do it. They are spending one cent per member per week. Fifty cents per member per year.

I would like to come back to some of the things that he had to say, but presently I want to notice my chart No. 6, please. (Brother Inman speaking: What is the number of that one?) Which one? Chart No. 6. Now the other night, in my *first speech* on the cooperation question, in the introductory remarks, I gave seven points on what the Bible teaches about how churches may work together. Brother Inman said I did not cite any scriptures. Today I went back and counted how many verses I used. Brother Inman, I cited 58 *verses* of scripture in those seven points. If he wants to go back and count them, I would be glad to have him do so.

Now this evening, my argument, simply stated, is that *there is a pattern*. The Bible tells us to "build all things according to the pattern" (Hebrews 8:5). We have pointed out that there is a pattern in *worship*, there is a pattern

ACCORDING TO THE PATTERN - HEB. 8:5
SCRIPTURES COMPLETELY FURNISH US - 2 TIM. 3:16-17, 2 PET. 1:3

THE PATTERN:

WORSHIP
LORD'S SUPPER (ACTS 20:7)
SINGING (1 COR. 14:15)
PRAYER (ACTS 2:42)
GIVING (1 COR. 16:1-2)
TEACHING (1 THES. 5:27)

WORK
EDIFICATION - (EPH. 4:16)
EVANGELISM -(1 TIM. 3:15)
BENEVOLENCE -(ACTS 6:1-4)

ORGANIZATION
PLURALITY OF ELDERS-(ACTS 14:23, PHIL. 1:1)
DEACONS - (1 TIM. 3:8 FF)
EVANGELISTS -(2 TIM. 4:5)
SAINTS - (EPH. 1:1-2)

COOPERATION
INDEPENDENT ACTION OF CHURCHES-(PHIL. 4:14-16)
(1THES. 1:7-8
NO OTHER ORGANIZATION THAN THE CHURCH·
(PHIL. 1:1)
ELDERS OVERSEEING WORK - ONE CONGREGATION
(1 PET. 5:2-3)
AUTONOMY OF EACH CHURCH·(SELF-GOVERNING)
(ACTS 20:28)

VIOLATIONS
BACON AND EGGS
THURSDAY NIGHT OBSERVANCE
INSTRUMENTAL MUSIC
COUNTING BEADS
CAKE SALES---- RUMMAGES

ENTERTAINMENT PARTIES ETC.
COMMERCIAL BUSINESS
BALL TEAMS, BOY SCOUTS
SUBSIDIZE HUMAN INST.

ONE PASTOR- BOARD OF DIRECTORS
STEWARDS,
BOARDS, SYNODS, ETC.

JOINT ACTION OF CONGR.
HUMAN ORGANIZATIONS
CATHOLIC POPE
CENTRALIZATION OF FUNDS
& WORK

OPPONENT JOINS THE SECTARIANS AND MODERNISTS WHO SAY THERE IS NO PATTERN !

in *work*, there is a pattern in *organization*, there is a pattern in *cooperation*. Now, I am also maintaining this evening that *there is a New Testament pattern in benevolence.* And here it is: *In the New Testament, when benevolent work was to be done, it was done by, through and within the local congregation according to divine instruction.*

You will remember the instance over in Acts the 6th chapter, in the Jerusalem church. They had some widows that were destitute. Some brethren in that congregation were appointed to see to that at the discretion of the congregation. In Acts 11:27-30 we have an instance of the churches in Judea being destitute. The brethren in Antioch sent money to relieve them, and they sent it to the elders. They did not send it to the board of directors, Brother Inman. They sent it to the elders. But in the modern plan, which Brother Inman is defending, the benevolent work of the church is done *by, through* and *within a human institution* according to *human wisdom.* He cannot find one of these human institutions in the word of God.

N.T. PATTERN VS. MODERN PATTERN IN BENEVOLENCE

NEW TESTAMENT PATTERN	MODERN PATTERN — VIOLATIONS
1. THE WORK WAS DONE BY THROUGH & WITHIN THE LOCAL CHURCH ACCORDING TO DIVINE INSTRUCTIONS. ACTS 6:1-6; 11:27-30	1. THE WORK IS DONE BY, THROUGH & WITHIN A HUMAN INSTITUTION ACCORDING TO HUMAN WISDOM.
2. EACH LOCAL CHURCH CARED FOR ITS OWN NEEDY IF ABLE. ACTS 6:1-6	2. LOCAL CHURCHES SEND THEIR NEEDY TO A HUMAN INSTITUTION NOT KNOWING IF THEY ARE ABLE TO CARE FOR THEM OR NOT.
3. WHEN LOCAL CHURCH UNABLE TO CARE FOR ITS NEEDY SISTER CONG.'S SUPPLIED THAT WHICH WAS LACKING. ACTS 11:29,30 ; 2 COR. 8:18-21	3. LOCAL CHURCHES SEND THEIR OWN NEEDY TO A HUMAN INSTITUTION AND SEND $10. A MONTH CONTRIBUTION.
4. IN UNAVOIDABLE EMERGENCIES ONE CHURCH SENT TO ANOTHER TO HELP MEET THE EMERGENCY. NOT ON A PERMANENT BASIS. ACTS 11:27-30	4. LOCAL CHURCH OR GROUP OF INDIVIDUALS CREATES AN EMERGENCY. AND CALLS UPON THE CHURCH IN GENERAL TO SUPPORT THEM ON A PERMANENT BASIS.
5. WHEN ONE CHURCH ASSISTED ANOTHER IN MEETING AN EMERGENCY SUCH ASSISTANCE WAS SENT TO THE ELDERS OF A CHURCH. ACTS 11:30	5. THE LOCAL CHURCHES SEND ASSISTANCE TO THE BOARD OF DIRECTORS OF A HUMAN INSTITUTION.

LET'S FOLLOW THE N.T. PATTERN

In the early church, each local church cared for its own needy, if able. Acts 6:1-6 shows that. And Acts 2:44-45 shows that, and Acts 4:34-35 shows that. They took care of their own needy. Distribution was made to every man according as any man had need. Now in the modern pattern, local churches send their needy to a human institution, not knowing if they are able to care for them or not. Send them down to Potter and you do not know whether they are going to be able to see to them or not. How much time, Brother Needham? (Brother Needham: You have six minutes.)

When the local church was unable to care for its needy, other congregations supplied that which was lacking. In Acts 11:27-30, Antioch sent to the brethren in Judea, and they sent the money by the hands of Paul and Barnabas to the elders. From 2 Corinthians 8:18-21 we learn that Galatia, Macedonia, and Achaia sent money, by the hands of messengers, unto the brethren in Jerusalem. And so that is how it was done in the Bible. But in the modern plan which Brother Inman is defending, what do local churches do? Do they take care of their own needy? No! You bag them up and you send them to a human institution, and then send the human institution $10.00 a month, and then you hang up your chart and say, "We like the way we are doing it." And you boast about how much you are doing, *fifty cents per member per year.*

In unavoidable emergencies, one church sent to another to help relieve the emergency, not on a permanent basis. And again we cite to you Acts 11:27-30. Antioch sent to the brethren who were destitute in Judea. What happens today? The local church or a group of individuals, in the sponsoring church arrangement, create an emergency. They are creating one for you right now. They are starting Mid-Western Children's Home and soon now, they are going to try to drum up some orphans, and then they are going to call upon the church in general to support them on a *permanent* basis. That is not the way it was done in the word of God.

When one church assisted another in meeting an emergency, such assistance was sent to the elders of the church (Acts 11:30), but in the modern arrangement defended by Brother Inman, the local churches send assistance to the board of directors of a human institution. And I say again, that is human wisdom, and I am calling upon him to follow the pattern.

Now, Brother Inman, do not get up and say now that I did not suggest to you the pattern. I am suggesting it to you right now, and here are the points (pointing to chart) in the pattern. And I want him to deal with that when he comes to speak in just a few minutes.

Now let us notice what he had to say about James 1:27. And I believe chart No. 23 is the one I want. James 1:27 says, "Pure religion and undefiled before God and the Father is this, To visit the fatherless and widows in their affliction, and to keep himself unspotted from the world." Now, if "visit the fatherless" in James 1:27 authorizes a human institution, a church orphanage, then we ought to have church widowages also, because it also says, "visit the widows in their affliction." So we ought to have church widowages.

Hebrews 13:2 says we ought to entertain strangers. If you can transfer individual responsibility to church responsibility, we ought to have *church* motels. Matthew 25:26 says to "clothe the naked." We ought, then, to have church haberdasheries. It says "visit the sick"; we ought to have church hospitals. It says "feed the hungry." Then

JAMES 1:27

IF THIS SCRIPTURE AUTHORIZES CHURCHES OF CHRIST TO BUILD AND MAINTAIN BENEVOLENT INSTITUTIONS, THEN SUCH A CONCLUSION WOULD ALSO AUTHORIZE THE FOLLOWING:

JAS. 1:27 ---- VISIT THE FATHERLESS ---- CHURCH ORPHANAGES
JAS. 1:27 ---- VISIT THE WIDOWS ------- CHURCH WIDOWAGES
HEB. 13:2 ---- ENTERTAIN STRANGERS --- CHURCH MOTELS
MT. 25:36 --- CLOTHE NAKED ----------- CHURCH HABERDASHERS
MT. 25:36 --- VISIT THE SICK ----------- CHURCH HOSPITALS
MT. 25:35 --- FEED THE HUNGRY -------- CHURCH CAFETERIAS
MT. 25:36 -- VISIT PRISONERS --------- CHURCH JAILS
I COR. 16:2 -- PUT MONEY IN TREASURY -- CHURCH BANKS
MT. 28:19,20. TEACH ALL NATIONS ------ CHURCH COLLEGES

we ought to have institutions that maintain church cafeterias. We are told to visit those in prison. Brother Inman, does that mean we ought to have church jails, too? If we can transfer individual responsibility to a congregation, then we ought to have church jails. And since we are to "lay by in store" on the first day of the week, put that money in a treasury, then we ought to have church banks. Shouldn't we? We are also to "teach all nations." And since we can have a human institution up here to do the benevolent work, then we could have church colleges down here to teach them, couldn't we, Brother Inman? Or could we have a church missionary society down here to teach them, Brother Inman? Now I want him to give some attention to that when he gets up to speak.

    Also he said, concerning Galations 6:10, we have an obligation to do good unto all men. He knew the truth on that passage. That passage is talking about individual responsibility. In fact, just before that it says, "whatsoever a man soweth, that shall he also reap." And it says that "in due season we shall reap, if we faint not." Brother Inman, are *churches* going to reap? At the judgment day, is God going to say, "Come up here now Marrtown Road church; you are going to reap what you have sown"? Or does the Bible say that every man (Romans 14:12) shall "give an account of himself" unto God?

Now really, that passage in Galatians 6 is simply saying that you have some *individual* responsibility, and these brethren are fussing about who is going to do it. The truth of the matter is, they are trying to shove it off on somebody else; they are trying to shove it off on a human institution. And this thing that he is defending is perversive, in that it causes people to neglect their personal responsibility and to think that they can discharge their obligation to God in benevolence by making a mere pittance of a donation to an organization that is never found in God's word.

Now, that is what we are talking about. This evening we are talking about whether the church is going to do the work, or whether the church can build a human institution *through* which to do it. And I want him to tell us *why* the church can build a human institution through which to do its benevolent work, but it cannot do its educational work, its edifying, through a human institution. Or why cannot it do its evangelistic work, its gospel preaching, through a human institution? I want him to tell us concerning that when he comes to the speaker's stand.

Now he has taken several passages this evening, 1 Timothy 5:16 and these others that I cited, and has tried to make those refer unto *congregational* responsibility. He has had several kinds of passages. Some refer to individual responsibility, and some unto congregational responsibility. But which one of them Brother Inman, has a *human institution* in it? I can read about *churches* in the Bible doing benevolent work. I can read about individual Christians in the Bible doing benevolent work. But I want to see in the Bible where we can read about churches doing their benevolent work *through a human institution*. That is what we are debating.

INMAN'S SECOND AFFIRMATIVE

I can never understand why in a discussion such as this, when affirmative arguments are made, they cannot be responded to and taken up as they were given so we may really have an examination, rather than two people going in two different directions. I do want to notice a few things. I do not know either why we have to go back to last night's discussion on another issue, but some things were said about this that I suppose we will have to notice.

First of all: how are we doing it? He ridicules the idea of our giving fifty cents, averaging fifty cents, per member. Now really, Brother Willis, those who stand with you, will you match that figure? I would like to see the figures. I would just like to see those. Are you caring for as many orphans? I would like to see the figures.

He said I said I was a man of one book. Well, it seems he cannot quote anything straight. He cannot even read it and then get it like it is. Last evening I did say that someone said to me, "Brother Inman, are you prepared for this debate?" I said, "Well, I have the advantage of Brother Willis. In preparing for this debate I just have one book that I have to study, the word of God. But he is going to go back and dig into old papers, financial statements and a multitude of other things, and I am not going to waste my time with this because we are discussing a scriptural issue and I am going to spend my time studying the word of God."

Now tonight when I came in, he asked me about another book over there that I did not hold up here last night. That book happened to be *Reflections*, a book by R. L. Whiteside. It so happens that in preparation for this discussion I did not even look into it, but when it first came out, because of my love for Brother Whiteside and appreciation for his scholarship, I read the book and I read it through. Yes, I read other books. I do have a book store. I am glad he is advertising it. I had read this book, and I had noticed something that he had said about helping people who are not members of the church. I noticed also that *Truth Magazine (I read that too sometimes)* complimented Brother Whiteside very highly. So I just had the book here in case there happened to be a quotation from Brother Whiteside. But all I needed to study was the word of God, and that is the place where I have tried to pitch the discussion.

He said that I said that the preacher the other day said he had an affinity for Brother Willis and his position. No, I said the preacher seemed to have an affinity for Brother Willis and his position. The thing that was bothering that fellow was the same thing that was bothering Julian Hunt when I made the same kind of arguments.

As a matter of fact, he has referred to the *Hunt—Inman Debate* several times, and our last proposition was worded something like this: "Resolved that I may consistently condemn the use of a mechanical instrument of music and still use a radio, song book, tuning fork, etc." In that discussion I made the same arguments that I have made here, and pointed out the same things that I pointed out during this discussion, and Hunt made the same arguments in return that he has been making. And so, this fellow the other day felt pretty good about it. He had someone who agreed with Julian Hunt and him. This is the thing that was "bugging" him. It was "bugging" him so much that he had to come in and tell me about it. They were not Christian Church arguments, or he would not have been bothered that much by them.

I had pointed out in my discussion the other evening that I was not calling for a prohibition and Paul did not say, "Where there is no prohibition there is no transgression." I did make a slip of the tongue and I suppose that makes me an unpardonable sinner.

He said that if I did not make some argument (I do not know what it was), he misunderstood me for two nights. Well, he certainly did. I thought that. He never did get what I was saying. This is the reason he never did try to answer. I suppose he misunderstood me for two nights. And it seems tonight that he still is not getting the issue and facing up to it.

He said that I contended that the Herald of Truth was not a separate organization. We did not even talk about

Third Night, Benevolent Institutions 149

that, or I did not. I do not remember even discussing whether it is a separate organization or not.

Then he wants to know what about the orphan home. Is it a separate organization? Yes, Sir! The home of a wife and husband is a separate organization from the church. I have not claimed that the orphan home is the church.

But now let us again notice the arguments that we may keep them before us. I pointed out the things that are authorized may be in three categories. Now, the things that we were talking about last night, and the things that we are talking about tonight, are the things which may or may not be done. He wanted to know where they are. What place do they fit? That is where they fit. An orphan must be visited. When there is an orphan child, we must visit that child. But who has legal custody of that child is a matter that is indifferent. The Bible does not say.

He wants to know, "Does that make the missionary society?" Now Paul said it is an indifferent thing whether you lead about a husband or wife. Can you lead about a missionary society? Now what does that have to do with the issue? Why not face up and answer the argument that is being made? We are enjoined to care for orphans (James 1:27). We are not told whether we are to care for those orphans individually or conjointly, by an individual visitation and contribution, or whether we can put it all together in a common treasury and from that help the orphans. If we are told, give chapter and verse please. "Where there is no law, there is no transgression." Jesus said that people will be judged individually by whether they visited the hungry.

By the way, while we are talking about that, will churches have to give an account for what they do? If not, Brother Willis has given up his whole position. If the church does not have to give responsibility, use that treasury any way you want to, and you will not have to answer for it. I never expected Brother Willis to get that liberal, did you? Just use it any way you want to; the church does not have to give an account. It will not reap what it sows. Let it sow any way it wants to. The apostles activated this command of Jesus.

Now let us notice that Brother Willis agreed and he emphasized that Matthew 25 is an individual matter. Let us notice that when the apostles interpreted this to carry out as recorded in Acts, they sold their possessions and brought it together and laid it at the apostles' feet, and distribution was made to each as he had need. When they carried this out (which Brother Willis says is individual, just like he said James 1:27 is an individual thing), they interpreted this to mean that they could carry this out and fulfill this from a common treasury. This is the way they understood it. This is the way they interpreted it. This is the way they carried it out.

Then a principle is set forth in 1 Timothy 5:16. No, sir, I do not believe that everything the individual does is the church doing it. I think if you will read that same article, in fact, I know if you read the same article just a little bit further down, you will find that I dealt with this passage and dealt with it just as I am dealing with it tonight, though I have gone into it a little further tonight. I pointed out that this individual is to do something to keep the church from doing it. But there is something else implied, and I pointed that out at the time, and said I am not

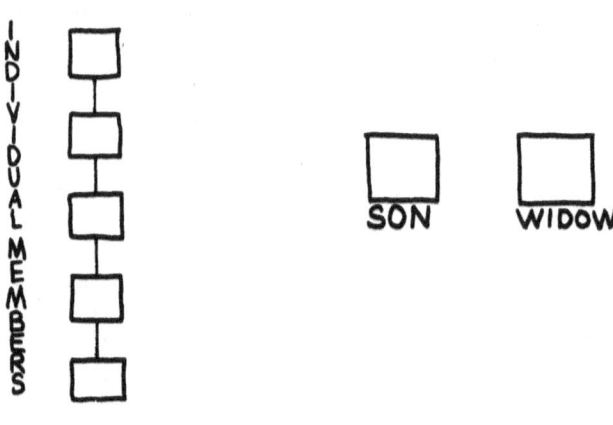

going to deal with that because it was not the point I was discussing then. But remove the son, remove this one that has the prime responsibility, and these do have the responsibility. When each bears an equal responsibility, this one cannot say "it's yours", and this one say, "it's yours." But each must accept his responsibility, and so they may each from their common treasury fulfill this obligation to a widow or orphan, or whomsoever it may be, because they are equally related to the need.

Now who must have legal custody of one who is helped, that is an orphan? Husband and wife? We did not have an answer to that. The church? A corporate home? These may. "Does the Bible set forth a pattern for helping in different ways if different agencies have custody? If so where?" And let us point out again that this act of helping or sending from the treasury to an orphan is not that of helping an institution. The institution is already built. It is already formed and chartered. Help is sent, not to help them in their need, as he suggests in one of his charts, but to help the orphans who are in need.

And we asked him some questions: "Is any specific manner for caring for orphan and forsaken children set forth in the New Testament?" Now we are enjoined to care for them in James 1:27. If care is enjoined and the manner is not specified, then any manner may be used which does not violate some other New Testament principle.

Now some questions: "Is it wrong for a group of brethren to form a corporation for the purpose of maintaining a home for orphaned and forsaken children?" I would like to have an answer to that, Brother Willis. "Is the forming of the home, is this in itself a sin? Is it right to take funds from a church's treasury to help orphaned or forsaken children at all?" If they are out here in a home adopted by a husband and a wife, is it a sin for the church to take money from the treasury, and help them? I would like to know about this. "Is it right to help orphaned and forsaken children at all? Or if right to help them at all, is it possible to help them in any way, if they happen to be in a corporate home?" Can we help them individually? Can you give individually, if they are in a corporate home? Is there any way that we can help? Is it possible to help an orphan or forsaken child who has been adopted by a man and his wife? Is it possible for the church from its treasury to give money directly to the man and wife? Now if you can, from the treasury, help in the case of adoption by man and wife, can you take it from the church treasury or must it be given to the child directly? Is it right or wrong to take funds from the treasury of the church to help one who is not a member of the church?

Now, let us have chart No. 8. We have "build an ark; build of gopher wood, oak, cedar, or pine." These would be perversions, these would be inclusions, or that which is included. These are perversions, these are incidentals and

GENERAL AND SPECIFIC AUTHORITY

COMMANDS	INCLUSIONS	PERVERSIONS	INCIDENTALS	ADDITIONS
BUILD AN ARK GEN. 6	GOPHER WOOD 3 STORIES	OAK, CEDAR, PINE TEN STORIES	TOOLS, SIZE OF TREES TRANSPORTATION	ANOTHER BUILDING
TEACH MT. 28:19	WHOLE COUNSEL THE TRUTH	HUMAN TRADITIONS DOCTRINES OF MEN	BLACKBOARD, T.V. CHARTS, RADIO	CHRISTIAN MISSIONARY SOC.
BAPTIZE MT. 28:19	WATER-BELIEVER BURIAL	WINE, INFANTS SPRINKLING	OCEAN, RIVER POOL, BAPISTRY	CHRISTIAN BAPTIZING ASSOCIATION
SING EPH. 5:19	SPIRITUAL SONGS MELODY IN HEARTS	WORLDLY SONGS MELODY ON HARPS	BOOKS, FORK VOICE PARTS	SINGING SAINTS SOCIETY
LORD'S SUPPER MT. 26	1ST. DAY, BREAD FRUIT OF VINE	MIDWEEK BEEF & MILK	PLATES, CUPS PLACE	CHRISTIAN COMMUNION CONFEDERATION
PRAY PHIL. 4:6	TO GOD IN FAITH	TO MARY IN PRETENSE	LENGTH OF PRAYER, POSTURE	CHRISTIAN PRAYING LEAGUE
GIVE I COR. 16	AS PROSPERED CHEERFULLY	SPARINGLY GRUDINGLY	COLLECTION PLATES, LAY ON TABLE	CHRISTIAN FELLOWSHIP FEDERATION
RELIEVE I TIM. 5:16	FOOD, CLOTHING SHELTER	OPPRESS VEX NEGLECT	HOUSE, TENT, CITY, COUNTRY	CHRISTIAN BENEVOLENT COOPERATION

these are additions (pointing to sections of chart). Now I want to know, does God teach for the church from its treasury to visit an orphan? Does He teach it at all? Would this be a perversion, if you help at all? Where would this fit in the category? Now, he comes to teaching and he says over here that this would be a perversion or this would be an addition. Would helping an orphan from the church treasury be an addition, an incidental, or a perversion? Just helping orphans, which would it be?

Well, let us ask another question? Is building a corporate home—just a group of us building it—is that an incidental or an addition? If we just go together and build one and it is not supported from the church treasury? What would this be? Which one of these categories would you put it in? I think we will have something interesting here if we can just get some answers. Which category would it fit in? All the way down here, where would it fit? Now, I am coming down to a benevolent corporation. We have relieve, food, clothing, shelter, oppress, vex, neglect, house, tent, city and country, etc. All these things in the various categories.

But now let us notice over here: He talked about the church relieving its own needy, and here is the reason we need some answers. If he says that an orphan who is not old enough to be a member of the church cannot be visited from the church treasury, I want to know, is that a church's needy? And if he says that they cannot be visited from the church treasury (This is what many contend; many of your brethren present here tonight contend that they cannot be visited from the church's treasury at all) then I want to know where they are to be visited from? If the church cannot from its treasury, how do they get to be the church's needy? And you are just about going to have to get a society.

And if they are not the church's needy, let us notice something else: What is the corporate home replacing? It is not replacing the church. You say they do not even belong to the church. They do not have anything to do with the church. They are not even the church's responsibility. Well, how in the world does the institution replace something that does not exist? You say it does not even exist. How does the church replace something that does not exist? How does this home taking the responsibility replace a responsibility you say does not even exist? You say the church does not have any responsibility. Now, Brother Willis may not take this position. This is the reason I wanted him to answer this awhile ago; so I can know. I do know that many brethren do argue this way. And if this be true, then this home does not take the place of the responsibility. It does not take the place of the church, because you say the church does not have any responsibility there. How much time do I have? (Brother Kessinger: You have about twelve minutes.) Twelve minutes.

I do want to get to his questions and be fair with these, and give him time to think about them before I get into the next chart. We got down to about the *Hunt—Inman Debate*. I said, "I know nothing of a Nashville Orphan Home. I will not defend it unless I find that its function is not contrary to New Testament principles." He says, "Since Brother Inman would not defend Nashville Orphan Home unless it is operated according to 'New Testament principles' would you please tell us what these 'New Testament principles' are that regulate the operation of Orphan Homes?" Well now, whether you think I am trying to escape something or not, I do not care, but this is an honest answer: I do not know what I had in mind back there when I wrote this. I just do not know what I had in mind. Now you can do with that whatever you want to, but that is an honest answer. I do not remember what my thinking was at that time. If you can remember back 27 years ago, remember all these things, well that is fine. But I do not have that good a memory in these things. I do not know just what I had in mind then.

"Please tell us how the Nashville Orphan Home could have been operated so as to be 'contrary to New Testament principles', and therefore to have elicited your opposition? What kind of orphan home would you not endorse?" Well, of course, we could start in naming a multitude of things. I would not want to endorse one that shot the children, and put them in a dungeon, and I could go ahead and name a multitude of things. But what does that have to do with the question tonight? You could just keep on and on and on making a list of things. And again I say, I do not remember just exactly what I had in mind at that time.

"Are there any of the institutional orphan homes today among us that you know about that are not operated according to 'New Testament principles'? If so, which ones are they?" That depends on what you mean by operated. I do not know, but I imagine that just about everyone of them somewhere along the line, like you and I as individuals, sometimes do some things that are contrary to New Testament principles. I just imagine sometimes they do. I know that I do not want to, but I am just human enough that I do that occasionally.

Now, he wanted to know about homes that are operated otherwise than what I was talking about in *Bible Herald*. Well, Boles Home, Potter Home, Mid-Western. He

Third Night, Benevolent Institutions 155

says "Please tell us when you decided the homes were scriptural about which you earlier had not reached any definite conclusions?" Now, the conclusion was not about whether they were scriptural or not, but whether they could be supported. The question was whether it was scriptural or not to support them in the way I think they could be tonight. I said I had not reached a conclusion then. I called upon all to study the Bible. This I have done. I cannot tell you the day nor the hour when I changed. That has nothing to do with it tonight. I have given the scriptures tonight that show why we may do it, and what we need to do is to look at these scriptures and see if I am misusing them. And when I changed my mind has nothing to do with it.

"What scriptural arguments convinced you these 'otherwise operated' homes (like the ones mentioned in your proposition) are right?" I was persuaded by the arguments that I gave in my first speech, which he did not notice. It is all right for a church from its treasury to visit or send money to these homes to be used to take care of the orphan children in them. I gave the scriptures and that was the whole argument.

"Is it possible (or probable) that twelve years from now you may be defending church support of colleges which you now contend must be 'privately owned and operated'?" Well, let us notice first of all: I said concerning the other item, I have not made up my mind. Let us notice another thing: There is a slight implication here or a sly implication that Brother Inman is just a little bit underhanded about this thing, and he is not really opposed to this matter of church support of colleges from the heart. Now if there is not this kind of thing meant in this question, what is the purpose of it? I do not really think that a question like this has any business being answered. This implies that I am just a little bit dishonest here, that I am being a little bit covert about this thing, and that I may be holding back something.

Now, if you want to know if I am going to change my mind twelve years from now, I do not know whether I will change my mind twelve years from now about anything or not. I had a man one time to send me a field report to the old paper I used to publish called *For Your Soul*, and he said, "I have been preaching for 60 years and I have never changed one position; what I believed back then I believe and teach today." I was a young fellow in my twenties then, and I had a hard time to keep from putting down at the end of that report when I put it in, "Never grown any, huh?" If I see scriptural reason for changing my mind on this or any other thing, I will change it. Now, Brother Willis, have you ever changed your mind about any scriptural position that you formerly occupied? How do I know that twelve years from now you will not possibly, or probably, decide that baptism is not essential to salvation? This has nothing to do with the proposition.

"Are the Orphan Homes mentioned in your proposition human institutions or divine institutions?" Human institutions.

Now let us look at the chart No. 6. New Testament pattern: "Work was done by, through and within the local church according to divine instruction." Now if you cannot

N. T. PATTERN VS. MODERN PATTERN IN BENEVOLENCE

NEW TESTAMENT PATTERN	MODERN PATTERN — VIOLATIONS
1. THE WORK WAS DONE BY THROUGH & WITHIN THE LOCAL CHURCH ACCORDING TO DIVINE INSTRUCTIONS. ACTS 6:1-6; 11:27-30	1. THE WORK IS DONE BY, THROUGH & WITHIN A HUMAN INSTITUTION ACCORDING TO HUMAN WISDOM.
2. EACH LOCAL CHURCH CARED FOR ITS OWN NEEDY IF ABLE. ACTS 6:1-6	2. LOCAL CHURCHES SEND THEIR NEEDY TO A HUMAN INSTITUTION NOT KNOWING IF THEY ARE ABLE TO CARE FOR THEM OR NOT.
3. WHEN LOCAL CHURCH UNABLE TO CARE FOR ITS NEEDY SISTER CONG.'S SUPPLIED THAT WHICH WAS LACKING. ACTS 11:29,30; 2 COR. 8:18-21	3. LOCAL CHURCHES SEND THEIR OWN NEEDY TO A HUMAN INSTITUTION AND SEND $10. A MONTH CONTRIBUTION.
4. IN UNAVOIDABLE EMERGENCIES ONE CHURCH SENT TO ANOTHER TO HELP MEET THE EMERGENCY. NOT ON A PERMANENT BASIS. ACTS 11:27-30	4. LOCAL CHURCH OR GROUP OF INDIVIDUALS CREATES AN EMERGENCY, AND CALLS UPON THE CHURCH IN GENERAL TO SUPPORT THEM ON A PERMANENT BASIS.
5. WHEN ONE CHURCH ASSISTED ANOTHER IN MEETING AN EMERGENCY SUCH ASSISTANCE WAS SENT TO THE ELDERS OF A CHURCH. ACTS 11:30	5. THE LOCAL CHURCHES SEND ASSISTANCE TO THE BOARD OF DIRECTORS OF A HUMAN INSTITUTION.

LET'S FOLLOW THE N.T. PATTERN

support an orphan from the church treasury because he is not a member of the church, does he fit here? Was that done through the church? You say it should not be. "The work is done by, through and within a human institution according to human wisdom." Well, he said it had to be. It is individual. He said James 1:27 is individual. An individual would have to use human wisdom about how much food to take, how much to buy, and when to go, and all of this, wouldn't he? He could not use his human wisdom as to whether he did go or not, but he could use it about the time, etc.

"Each local church cared for its own needy." Well, is this orphan needy? Is it or isn't it?

"Local churches send their needy to human instituiton, not knowing if they are able to care for them or not." Now, actually, the church does not control the matter of who has the legal custody of the child. The State controls that. The church may have something to do sometimes with where the State places them. They may be able to persuade them to do certain things here. But actually the church does not control this; the State does.

"When the local church was unable to care for its needy, sister congregations supplied that which was lacking." Well, they sent something. By the way, this matter he talked about last night. He stopped before he got through with that sentence about Jerusalem. I went ahead and said "or Judea as the case may be, if you want to talk about that." I think you will find that on the tape too. I did not say that they went ahead and sent it out from Jerusalem to somewhere else. He said I did, but even what he read a moment ago did not say that. That statement just says Jerusalem. I did not say they sent it from Jerusalem to somewhere else, Brother Willis. We want to know: does he say this church is needy? We would like to know about that so we can discuss it tomorrow evening.

"In unavoidable emergencies, one church sent to another to help meet the emergency, not on a permanent basis." Well, how permanent is the loss of a father and mother? I lost my father when I was 18 months old. I can tell you it is very permanent! It is extremely permanent! He says you can just send over here one or two times. It is just an emergency and it is over.

"When one church sent to another to meet an emergency, such was sent to the elders of the church." To care for orphans?

"The local churches send assistance to a board of directors." They do not send assistance to them, that is they do not send that to assist them. They send that to assist orphans. They send it to the home. Now just put husband

and wife in here where he wants to put the home, and you have the same problem.

How much time do I have? (Brother Kessinger: You have a minute.) What was your other chart you had? I did have something that I wanted to see. Chart No. 23.

JAMES 1:27

IF THIS SCRIPTURE AUTHORIZES CHURCHES OF CHRIST TO **BUILD** AND **MAINTAIN** BENEVOLENT INSTITUTIONS, THEN SUCH A CONCLUSION WOULD ALSO AUTHORIZE THE FOLLOWING:

JAS. 1:27 ----- VISIT THE FATHERLESS ---- CHURCH ORPHANAGES
JAS. 1:27 ---- VISIT THE WIDOWS ------- CHURCH WIDOWAGES
HEB. 13:2 ---- ENTERTAIN STRANGERS --- CHURCH MOTELS
MT. 25:36 --- CLOTHE NAKED ----------- CHURCH HABERDASHERIE
MT. 25:36 --- VISIT THE SICK ---------- CHURCH HOSPITALS
MT. 25:35 --- FEED THE HUNGRY ------- CHURCH CAFETERIAS
MT. 25:36 -- VISIT PRISONERS ------- CHURCH JAILS
ICOR. 16:2 -- PUT MONEY IN TREASURY ---CHURCH BANKS
MT. 28:19,20. TEACH ALL NATIONS ------ CHURCH COLLEGES

Church haberdashery. Many congregations have the haberdashery in their basement. When people do not have clothes, they ask them to come in and take their pick. It is all right as long as they do not start a business and do not start charging. Our brethren all of this time have understood this is all right, and many of the preachers here tonight who stand with Brother Willis encourage the congregation to do exactly this. Would it be right then for them to go out and start selling? No.

Now to this matter of teaching down here. Brother Willis has wanted very badly to do something to get at Ohio Valley College for some reason or other; I do not know just why. But the thing that is to be taught to all nations, Brother Willis, is the gospel. Now we go out here and the church may support the preaching of the gospel and the teaching of the gospel. But when you form a college and begin teaching some other things and have a business, that is a different matter. Thank you.

WILLIS' SECOND NEGATIVE

I might just as well refer in the beginning to some of the things with which Bother Inman closed. In the conclusion of his speech he said that some churches have haberdasheries in their basements, but he says, they cannot charge for the items. I wonder, Brother Inman, if you are opposed to these orphan homes that *charge* $60.00 a month to take care of orphans. I wonder if you are opposed to these old folks' homes that *charge* $60.00 per month to take care of old people.

Now he said you can have a haberdashery; just do not charge. I am maintaining you could send to the church haberdashery on the same basis you could send to the church orphanage. But he says you cannot charge, but they do charge in these church orphanages.

But also, I want to notice that Brother Inman, thus far in his presentation of proof tonight, has cited two passages that relate to *congregational* benevolence. Now that is what we are talking about tonight, Brother Inman. We are not talking about what an individual Christian can do. Now he cited a good many passages that relate to that, like James 1:27. He said James 1:27 is congregational, you remember. All you have to do is read a little bit in the context. Somebody said that a text without a context is a pretext. That is what Brother Inman has; he has a pretext. He has taken James 1:27, but he has not read what is in the context of it. The preceding verse says "if any *man* thinketh *himself* to be religious, while *he* bridleth not *his* tongue but deceiveth *his* heart, this *man's* religion is vain." Does that sound like a church, Brother Inman?

Then James says, "Pure religion and undefiled before our God and Father is this, to visit the fatherless and widows in their affliction, and to keep *oneself* unspotted from the world." Does that sound like a church? "Keep *oneself* unspotted from the world." I wonder if we could set up an institution, and get church donations, to keep us unspotted from the world. That is in the same verse. And if you could set up one to visit the widows and orphans in their affliction, then it looks like we ought to be able to set up one to keep us unspotted from the world. But the truth of the matter is that that passage is not talking about congregational benevolence at all. He cited several passages that relate to individual benevolence.

He told us that some of these congregations are going to have to answer for how they use money. I tell you, some of the *individuals* in those congregations are going to have to answer as to how they use the Lord's money, and they ought to keep that before them, in sending it to a human institution. The Lord they are going to have to face said, "Whatsoever you do, in word or in deed, do all in the name of the Lord Jesus." Some of these brethren in some of these churches are taking the church's money and sending it to a human institution. When God calls on the judgment day, he is not going to say for a certain church to come up here. I gave you the passage: Romans 14:12, "So then each *one* of us . . ." Now, Brother Inman would have that to read *"each church* shall give an account of *itself* to God." That is not what it says, brethren. It says "each one of us shall give an account of *himself* un-

N. T. PATTERN VS. MODERN PATTERN IN BENEVOLENCE

NEW TESTAMENT PATTERN	MODERN PATTERN — VIOLATIONS
1. THE WORK WAS DONE BY THROUGH & WITHIN THE LOCAL CHURCH ACCORDING TO DIVINE INSTRUCTIONS. ACTS 6:1-6; 11:27-30	1. THE WORK IS DONE BY, THROUGH & WITHIN A HUMAN INSTITUTION ACCORDING TO HUMAN WISDOM.
2. EACH LOCAL CHURCH CARED FOR ITS OWN NEEDY IF ABLE. ACTS 6:1-6	2. LOCAL CHURCHES SEND THEIR NEEDY TO A HUMAN INSTITUTION NOT KNOWING IF THEY ARE ABLE TO CARE FOR THEM OR NOT.
3. WHEN LOCAL CHURCH UNABLE TO CARE FOR ITS NEEDY SISTER CONG.'S SUPPLIED THAT WHICH WAS LACKING. ACTS 11:29,30; 2 COR. 8:18-21	3. LOCAL CHURCHES SEND THEIR OWN NEEDY TO A HUMAN INSTITUTION AND SEND $10. A MONTH CONTRIBUTION.
4. IN UNAVOIDABLE EMERGENCIES ONE CHURCH SENT TO ANOTHER TO HELP MEET THE EMERGENCY. NOT ON A PERMANENT BASIS. ACTS 11:27-30	4. LOCAL CHURCH OR GROUP OF INDIVIDUALS CREATES AN EMERGENCY. AND CALLS UPON THE CHURCH IN GENERAL TO SUPPORT THEM ON A PERMANENT BASIS.
5. WHEN ONE CHURCH ASSISTED ANOTHER IN MEETING AN EMERGENCY SUCH ASSISTANCE WAS SENT TO THE ELDERS OF A CHURCH. ACTS 11:30	5. THE LOCAL CHURCHES SEND ASSISTANCE TO THE BOARD OF DIRECTORS OF A HUMAN INSTITUTION.

LET'S FOLLOW THE N.T. PATTERN

to God." We are going to be judged individually. That just shows further, if you will take Galations 6:10 in its context, that Paul is talking there about individual responsibility, and not about congregational responsibility.

The first of the two passages he cited tonight that relates to congregational benevolence is Acts 2:44-45, where we read about the church in Jerusalem relieving its own needy. Brother Inman, that is my passage; that is not yours. It says the *church* relieved its own needy. On the pattern chart I had before us awhile ago, I said "It was done *by, through* and *within* the local church." That is what that passage teaches, and he wants to read into it a human organization.

And then the other passage (I Timothy 5:16) says that the church "may relieve them that are widows indeed." Who may relieve them? The board of directors may

I TIMOTHY 5:16

relieve the widows indeed? That is what the passage is *supposed* to read, if you let Brother Inman interpret it for you. He would have it say that the board of directors may relieve them that are widows indeed. Instead, it said that the *church* may relieve them that are widows indeed.

I have an obligation to answer the passages that are relevant to his argument, and there are two passages that are relevant to his argument. He used some other passages, but they relate to individual benevolent responsibility, and Brother Inman, we are not debating that. That is not our question this evening. Our question this evening is what *churches* can do with their money. I do not see in either of those passages a human institution or a church sending any money to a human institution.

Now, let us notice his questions. He said that perhaps I had not dealt satisfactorily with them. "Is there any specific manner of caring for these set forth in the New Testament?" No, we are not talking about the manner or method. Brother Inman would like to have you think this is what we are talking about. But that is not what we are talking about tonight. We are talking about: *"Is there an institution specified in the Bible that is to do the work of benevolence that God has assigned the church?"* And the answer is, yes! And it is not Mid-Western Children's Home. It happens to be a local church. That is what is specified. And the same thing is wrong, good people, when you add another institution, that is wrong when you add another kind of music to worship. That is what is wrong with it. The organization that is to do that work is specified.

You might also keep in mind that the organization that you brethren are building has to use methods also. It has to have methods. It has to decide whether it is going to use a brick building or a frame building. So the organization is specified.

Then he says, "Are we enjoined to care for them? See James 1:27." That is talking about individual responsibility: "Keep *oneself* unspotted from the world."

"If care is enjoined and the specific manner is not, then any manner may be used which does not violate some other New Testament principle." I have already answered that. The organization *is specified*. What we are debating is "what organization is to do this work?"

THIRD NIGHT, BENEVOLENT INSTITUTIONS 163

He said, "Is it wrong for a group of brethren to form a corporation for the purpose of maintaining a home for orphaned and forsaken children?" Do you want the answer, Brother Inman? It is "no", "NO!" "so long as" (quoting Clifton Inman now) "it is *privately* owned and operated." I do not object to that. It is just like operating *Bible Herald* as a private endeavor. I do not object to that. A group of brethren could build and establish a Shell Oil station. But could a church contribute to it? That is what he is defending tonight—*church* contributions to institutions that brethren themselves by their own human wisdom form.

Oh, he said awhile ago, "They can use good judgment." Brother Inman, I said your authority is not divine wisdom; it is human wisdom. And unless he finds some passages tomorrow night that he has not cited tonight, he is going to have to close this debate saying his authority is human wisdom. He cited two passages. I want you to go home and get your Bible and look over those verses. Acts 2:44-45 and I Timothy 5:16 are the only two passages he cited that relate to congregational benevolence. See if you can find a board of directors in either one of them. And if you can, I would appreciate you letting me know about it tomorrow.

I also would say, Brother Inman, that a group of individuals could form a school like Ohio Valley College, (But I would not say a church could send to it) just like I would say a group of brethren could form a home to care for orphans. In fact, I know of one brother that owns and operates a home for the aged. I do not have any objection to that. That is his business enterprise. It is perfectly all right. But if he starts trying to get the church to subsidize his business enterprise, brother, he is going to run into some objections. That is where these brethren have run into their objections.

"Is it right to take funds from a church's treasury to help orphans or forsaken children at all?" Brother Inman asked this question again in number "F" at the bottom of the sheet. "Is it right or wrong to take funds from the treasury of the church to help one who is not a member of the church?" Brother Inman knows that this is a separate issue. Actually, I would be real happy to sign another proposition with him and debate the question of "to whom does a congregation have benevolent responsibility?" I would be glad to debate that with him.

However, you can just write down a couple of things here: Either a congregation has *limited* benevolent responsibility, or it has *unlimited* benevolent responsibility. Does it have benevolent responsibility to atheists and infidels? Does it have benevolent responsibility to lazy people? Let me tell you, Brother Inman, the Bible says in 2 Thessalonians 3:10, "if any will not work, neither let him eat." Now that limits it, doesn't it?

But if you want a more specific answer to your question, *I do not know of any passage where any church in the New Testament ever supplied benevolence to anybody other than to a saint.* I am trying to be candid about the thing. That is all I know about it.

Brother Inman asked me if I would change if I found out I was wrong. That is one point I changed on, Brother Inman. At one time I preached what Brother Inman now says about that. I taught at one time that the church could help just anybody, until a fellow came and said, "Where is the scripture for it?" I started hunting and I have been hunting a good many years, and I have not found it yet. If Brother Inman can cite some passage where a church helped someone other than a saint, I would be glad to have the passage.

He said further: "Is it right to help orphaned or forsaken children at all? Is it possible to help them any way if they happened to be in a corporate home?" What does he mean by that? Well, he means if they are in a corporate home, can the church send to the corporation? Now, Brother Inman, another question: Is it all right to help them if they happen to be in Ohio Valley College too? If they are in a corporate home, according to him the church can send to the corporation. Suppose they happen to be in Ohio Valley College. Can they send to Ohio Valley College to help them? And suppose they happen to be in a hospital. Can the church make a donation to a hospital? Now, we are not talking about buying services; we are talking about contributions. Can the church make a donation to them in a hospital by sending it to the board of directors?

"Is it possible to help an orphan or forsaken child who has been adopted by a man and his wife?" When they adopt him, he becomes the parents' responsibility. 1 Timothy 5:8 says, "if any provideth not for his own, and specially his own household, he has denied the faith, and is worse than an unbeliever." That is their obligation, and in the Bible when saints could not discharge their obligation, the church contributed to their relief.

Brother Inman made an inference this evening that the board of directors over there at Mid-Western Children's Home are the parents. I think that is the inference. If it is not, I would be glad to have him straighten it up. Now I want to know, what are those parents (the board of directors at Mid-Western Children's Home and at Potter who in nearly every instance have to be wealthy brethren before they get appointed to that board)? What are they if these are their children and they do not provide for their own? What does the Bible say about parents who do not take care of their own? It says they have "denied the faith" and are "worse than an infidel." Brother Inman tried to make the restored home argument. That home was destroyed, and they restored it. Now who are the parents? The board of directors? Is that who the parents are?

I asked him some questions awhile ago, and I now come to the questions that I gave him. I asked him the question: "Are the orphan homes in your proposition human or divine institutions?" And he answered that they are "human institutions." Now Brother Inman said he had not been reading much on this, and that is rather obvious, because if he had been reading much he would have learned by now that they are not human institutions. Brother Inman, when they restore them, they are divine institutions. You ought to have attended some of the debates some of these brethren have held. Or, at least, you ought to read the debates. Brother Guy N. Woods says "It is merely and solely the restoration of that which is lost. As such it enjoys the status of a *divine* institution." (*Gospel Advocate,* June 6, 1957, page 359.) Now Brother Inman says they are human institutions. The truth of the matter is they do not know what they are. It is something they made themselves; they do not know what they are.

He said he wrote some things a long while ago, and he has forgotten to what he had reference. And he has forgotten just when he changed. Well now, Brother Inman, I remember when I changed on the matter of whom the church can help, and I remember what changed me. I could not find any Bible passage for it. I want to know this evening what Bible passage changed your mind. And he has not cited the one that changed his mind.

He says, "Can you fellows match what we are doing?" He said we are giving fifty cents a year. I related that earlier. He said "Can you match that?" I tell you, I do not feel much like bragging about matching a penny per week a member! But I figured he might ask that. So I went to the Treasurer of the Brown Street church, where I work, just before I left and said, "Would you run down through our financial report for the last few years and see how much we spent in benevolence?" He gave me the persons and the totals, and it happened to be *three times* as much as you brethren are spending! Now I am not bragging about it; I am not very proud about how much we gave. But I will tell you what we have done, Brother Inman. *Every single needy person that has been the responsibility of Brown Street church has been taken care of,* and that is what we are supposed to do. And if you do not believe that is so, you name one that is the obligation of the Brown Street church that we have not taken care of, and we will be glad to see that he is attended to. Fifty cents per member per year, and "look what we are doing!" "We like the way we are doing it better than the way you are not doing it."

Now, let us notice some other charts that really pinpoint the issue. (Give me the pointer please.) I want chart No. 3, please. We want to discuss "What are we having this debate about?" About a 100 years ago we had an issue in the church, and it entailed a human institution. The issue back then, Brother Inman, was not simply a matter of how to preach the gospel. That is what he is trying to make it tonight. And the issue was not "Should the gospel be preached?" That is what he is trying to make it tonight. The issue was not "Should we take care of these people?" Or "Was the church obligated?" Or, "Could churches cooperate?"

And I might just pause here. Brother Inman, you said I misunderstood you. Did you say that there *is* a pattern in congregational cooperation the first two nights? Is that what you said? He said I misunderstood him. I

THE ISSUE THEN AND NOW

THE ISSUE THEN WAS NOT
1. SIMPLY A MATTER OF "HOW."
2. SHOULD THE GOSPEL BE PREACHED?
3. WAS THE CHURCH OBLIGATED?
4. COULD CHURCHES CO-OPERATE?
5. COULD A PLACE BE MAINTAINED?
6. SYSTEMATIC ARRANGEMENT?

THE ISSUE THEN WAS
COULD CHURCHES BUILD AND MAINTAIN MISSIONARY SOCIETIES THROUGH WHICH TO DO THEIR WORK OF EVANGELISM

THE ISSUE TODAY IS NOT
1. SIMPLY A MATTER OF "HOW."
2. SHALL THE NEEDY RECEIVE CARE?
3. IS THE CHURCH OBLIGATED?
4. CAN CHURCHES CO-OPERATE?
5. CAN A "HOME" BE MAINTAINED?
6. SYSTEMATIC ARRANGEMENT?

THE ISSUE TODAY IS
CAN CHURCHES BUILD AND MAINTAIN BENEVOLENT SOCIETIES THROUGH WHICH TO DO THEIR WORK OF BENEVOLENCE

---

understood him to say that there are some patterns in the Bible, but there is not any pattern for congregational co-operation. That is what I thought he said. And he said I misunderstood him. We will have to find out about that. I will listen to the tapes later.

And the issue was not "Could we maintain a place to preach the gospel?" Or "Could we have a systematic arrangement to preach the gospel?" Brethren, the issue a 100 years ago was simply this: *Could churches of the Lord Jesus Christ build and maintain missionary societies through which to do their work of evangelism?*

Now we are in the throes of another period of trouble. And the issue today, brethren, is not simply a matter of "How are we going to take care of the needy for whom the church has benevolent responsibility?" The issue is not "Shall the needy receive care?", or "Is the church obligated to these?", or "Can churches cooperate in relieving these?", or "Can a home be maintained?", or "Can we have a systematic arrangement by which we attend to this responsibility?" Brethren, the issue today is, "*Can churches of Christ build and maintain benevolent societies through which to do their work of benevolence?*" That is really what we are having this debate about.

Chart No. 4. Then chart No. 7 after that. The issue, brethren, is "*Which organization shall perform and control the work God commands the church to do?*" That

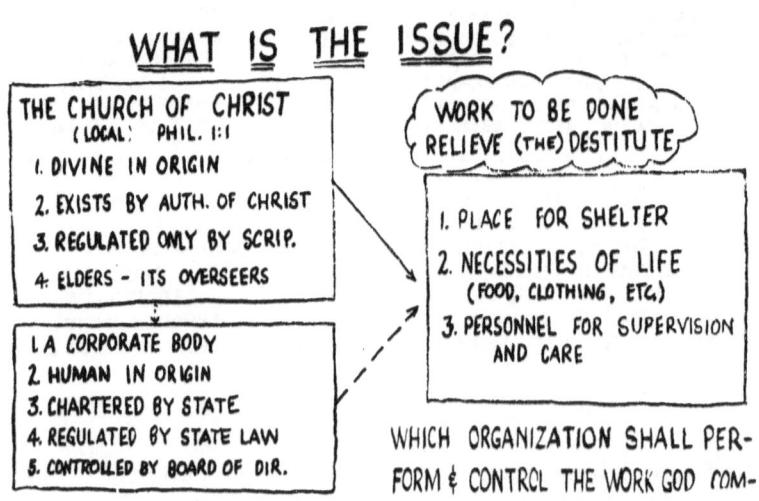

is what we are debating. Which organization is going to control it? On one hand you have the church of the Lord Jesus Christ. It is divine in origin. It exists by the authority of Christ. It is regulated only by the scripture, and it has elders as overseers.

There is some work to be done. There are certain ones whom the church is to relieve. They need a place for shelter. They need the necessities of life, like food and clothing, etc. And, in some instances they may need personnel for supervision and care. And the issue is: *Shall the church of Christ attend to this matter of benevolence, or shall corporate bodies attend to it?* He calls it a corporate home, a human institution, human in origin. He admitted it is a human organization. It is chartered by the State. It is regulated by State law, and it is controlled by a board of directors. Shall this human institution attend to this obligation, or shall the blessed church of the Lord Jesus Christ do the work that God gave it to do?

Chart No. 7, please. This covers the same thing again, but I want to be sure that you understand what we are talking about. All I am to do tonight is to examine Brother Inman's proof. He cited two passages that talk about congregational benevolence, Acts 2:44-45 and 1 Timothy 5:16. It is scriptural, brethren, for the church under Christ, through its elders and its deacons, to build a home (a house), buy a home, rent a home, buy clothes, pay for

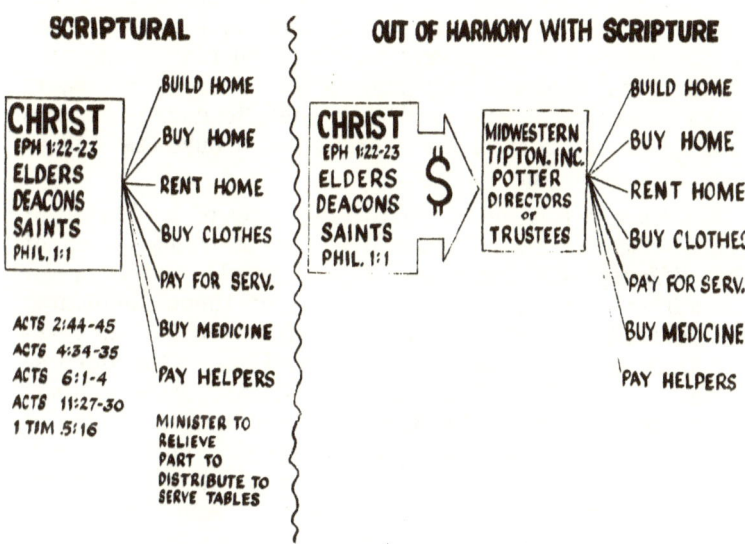

services, buy medicine, pay helpers in order to minister to, or relieve, or part to, or distribute to, or to serve tables. And here are the passages that say that (pointing to scriptures on chart). These are the passages: Acts 2:44-45. The *church* did it, not a *board of directors*, Brother Inman; a church did it. That is the same passage he has been trying to use. That is the church in that passage; not a board of directors. (Acts 4:34-35; Acts 6:1-4; Acts 11:27-30; 1 Timothy 5:16.) The church is to do that.

Now this is out of harmony with the scriptures (pointing to right side of chart). This is what Brother Inman is defending tonight. Is it scriptural for the church under Christ, through its elders and its deacons, to relinquish its funds to a human institution whether it be called Mid-Western Children's Home or Tipton Home, Inc.? Is it scriptural to turn these funds over to the board of directors who in turn uses some methods? They may buy a home. They may build a home. They may rent a home. They may buy clothes. They may pay for services. They may buy medicine, or they may pay helpers.

Let us talk now just a little about, "What is a corporate home?" Brother Inman is talking about a "corporate home." A corporation is an ideal body. It subsists only in contemplation of law. But as such, it has real existence. It has legal entity the same as a person. It has most of the property rights of an individual, such as the right to hold property, to buy and sell goods, to make contracts, to sue and to be sued, to engage in, and to conduct and control the operation of a business, and as such it is not a part of anything.

I have before me a photostatic copy of a charter of one of the corporate homes. We have a whole bunch of the different charters here, if you would like to know something about them. Here is one of them. Remember his proposition said, "Mid-Western Home, etc." I am reading from one of these charters now. Here is the purpose of this body politic, this human institution: "The support of any benevolent or charitable undertaking, as a lodge of Masons, Odd Fellows, hospitals for the sick, houses of refuge or correction, orphan asylums and all other objects of like nature; testing for public safety." And then it lists a whole bunch of other objects. And they say, it is for "*white* children of school age." (Charter of Greater Chattanooga Children's Home, Inc.). It is strange that these little black children do not ever get hungry, and their parents do not ever die. But Potter orphan home and the Greater Chattanooga Orphan Home are for white children.

Here are the qualifications for the board of directors from the Greater Chattanooga home charter. One must "believe in the support, either by individuals or churches from their treasuries, of organizations which care for orphans, dependent children, the aged and the *sick*." Brother Inman, can a church make a donation to a hospital? Are you ready for church hospitals? Now you have to believe that to be on the board. Furthermore, I told you the other night they are writing their creeds in their deeds. One must "believe in the right of congregations to practice cooperation among themselves in the performance of any good work."

Let us turn to another chart please, Chart No. 16. Brother Inman does not like to talk about this college issue. It is rather touchy. I know why it is touchy too, because a college is a human institution like an institutional orphan home.

COLLEGE	ORPHAN HOME
1. OPERATED BY A CORPORATE BODY	1. OPERATED BY A CORPORATE BODY
2. CHARTERED BY THE STATE	2. CHARTERED BY THE STATE
3. MAKES OWN CONTRACTS	3. MAKES OWN CONTRACTS
4. BOARD HIRES AND FIRES PERSONNEL	4. BOARD HIRE AND FIRES PERSONNEL
5. COLLEGE OPERATES FARMS, PRINT SHOPS. RECEIVES PROFITS FROM OIL WELL ROYALTIES	5. ORPHANAGES OPERATES FARMS, PRINT SHOPS RECEIVES PROFIT FROM OIL WELL ROYALTIES
6. HAS OWN TREASURY	6. HAS OWN TREASURY
7. COLLEGES LOAN MONEY	7. ORPHANAGES LOAN MONEY
8. HUMAN ORGANIZATION TO TEACH	8. HUMAN ORGANIZATION TO TEACH
9. ORPHANS GIVEN HELP ON TUITION	9. ORPHANS GIVEN HELP ON TUITION
10. CLAIMS TO BE AN ADJUNCT OF HOME	10. SOME CLAIM ORHANAGE DOING WORK OF HOME AND NOT THE CHURCH

"THEY STAND OR FALL TOGETHER"
IF CHURCHES OF CHRIST CAN BUILD, MAINTAIN AND REGULARLY CONTRIBUTE TO A BENEVOLENT ORGANIZATION, WHY NOT AN EDIFICATION ORGANIZATION?

I want you to notice now, that the church support of colleges and the church support of institutional orphan homes are parallel. They stand or fall together, as some of the brethren who agree with Brother Inman have said. Let us notice how they are parallel.

The colleges are operated by corporate bodies; orphan homes are operated by a corporate body. The college is chartered by the State; orphan homes are chartered by the State. A college makes its own contracts; the board of the orphan home makes its own contracts. The college board hires and fires personnel; the board of the orphan home hires and fires personnel.

The colleges operate farms, print shops, receive profits from oil well royalties, and he says that is why the church cannot support them. Brother Inman, orphanages operate farms, print shops, and receive profits from oil well royalties, and if you want the proof, just ask for it, and I will be glad to show it.

Boles Home owns and operates a 2350 acre farm. The Maude Carpenter Children's Home operates an 800 acre wheat farm. He says that is why you cannot make a church donation to a school, because they are in business enterprises. The Childhaven Orphan Home raises and markets 1000 hogs and 100,000 chickens every year, and that is a business enterprise. The Tipton Orphan Home owns a cotton farm. He says that is why you cannot contribute to the college, because they operate farms. Orphanages operate farms, print shops, receive profits from oil well royalties.

Colleges have their own treasury and the orphan home has its own treasury. Colleges loan money; orphanages loan money. Morrilton Orphan Home loaned a Little Rock, Arkansas church $40,000.00 a few years ago. So they are in the loaning business. The college is a human organization to teach; and this one over here is a human organization that also teaches. Potter Orphan Home operates a school. In fact its name is "The Potter Home and School." Brother Inman says a church cannot support a school, but it does if it sends its money to the board of directors of Potter, or Schults-Lewis, or Mt. Dora. Inman infers if you will send the money through the board of directors of an orphan home, the church then can support a school.

I said this one (college) is a human organization to teach, and this one (orphan home) is a human organization to teach. Orphans are given help on tuition by the college; orphans are given help on tuition by the orphan homes. The college claims to be an adjunct to the home, and some claim that the orphanage is doing the work of the home, and not of the church. Now, if the churches of Christ can build, maintain, and regularly contribute to a human benevolent organization, why cannot they also build, maintain, and regularly contribute to an educational organization? If Brother Inman knows some differences in two, I would like to have them pointed out.

While we are talking about that, let us just mention another point or two. Brother Inman wrote several years ago about Ohio Valley College. And he wants to know why am I picking on them. I am not picking on them. I am trying to get Brother Inman to see that his arguments are inconsistent. That is what the Christian Church man said about it. He said Inman was inconsistent. Inman maintains that a church can donate to this institution (orphan home), but cannot donate to that human institution (college). That is where he is inconsistent.

What about some of these colleges like David Lipscomb College and Freed-Hardeman College, that do take money from churches? What about these? How does Brother Inman feel about these? Here is how he feels. He is real "strong" on this. Listen. He said: "Though our *philosophy* of obtaining support may vary from them, we are not intending to start any crusade against these schools, but shall give them our prayers and blessings." (*Gospel Advocate*, June 11, 1959, page 373.) What are they doing? They are doing something that is *sinful*, Brother Inman says. They are taking money from churches. What are you going to do for them, Brother Inman? I am going to give them my blessing and my prayers. That sounds real strong, doesn't it? He really has conviction on this thing. He is going to give them his prayers and his blessings, while they engage in that which he said is sinful.

Brother Inman needs to do a little reading on the college question. He will find out some things. Brother Batsell Barrett Baxter is the speaker on the Herald of Truth program and here is what he said. He is just drawing Brother Inman's picture. You listen to him. He said, "Some who are agreed that the church can contribute to an orphans' home are not convinced that the church can contribute to a Christian school. It is difficult to see a significant difference so far as principle is concerned. *The orphans' home and the Christian school must stand or fall together."* (*Questions and Issues of the Day*, page 29.) That is why Brother Inman does not want to talk about it. Brother Baxter says, "They stand or fall together." Brother W. L. Totty said, "All these institutions" (And he mentions Potter Orphan Home and David Lipscomb College) "must stand or fall together." (Letter to Robert Welch, December 6, 1950.) "The orphan homes are parallel with the colleges." (W. L. Totty, *Miscellaneous Discussions of Bible Colleges*, page 19.)

Brother Bill Heinselman, who moderated for Brother Clifton Inman in his debate with Brother Emerson Flannery a few years ago, told me in Brother Inman's presence, that he believed that the right of a church to make a donation to an institutional orphan home also justified the college receiving donations from churches.

Brother N. B. Hardeman also says he believes they are parallel. He said, "Note the parallel: 1. The school is a human institution; it has a board of directors; it teaches secular branches in connection with the Bible. 2. An orphan home is a human institution." This is Brother N. B. Hardeman. These are not conclusions drawn by me. ". . .it has a board of directors; it teaches secular branches in connection with the Bible. *The same principle that permits one must also permit the other. They must stand or fall together. The right to contribute to the one is the right to contribute to the other."* (Firm Foundation, October 28, 1947.)

Now what am I maintaining tonight in this discussion? My obligation tonight is to examine the proof given by Brother Inman. He has given me two verses. Neither one

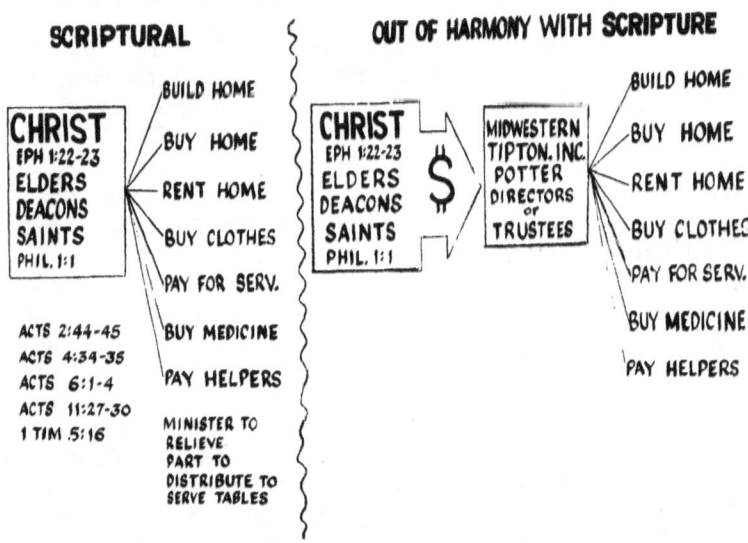

of them says a thing on earth about a board of directors or about a human institution. I maintain that a local church ought, under the direction of its elders and through the activity of its members, to attend to all of its benevolent responsibility. And when it has some calamity, such as the dearth which came to pass in the Bible times, that makes it unable to care for its own needy, then other churches should send to the elders of that church in need in order to enable it to relieve its own needy.

Our argument this evening is, shall the church do it, this side over here (referring to chart No. 7)? Or shall a human institution do it? And if a human institution can do the church's benevolent work, why cannot the church do its edifying through Ohio Valley College? And if it can do the benevolent work through a human institution, why cannot the church do the evangelistic work through a human institution like the United Christian Missionary Society? Now, people, that is really where we stand this evening.

PROPOSITION

"RESOLVED THAT IT IS UNSCRIPTURAL FOR A CONGREGATION, OR CONGREGATIONS, TO TAKE MONEY FROM THEIR TREASURIES AND SEND IT TO A CORPORATE HOME (SUCH AS MID-WESTERN, POTTER, SCHULTS-LEWIS, MAUDE CARPENTER, LUBBOCK, ETC.), WHICH IS ORGANIZED FOR THE PURPOSE OF PROVIDING A HOME FOR ORPHANED OR FORSAKEN CHILDREN."

Affirmative: Cecil Willis
Negative: Clifton Inman

WILLIS' FIRST AFFIRMATIVE

It is a pleasure to stand before you this evening, and to have an opportunity to continue my part in this discussion. This evening we are discussing virtually the same proposition that we discussed last evening, with the exception of the fact that we just have it turned around. Brother Inman last night maintained that is *scriptural* (By scriptural he said he meant that it was not contrary to the scripture; tonight I am affirming that it *is* unscriptural, and by that I simply mean that it *is contrary* to the scripture) for a congregation or congregations to take money from their treasuries and send it to a corporate home, such as Mid-Western, Potter, Schults-Lewis, Maude Carpenter, Lubbock, etc., which is organized for the purpose of providing a home for orphaned or for forsaken children.

Now in order somewhat to bring to focus clearly the issue that we have before us, I want to read some questions that I presented to Brother Inman a little while ago. These are some questions to which I would appreciate Brother Inman giving attention. (1.) *"Last night you made the 'restored home' argument."* The orphan lost his home and so these brethren are going to restore it now.

"*When you 'restore' the child's broken home, who then are his parents? The board of directors? The superintendent? The matrons? The contributors, or someone else?*" (2.) "*Which 'restored home' can the church contribute to? The home restored by Christians (Mid-Western)? The home restored by Baptists (Buckner Orphan Home)? The home restored by Catholics (Sacred Heart Children's Home, Inc.)? The home restored by Methodists (Methodist Children's Home)?*"

I want to get this point before you, and I want Brother Inman to tell us to which one or ones of these homes a church can donate. Now up here we have a home that

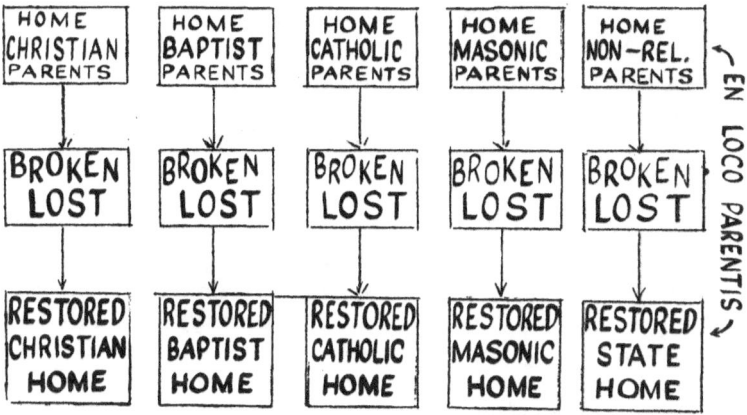

consists of parents that are Christians. This home is broken and so they restore it. Brother Inman says then we have a restored Christian home. That is Mid-Western Children's Home. But, we have another type of home over here. This is a home that consists of Baptist parents. This home is broken or lost and it is restored by Buckner Home. We have another home over here consisting of Catholic parents. It is broken and it is restored. We have another one over here that might consist of Masonic parents. It is broken and it is restored. And then we might have over here a State home. We have non-religious parents. It is broken and it is restored by a State home. Now what I want Brother Inman to tell us is: *"Unto which one or ones of these 'restored homes' can churches of Christ contribute?"*

Now he has said considerable so far about limited benevolence. I have a third question. (3.) *"Do you believe in limited or unlimited benevolence?"* Now he seemed a little bit excited last night that I said I believed in limited benevolence. Now we are going to see if Brother Inman believes in limited benevolence. Now remember, this restored home is just like this original home. It has been restored, according to his argumentation. His inferences were last night, in fact his plain argument last night, was that the church can help all these people, aliens as well as saints. Now if you restore this Catholic home, I want to know: *can the church donate to it?* We will see if perhaps he also believes in limited benevolence.

(4.) *"If the original home (a divine institution) is restored, how is it that the restored home is a human institution?"* I asked him last night: "Is Mid-Western Children's home a divine or human institution?" He said, "a human institution." I want to know if you *restore* a divine home, how does it turn out to be a human institution? I hope he does a better job of restoring the church than he does of that. One starts out with a divine body and he is going to restore it. He would have a human institution after it is restored, according to his argument.

(5.) *"If individual responsibility can be discharged through a common congregational treasury, then can our individual responsibility to educate our children be discharged through a common congregational treasury?"* Of course, he argued last night that individual responsibility could be discharged through a common congregational treasury.

Some of you people were not here last night. Brother Inman last night presented a number of scriptures, but he only presented two scriptures that had anything to do with *congregational* benevolence. Now we are not talking about what an individual can do. We are talking about what churches can do. That is what the proposition says. And he presented two passages last night, and only two, that pertain to congregational responsibility. He cited Acts 2: 44-45 and then he cited I Timothy 5:16. And those were all he gave last night that had a thing on earth to do with

FOURTH NIGHT, BENEVOLENT INSTITUTIONS   179

congregational benevolence, and neither of them says a thing about a human institution.

(6.) *"Which of the two Bible references that you presented last night pertaining to congregational benevolent responsibility convinced you that it is scriptural to support a benevolent society under a board of directors like Mid-Western Children's Home?"* Now until 1954 he was not convinced you could support such an institution, and became convinced, and so I want to know what convinced him. He said last night it was the scriptural argument he presented last night. But he gave only two scriptures. Thus I want to know: Which of those scriptures convinced him that churches could discharge their benevolent responsibility through a board of directors?

(7) *"What difference do you think you see between churches contributing to institutions like Ohio Valley College to do educational work, and churches contributing to institutions, like Mid-Western and Potter, to do benevolent work?"* And please be explicit, Brother Inman, when you answer that question.

(8.) *"If James 1:27 authorizes church supported institutional orphanages* (and that was his argument last night), *does Matthew 25:31, which says 'visit' those that are sick, justify church hospitals?* And if not, tell us why not.

(9.) *"What did the Jerusalem church do with the money sent by Antioch by the hands of Barnabas and Saul?"* I read from the tapes last night where Brother Inman said that the money was sent from Antioch *"to Jerusalem,"* but then he said, "I did not say that they sent it out to Judea." Well now, if you did not, Brother Inman, *what did they do with it? Did they keep it?* Did they keep the money that belonged to all the churches in Judea, or did they send it out? That is what I want to know.

(10.) *"What features of orphan homes like Boles and Potter caused you to be undecided whether they were scriptural before 1954?"* I also asked him a question about his previous position, and he said he could not remember last night. But if he can remember what it was that he thought was unscriptural about these institutions before 1954, I want him to tell us what those objectionable features were.

(11.) *"Why would it be unscriptural to incorporate as a separate institution the Herald of Truth to do evangelistic work* (He said it would be last night),*but is scriptural to incorporate a separate institution through which to do benevolent work?"*

And then this is a question I gave Brother Inman last night, and he overlooked it through two speeches. I over-looked one of his questions the other night. I suppose that oversight was inadvertent. That happens sometime. So, I am asking the question again. (12.) *"If the board of directors of Mid-Western Children's Home Inc. were to alter or expand its program of work so as to include evangelistic work, would you object to it?"* Now do not change anything else; operate it just like it is. Just suppose they decided *also* to start doing evangelistic work. Would you object to it? And if so, tell us why.

(13.) *"If the church cannot do what an individual Christian can do* (Brother Inman said there is a difference between individual action and congregational action), *then why did you last night say that individual benevolent responsibility can be 'implemented' through the common church treasury?"* Now I ask these questions in order to get the issue further defined.

Brother Inman cited last night Matthew 25:31-46; James 1:27; the first part of I Timothy 5:16; Luke 10:25-27; and Luke 4:25-27, but all of these related to individual responsibility. Yet he cited these as authority for the church functioning through a human institution. Now, Brother Inman, if I were to concede to you what I am not going to concede, that those passages were talking about church obligation, there is not a thing on earth in a one of those passages that authorizes a human institution. I can read over in Acts 8:4 that the early church went everywhere preaching the word. I might just as well say those individuals were supposed to preach, and that therefore is the passage that authorizes the missionary society. He showed us some passages that pertain to individual benevolent responsibility, and then said, those passages authorize the church to function through a benevolent society.

He got confused on James 1:27. The preceding passage says, "If a *man* thinketh himself to be religious, while *he* bridleth not *his* tongue but deceiveth *his* heart, this *man's* religion is vain." Brother Inman tried to make that "man" become a congregation. Now that is a sectarian argument. I charged him with making Christian Church arguments, but now he is making a sectarian argument. The sectarians turn to John 15:5-6 and they read about "the vine" and "the branches." John 15:6 says, "If a MAN abide not in me...." You know what they do with that? They say that is talking about different churches. They try to make a church out of "a man" in John 15:6. Brother Inman tries to make the "MAN" into a church in James 1: 26-27.

Let us look at Galatians 6:10 just a minute, please. I want chart No. 25. Brother Inman gave the passage last night, "So then, as we have opportunity, let us work that which is good toward all men, and especially toward them that are of the household of faith." Now we want to know

THE "WE" AND "US" IN GALATIANS

IS PAUL TALKING ABOUT CHURCHES OR CHRISTIANS?
IF WE ARE TO UNDERSTAND GAL. 6:10, WE MUST KNOW
1. GAL. 3:13 – REDEEMED "US", BEING MADE A CURSE FOR "US".
2. GAL. 5:1 – CHRIST HATH MADE "US" FREE.
3. GAL. 5:25 – IF "WE" LIVE IN THE SPIRIT, LET "US" WALK.....
4. GAL. 5:26 – LET "US" NOT BE DESIROUS OF VAIN GLORY.
5. GAL. 4:28 – NOW "WE" ARE THE CHILDREN OF PROMISE.
6. GAL. 4:31 –"WE" ARE NOT CHILDREN OF THE BONDWOMAN.
7. GAL. 5:5 – FOR "WE" WAIT FOR THE HOPE OF RIGHTEOUS.
8. GAL. 6:9 –"WE" SHALL REAP IF "WE" FAINT NOT.
9. GAL. 6:10 – AS "WE" HAVE OPPORTUNITY, LET "US" DO GOOD.

THE CHURCHES OF GALATIA WERE COMMANDED TO ASSIST THE SAINTS. I COR. 16:1-2

if Paul is talking about churches in this passage, or if this is referring to individual responsibility. Now notice the "we" and the "us" in Galatians. Galatians 3:13, "Christ redeemed *US* from the curse of the law, having become a curse for *US*." I want to know, did Christ redeem the congregation *as a unit?* Or, did he redeem us as individuals? Galatians 5:1, "For freedom did Christ set *US* free." Does he free us as bodies of people, or as individuals? Galatians 5:25, "If *WE* live in the Spirit, by the Spirit let *US* also walk." Paul here was talking about individual responsibility. Galatians 5:26, "Let *US* not become vainglorious." Galatians 4:28, "Now *WE*...are children of promise." This is talking about individual action all the way through. Galatians 5:5, "For *WE*...wait for the hope of righteousness." And Galatians 6:9, "*WE* shall reap, if *WE* faint not." I asked last night, in the judgment day is God going to say "all right, this congregation come and be judged", or will every *MAN* give an account of himself unto God? Now he says, "As *WE* have opportunity, let *US* do good." It is the same "we" and the same "us" who are going to reap what we sow, and who are going to have to answer unto almighty God.

Now let us notice another thing or two. He said last night that he only studied one book in preparation for this debate. Chart No. 10. And perhaps his study will help him a little bit now. Let us see if it will. He said he did not study any other books; he just studied the Bible. Now we will see if his study did him very much good. What I want to know, Brother Inman, is where we can find what you are defending? He has been arguing that we are making laws where God did not make any. He just studied the Bible—

WHO MADE LAWS WHERE GOD MADE NONE?
THERE IS NO COMMAND, EXAMPLE, or NECESSARY INFERENCE:

1. WHERE CHURCHES of CHRIST EVER BUILT A BENEVOLENT ORGANIZATION
2. WHERE CHURCHES of CHRIST EVER SENT A CHILD TO A BENEVOLENT ORGANIZATION
3. WHERE CHURCHES of CHRIST EVER CONTRIBUTED TO A BENEVOLENT ORGANIZATION
4. WHERE CHURCHES of CHRIST EVER HEARD OF A BENEVOLENT ORGANIZATION

OPPONENTS CASE RESTS UPON THE SUM TOTAL of ABSOLUTELY NO SCRIPTURE!!!

"Lawlessness"(Gr. anomia)-- the condition of one without law,-- either because ignorant of it, or because violating it."
(THAYER p.48). MATT. 7:21-23; 1JNO.3:4; 2JNO. 9.

FOURTH NIGHT, BENEVOLENT INSTITUTIONS   183

that is all he studied. Now I want him to show us a command or an example or a necessary inference, either general authority or specific authority, where churches of Christ ever *built* a benevolent organization, or where churches of Christ ever *sent a child* to a benevolent organization. Now he studied that book he said, and that is all he studied, and he ought to have the passage. I want the passage where churches of Christ ever *contributed to* a benevolent organization. Really my opponent's case rests upon the sum total of absolutely *no* scripture. If he has some scripture, I want him to ask for this chart (Chart No. 10), and say "here is the scripture where you can read about that benevolent organization."

He asked me a question last night that I missed: "Who must have legal custody of the one who is helped?" Brother Inman handed out his paper last night, and if you will take a look at it you will notice that he has arguments and questions all mixed up together. Frankly, when I looked it over I could not differentiate between arguments and questions, and I therefore overlooked one. But Brother Inman, we are not debating the question of who must have legal custody. Actually, I am not greatly concerned about who has the legal custody. But, I am concerned about the fact that the elders of the church must maintain the oversight of the relief that is being rendered by the church. That is what I am maintaining. And when elders turn this work over to a benevolent organization, a board of directors, they do not maintain their oversight.

Now, let us notice another thing or two about what we are not debating. Notice what is *not* the issue. The issue tonight is not whether needy persons must be cared for. We all believe that they should be. The issue is not whether benevolent organizations have a right to exist. We all believe that they do have the right to exist as private institutions, private business enterprises. The issue is not whether churches may cooperate in benevolence. We all believe that they may. Brother Inman believes that, and I do too. The issue is not can churches buy goods or services from human institutions in doing their work. Churches might buy groceries from a grocery store. I believe that is all right.

But here is what the real issues are: (1) *May a church scripturally donate her funds to a human organization do-*

184   THE WILLIS-INMAN DEBATE

ing benevolent work? That is what we are talking about, and on this we disagree. He says they may; I say they may not. (2) *May a church scripturally turn over to another organization the control and the oversight of her benevolent work?* On this we disagree. (3) *Is the church her own benevolent society?* On this we disagree. (4) *May the church centralize her benevolent work, either under the eldership of a sponsoring church or under an institutional board?* On this we disagree. (5) *May the church effect any arrangement, scripturally, to do a brotherhood work either in benevolence or evangelism?* And on this we disagree.

Chart No. 5, please. I want to show you that when you do not have anything in the word of God about a human institution, you cannot find any Bible way to operate that thing. And since it is not in the word of God, Brother Inman and the brethren who defend these institutions are all confused about how they ought to be operated. There is a lot of disagreement. I want to know now, *where do you*

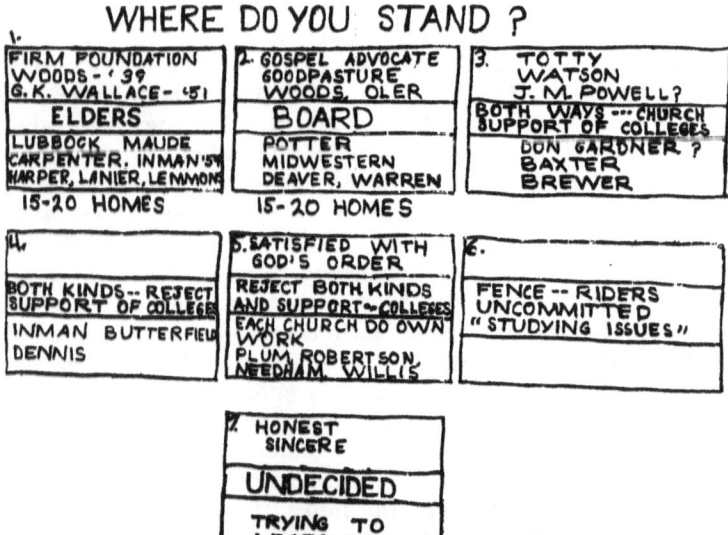

stand? I am trying to put some of these brethren in their relative positions in order that you might understand this issue.

Some people say there are about 15 or 20 orphan homes that are under elders of churches, that are operated according to the sponsoring church arrangement. We have two of them in the proposition, the Lubbock home, and Maude Carpenter home. They are under the elders of the church. And the FIRM FOUNDATION, Brother G. K. Wallace, Brother Guy N. Woods *several years ago*, Brother Inman until 1954, Brother E. R. Harper, Brother Roy Lanier and Brother Reuel Lemmons even today, say that they *must be under elders*.

Now the GOSPEL ADVOCATE on the other hand, Brother Goodpasture, Brother Guy N. Woods *today*, and Gayle Oler, Roy Deaver and Tom Warren say, "No, *they must* be under a board of directors." Now talk about division. They have it right there. One half of them say they *must* be under elders, and the other half say they *must not* be under elders but they *must* be under a board. And there are about fifteen or twenty of these institutions that are operated that way, and two of them are in my proposition, Potter and Mid-Western.

And there are other brethren that say, "Well, it does not really make any difference. You can have them both ways." You can put them under elders or under a board, but they also endorse church support of colleges. Brother W. L. Totty, Brother Sterl Watson, and I think Brother J. M. Powell, President of the Ohio Valley College, would fit into this category here. I think Brother Don Gardner, the former President of the Ohio Valley College also fitted into this category. If Powell and Gardner do not fit here, I would be glad to put them in the category into which they say they do fit. However, if Brother Powell says this is not where he belongs, I am going to get his brother-in-law, B. C. Goodpasture, on him. Goodpasture says you are a Sommerite if you do not go along with church support of colleges. And the man speaking on the Herald of Truth Radio and Television program (Batsell Barrett Baxter) and Brother G. C. Brewer have said you can have orphan homes both ways and you also can support colleges out of the congregational budget.

Now there are some who say you can operate these homes both ways, either under elders or under a board, but they reject the church support of colleges. This is where Brother Inman is, and Brother Tom Butterfield and Brother Fred Dennis.

And there are others who are satisfied with God's order. They reject the super-eldership of a sponsoring church and a human institution. They maintain that churches must not donate to Bible colleges, and they maintain that each church ought to do its own work. That is where you find fellows like C. D. Plum, Earl Robertson, James Needham and Cecil Willis. We reject both of these kinds of "homes", but for different reasons. But we reject both the sponsoring church type "home" and the institutional "home."

And here are some others over here (points to section 6 on chart), and we might have some of these fellows in the audience. They are on the fence; they are uncommitted. They say, "I am just studying the issues." I have wondered if some of those fellows are *studying* or if they are *stalling*. They have had a good while to study. These things have been around a good while, and I think it is about time these fellows made up their minds on these issues. And there are some other people who are honest and sincere and undecided, and they are trying to learn. I imagine there are some of those in this assembly this evening.

Now then, I would like to have chart No. 6 please. We noticed last night the Bible pattern of how churches took care of their own needy, and the pattern was that the work was done *by, through* and *within* the local church according to divine instructions (Acts 6:1-6; Acts 11:27-30). But the modern pattern is that the work is done *by, through* and *within* a *human institution* according to *human wisdom*. The pattern in the New Testament was that each local church cared for its own needy, if able (Acts 6:1-6). The modern pattern is that the local churches send their needy to a human institution, not knowing if they are able to care for them or not. (Get chart No. 6 on the large chart roll ready, please.) When the local church was unable to care for its own needy, sister congregations supplied that which was lacking (Acts 11:27-30; 2 Corinthians 8:18-21). But instead today local churches send about $10.00 a month donation to a human institution, and that is how

N. T. PATTERN VS. MODERN PATTERN IN BENEVOLENCE

NEW TESTAMENT PATTERN	MODERN PATTERN – VIOLATIONS
1. THE WORK WAS DONE BY, THROUGH & WITHIN THE LOCAL CHURCH ACCORDING TO DIVINE INSTRUCTIONS. ACTS 6:1-6; 11:27-30	1. THE WORK IS DONE BY, THROUGH & WITHIN A HUMAN INSTITUTION ACCORDING TO HUMAN WISDOM.
2. EACH LOCAL CHURCH CARED FOR ITS OWN NEEDY IF ABLE. ACTS 6:1-6	2. LOCAL CHURCHES SEND THEIR NEEDY TO A HUMAN INSTITUTION NOT KNOWING IF THEY ARE ABLE TO CARE FOR THEM OR NOT.
3. WHEN LOCAL CHURCH UNABLE TO CARE FOR ITS NEEDY SISTER CONG.'S SUPPLIED THAT WHICH WAS LACKING. ACTS 11:29,30; 2 COR. 8:18-21	3. LOCAL CHURCHES SEND THEIR OWN NEEDY TO A HUMAN INSTITUTION AND SEND $10. A MONTH CONTRIBUTION.
4. IN UNAVOIDABLE EMERGENCIES ONE CHURCH SENT TO ANOTHER TO HELP MEET THE EMERGENCY. NOT ON A PERMANENT BASIS. ACTS 11:27-30	4. LOCAL CHURCH OR GROUP OF INDIVIDUALS CREATES AN EMERGENCY. AND CALLS UPON THE CHURCH IN GENERAL TO SUPPORT THEM ON A PERMANENT BASIS.
5. WHEN ONE CHURCH ASSISTED ANOTHER IN MEETING AN EMERGENCY SUCH ASSISTANCE WAS SENT TO THE ELDERS OF A CHURCH. ACTS 11:30	5. THE LOCAL CHURCHES SEND ASSISTANCE TO THE BOARD OF DIRECTORS OF A HUMAN INSTITUTION.

LET'S FOLLOW THE N.T. PATTERN

they propose to discharge their obligation. In unavoidable emergencies in New Testament days, one church sent to another church to help meet the emergency, but not on a permanent basis. But we have today a church or a group of individuals creating an emergency and then calling upon the church in general permanently to support them. When one church assisted another church in meeting an emergency in the New Testament, such assistance was sent to the elders of the church. But today the local churches send assistance to the board of directors of a *human institution.*

I pointed out last night, by using another chart, that on the same basis that Brother Inman can maintain the defense of church support of these human institutions in benevolence, he will have to go along with the church support of a human institution, like Ohio Valley College, in education.

Now I want us to notice another thing wrong with this institutional benevolence. In Ephesians 3:21 the Bible says, "Unto him be the glory in the church and in Christ Jesus unto all generations for ever and ever. Amen." In Matthew 15:13, the Bible says: "Every plant, which my heavenly Father hath not planted, shall be rooted up." The institution that God put here to do the work that he as-

COLLEGE	ORPHAN HOME
1. OPERATED BY A CORPORATE BODY	1. OPERATED BY A CORPORATE BODY
2. CHARTERED BY THE STATE	2. CHARTERED BY THE STATE
3. MAKES OWN CONTRACTS	3. MAKES OWN CONTRACTS
4. BOARD HIRES AND FIRES PERSONNEL	4. BOARD HIRE AND FIRES PERSONNEL
5. COLLEGE OPERATES FARMS, PRINT SHOPS. RECEIVES PROFITS FROM OIL WELL ROYALTIES	5. ORPHANAGES OPERATES FARMS, PRINT SHOPS RECEIVES PROFIT FROM OIL WELL ROYALTIES
6. HAS OWN TREASURY	6. HAS OWN TREASURY
7. COLLEGES LOAN MONEY	7. ORPHANAGES LOAN MONEY
8. HUMAN ORGANIZATION TO TEACH	8. HUMAN ORGANIZATION TO TEACH
9. ORPHANS GIVEN HELP ON TUITION	9. ORPHANS GIVEN HELP ON TUITION
10. CLAIMS TO BE AN ADJUNCT OF HOME	10. SOME CLAIM ORHANAGE DOING WORK OF HOME AND NOT THE CHURCH

"THEY STAND OR FALL TOGETHER"
IF CHURCHES OF CHRIST CAN BUILD, MAINTAIN AND REGULARLY CONTRIBUTE TO A BENEVOLENT ORGANIZATION, WHY NOT AN EDIFICATION ORGANIZATION?

signed his people to do is the church. How much time, Brother Needham? (Brother Needham: Eight minutes.) The Bible tells us in Ephesians 3:11 that the church is the manifold wisdom of God and that it is the eternal purpose of God. In Hebrews 8:2 the Bible tells us that the church is a spiritual tabernacle which the Lord built and not man; the Lord pitched it and not man. So when we think about the church, brethren, we need to remember that the church was planned in God's mind, that it was built by the Son of God. God is infinite; God is perfect. His Son is infinite; his Son is perfect. Therefore, that which God provided is perfect for that for which God provided it. In Psalms 18:30, the Bible says "As for God, his way is perfect." In Colossians 2:10 the Bible says, "Ye are complete in him." Now that which God has provided, brethren, is perfect.

We do not need any human organizations. And all I am defending tonight, and I want you to understand what I am defending, is that *every work that God assigned to the church must be done by, through and within the church, under the direction of the elders of that church.* That is what I am defending. Brother Inman is saying you can turn it over to a board of directors in benevolence, but he says this cannot be done in education. He says the church's educational work cannot be turned over to the board out there at Ohio Valley College. And Brother Inman is saying you can turn the work over to a board in benevolence, but you cannot permit the board to do your missionary work. That is really what a missionary society is. It is a human institution, in organization like Mid-Western Children's Home or Potter Orphan home, through which churches attempt to preach the gospel.

Now a number of brethren have realized that the benevolent society and the missionary society are very similar. Let us note a number of points of similarity: (1) *Both originated in the mind of man,* and hence are human institutions. If you were here last night, you heard Brother Inman say that the institution he is defending is a human institution. Both of them are human institutions. (2) *Both are organizations separate and apart from the church.* You have heard him say that too, haven't you? You have heard him say that this institution I am defending is not a church—it is apart from the church.

MISSIONARY AND BENEVOLENT SOCIETIES

1. BOTH ORIGINATED IN THE MIND OF MAN. HENCE ARE HUMAN' INSTITUTIONS.
2. BOTH ARE ORGANIZATIONS SEPERATE AND APART FROM THE CHURCH.
3. BOTH SOLICIT AND ACCEPT CHURCH CONTRIBUTIONS.
4. BOTH COMPOSED OF PRESIDENT OR SUPT., BOARD OF DIRECTORS, SEC. AND TREAS., ETC.
5. BOTH CLAIM TO PERFORM A WORK OF THE CHURCH.
6. BOTH ARE ORGANIZATIONS LARGER THAN THE LOCAL CHURCH BUT SMALLER THAN THE UNIVERSAL CHURCH.
7. BOTH HAVE THEIR OWN CONSTITUTIONS AND BY-LAWS.
8. BOTH DESIGNED TO GIVE MISSION OF CHURCH GREATER EFFICIENCY
9. BOTH CONTROL PORTION'S OF THE CHURCH'S TREASURY.
10. BOTH CONSIDERED BY WORLD AS OFFICIAL FUNCTIONING ORGANS OF THE CHURCH.
11. BOTH PROPOSE TO DO WHAT THE CONGREGATIONS CANNOT DO THEMSELVES.
12. BOTH CLAIM TO BE EXPEDIENTS.
13. BOTH CAUSE DIVISION IN THE CHURCH.
14. BOTH HAVE TO PROVIDE MEANS AND METHODS.
15. BOTH ACTIVATE THE CHURCH UNIVERSAL.
16. BOTH ARE DEFENDED BY THE SAME ARGUMENTS.

(3) *Both solicit and accept church contributions.* (4) *Both are composed of President or Superintendent, Board of Directors, Secretary and Treasurer, etc.* (5) *Both claim to perform a work of the churches.* (6) *Both are organizations larger than the local church, but smaller than the universal church.* (7) *Both have their own constitution and by-laws.* (8) The missionary society, and the benevolent society Brother Inman is defending, are *both designed to give the mission of the church greater efficiency,* or implementation. (9) *Both of them control portions of the church's treasury.* (10) *Both are considered by the world as official functioning organs of the church.* You get your newspaper and see who is running Mid-Western Children's Home. The world thinks the Church of Christ is running that. (11) *Both propose to do what they say the congregations themselves cannot do.* The churches alone will never get the job done. (12) *Both claim to be expedients.* We have heard a good bit about expediency. (13) *Both cause division in the church.* (14) *Both have to provide means and methods.* They both are *institutions.* They both have to use means and methods. (15) *Both of them activate the church universal.* That which they are doing is not the work of the *local* church. It is the action of the church universal. (16) And *both are defended by the same arguments.*

So I have given you on this chart a number of points of similarity between the missionary society and the benevolent society. I would like for Brother Inman to show us the difference between a church supported benevolent society and a church supported missionary society. Now, Brother Inman, if I were in your position and trying to defend a church supported benevolent society, I would just apologize to the Christian church, and shut my mouth. If I were going to try to defend acting through a human institution in benevolence, I would not say a thing on earth about others acting through a human institution in evangelism.

The word "parallel", if you will look it up in the dictionary, means "with like direction or tendency; like in essential parts; anything equal to or resembling another in all essential particulars." Brother Inman, I would like for you to show me some "essential particulars" that are dif-

FOURTH NIGHT, BENEVOLENT INSTITUTIONS 191

ferent between the missionary society and the benevolent society.

Somebody says, "Oh, one is doing benevolent work and the other is doing evangelistic work." I knew that! What I am talking about is this, *Show me a difference in their organizational structure.*

Brother G. K. Wallace said in 1951, "There is a parallel between an orphan home that has a board of trustees other than the elders of a church to do the work of the church, and the United Christian Missionary Society" (*Gospel Guardian,* May 24, 1951). Brother C. R. Nichol said, "Brethren call me at times for debates, and occasionally the missionary society is brought into the discussion. It is an organization through which the congregations function." Now listen to his question: "On what grounds am I to oppose such organizations and then defend the organization of the _____ orphan home?" And he left out the name of the orphan home. Brother Nichol asked, "On what basis am I to oppose the missionary society and defend the separate organization of the orphan home?" (*Firm Foundation,* May 23, 1933). Brother Inman, that would be a good question for you to work on when you get up here.

Brother George Pepperdine said, "If a separate organization to own and operate a children's home is not unscriptural, then I do not understand why it would be unscriptural for the same board of directors to operate a missionary society" (*Gospel Advocate,* 1933, page 571). And that is what I was getting at when I asked him if the Mid-Western Children's Home board could alter its program of work to include evangelism. Brother Foy E. Wallace said, "If it were 'permissible to have a Bible college as an adjunct to the church in the work of education and an orphan's home in the work of benevolence', we quite agree that it would be 'permissible' to have a 'missionary society in the work of evangelization'. It seems to me the same principle which allows the one will allow all." (*Gospel Advocate,* July 2, 1931, page 804).

We showed last night that his arguments will force him to defend the church support of colleges. And I am showing him tonight, or at least trying to show him, that the same arguments he makes indict the all-sufficiency of

God's sacred provision for his people, and indicate that he does not believe that the congregation is sufficient. His arguments necessarily obligate him to say that the church can do its evangelistic work through a human institution in the same way that he says the church can do its benevolent work through a human institution.

So you keep in mind now, when Brother Inman comes to speak, that he is looking for a passage in God's word where churches worked through a human institution. What he wants to find is where they worked through human institutions that did benevolent work, but they did not work through the same kind of human institutions to do evangelistic work. And it is going to be interesting when he finds the passage that authorizes a human institution for benevolence, but that condemns a human institution for evangelistic work. I called attention awhile ago in connection with chart No. 10 that he said he studied just one book, and that is the book out of which I want the passage. Where can you read of a church sending a contribution to a human institution? Where in the Bible can we read where churches of Christ ever heard of a human institution through which to do their benevolent work? I thank you for listening. We will make further argumentation in my next speech.

INMAN'S FIRST NEGATIVE

Again, we appreciate the presence of each one. I want to express that appreciation as well as others have. We are thankful to our God for an opportunity to study his word. I want to say again that the matter before us is too serious and our care for one another too grave a matter for me not to spend my time in trying to find an answer from the word of God. I would like this evening, first of all, to go over the things that I noted last evening before going into the things that have been said this evening, because these are the background against which we can unweave a lot of things that have been said this evening.

Let us notice again that things that are authorized may be in one of three categories. Those that are demanded of all, as we have mentioned on our chart; those that are demanded of some, or under some circumstances; and then those things which we may or may not do. Paul said in I Corinthians 9:5, "Have we no right to lead about a wife that is a believer, even as the rest of the apostles, and the brethren of the Lord, and Cephas?" I have authority to do this; I do not have an obligation to do this. We noted concerning baptism that we are commanded to be baptized, if we would have salvation. It is not a matter of whether we want to be or whether we will be; we must be. But then whether we are baptized in an open stream or in an enclosed baptistry is a matter of choice, and depends upon the expediencies of the occasion.

We are enjoined to care for orphans, and I hope Brother Willis, that you will listen to this argument and get it. Do not just come up here and say "he said something about James 1:27." Notice what I say about James 1:27. In James 1:27, we are told, "Pure religion and undefiled before our God and Father is this, to visit the fatherless and widows in their affliction, and to keep oneself unspotted from the world."

(Mimeographed Sheet distributed by Brother Inman)

POINTS TO NOTE

1. Things authorized may be placed in 3 categories. See chart.
2. To be authorized a thing must not necessarily be bound.
3. Where there is no law, there is no transgression. Romans 4:15.
4. Paul had authority to lead about a wife, but he did not lead about a wife. I Corinthians 9.
5. We are enjoined to care for orphans. James 1:27.
6. We are not told to do this separately conjointly.
7. Where there is no law there is no transgression.
8. Jesus said that people will be judged individually by whether they visit the hungry. Matthew 25:31-46.
9. The apostles activated this command by forming a common treasury. Acts 2:44-45.
10. A principle is set forth in I Timothy 5:16 that when one member has prime responsibility he should not permit this responsibility to be shifted to all, but that when there is no prime responsibility, the whole church is to be responsible.
11. Who must have legal custody of the one who is helped?
    A. Three agencies who may have legal custody:
       a. Husband and wife
       b. Church
       c. Corporate home
    B. Does the Bible set forth a pattern for helping in different ways if different agencies have custody? If so, where?
12. The act of helping is not that of helping an institution but of helping a needy child.
13. Concerning those who are not members of the church. Luke 10:25-37; Luke 4:25-27.

CARE OF ORPHANED OR FORSAKEN CHILDREN

1. Is any specific manner of caring for these set forth in the New Testament?
2. Are we enjoined to care for them?   See James 1:27.
3. If care is enjoined and specific manner is not, then any manner may be used which does not violate some other New Testament principle. Romans 4:15.

4. Some questions to elicit exact point of difference:
   A. Is it wrong for a group of brethren to form a corporation for the purpose of maintaining a home for orphaned or forsaken children?
   B. Is it right to take funds from a church's treasury to help orphans or forsaken children at all?
   C. If right to help orphaned or forsaken children at all, is it possible to help them in any way if they happen to be in a corporate home?
   D. Is it possible to help an orphaned or forsaken child who has been adopted by a man and his wife?
   E. Is it possible for the church, from its treasury, to give money directly to the man and wife, or must it be given to the child directly?
   F. Is it right or wrong to take funds from the treasury of the church to help one who is not a member of the church?

I hope you are looking at the paper that you were handed this evening when you came in. Notice Point No. 6 on the side which says, "Points to Note." I made this yesterday in a hurry when I was trying to take care of the bookstore and do a little work too. This really should read like this, "We are not told whether to do this separately or conjointly." Here we are enjoined to visit the fatherless, but we are not told in this passage whether in visiting them we may visit them individually or conjointly. Now, since we are not told whether we are to visit separately, individually, or conjointly, then "where there is no law, there is no transgression" (Romans 4:15).

Now notice that James 1:27 says to visit the widows, and it also says to visit the fatherless. (And Bob would you hand me that chart I have over there, please). Now, Brother Willis, are you listening? When it comes to the matter of the widows in I Timothy 5:16 the apostle says, or the Holy Spirit through him says, that anyone who has a widow should take care of that widow, "and let not the church be charged." Here then is a principle. The principle is that when there is a widow (And we could put orphan in here at the same place, because this is an application of the principle set forth in James 1:27), who has a son or other relatives who bear the closer relationship to her than anyone else in the church, then he should take care of that

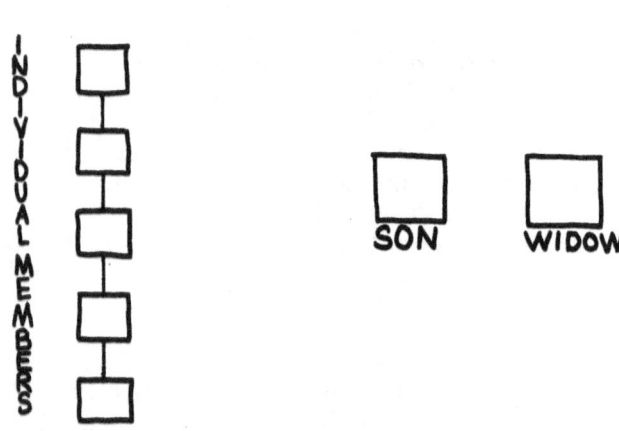

obligation. But when there is no one that bears that closer relationship, when we remove the son, who becomes responsible for that widow or that orphan? Each one bears the same relationship. So they all bear responsibility, and from the treasury of the church they may and should support that orphan or widow.

You not only missed the question last night, you just never paid any attention to the whole of this argument or any other. I would like some attention paid to it. When there is an orphan that does not bear a closer relationship to one individual in the church than to another, then the church is obligated to take care of that orphan. Each one has the same obligation. So from that treasury which is common to all, the church treasury if you please, they should take care of that widow or that orphan. That is the principle set forth.

Now he spends a lot of time with the individual argument, talking about this on James 1:27. Brother Willis, I

FOURTH NIGHT, BENEVOLENT INSTITUTIONS 197

want you to listen to this from Matthew 25, and then pay attention to what I say. Do not just get up here and say he mentioned a scripture that does not have anything to do with the case. Please note what I pointed out. Jesus said that people would be judged individually. And last night he agreed with me. He said that is an individual case; it does not have anything to do with it. But he did not notice what I had to say about it.

Jesus said that in the day of judgment we will answer individually as to whether or not we visited those who are hungry. When the apostles came to interpret this and to put into practice what Jesus taught and to activate it, this is the way they interpreted it. They who had possessions sold them, put them into a common treasury and divided to every man as he had need (Acts 2:44-45). This is the way the apostles, through the Holy Spirit, interpreted that which was given as an individual responsibility to each Christian. They then fulfilled their individual responsibility from the common or the church treasury. Now do not just get up here and say he mentioned some passages. Face up to the argument like a man, and tell us what is wrong with this. Or face up to it like a man and say "Well now I just misunderstood this." You want to know what caused me to change my mind? This kind of reasoning from the word of God, and this other kind of jumping from here to yonder, and not paying any attention to the word of God. That is what changed my mind.

A principle is set forth in I Timothy 5:16 that when one member has prime responsibility, he should not permit this responsibility to be shifted to all, but when there is no prime responsibility the whole church is to be responsible. That is what we illustrated a moment ago.

Then we asked, "Who must have legal custody of the one who is helped?" And he said that does not have anything to do with it. That is the whole problem here, really. This is the whole question. There are three agencies that may have legal custody: a husband and wife, the church, or a corporate home. Now, of course, he says the church cannot. He says it would be wrong if the church did it. Now, he may deny that, but he said that the church cannot help someone who is not a member of the church. Therefore, since the orphan is not a member of the church, the church cannot do it. That has been his whole argument.

Have you noticed how he has been arguing with himself? You know, really I am not even needed in this discussion. He has been arguing with himself ever since it started. He says the church cannot help this orphan who is not a member of the church. The church cannot take money from its treasury to help someone who is not a member of the church. And then he turns right around and says, "Inman, you have a human organization in there taking the place of the church and doing the church's work." No, you say it is not the church's work. You are saying the church would be sinning if it did it. You say, "the church has to do it; the church can't!" So he stands here and argues with himself all the time, "the church can, the church can't." "The church sins if it does; the church has to do it." Last night and tonight, all the time, just arguing with himself. "The church must do it; the church can't do it. The church must do it; the church can't do it." I think it is time that he quits arguing with himself and makes up his mind which way he is going. He has been carrying on a debate with himself all last night and tonight.

"Does the Bible set forth a pattern for helping in different ways if different agencies have custody?" Now, I want to point this out. He talks about a restored home argument—an argument about a restored home. You know, he had the idea that I was going to make a lot of arguments. He came here and had a lot of things built up and charts built up. When I did not go along with this, he just has to have me saying these things, and he is going to have me saying them whether I ever say them or not. But it is a plain fact that a home is a place where a baby is bathed, and fed, and put to bed and pampered and given all kinds of training and exercise. I do not believe it is the work of the church to do this. It is the work of the home to do this. When the home ceases to be, the home that the child had ceases to be, you never restore that.

As I pointed out last evening, my father passed on when I was 18 months old. He has not been restored, and anybody that has had that experience knows that does not happen. He is not restored. The home we had has not been restored. I do not feel bitter about this, but yet, at the same time, I missed something here. I think maybe I gained something from my mother, and from some hardship. Yet I lost something too. But that was never restored. Something else came along and made up for this. In my case, it was just a mother who had the grit to do it. In other cases it is other things. But something has to take the place of that which was lost. That other is not restored, but something does have to take the place.

Somebody does have to diaper and feed the baby. Somebody does have to bathe it and put it to bed. Somebody has to bounce it upon his knee. Now, if that child still has need, and those who give it shelter and food find themselves in financial difficulty and in straits so that they are unable to provide what the child needs, then everyone of us who has heart and who claims to serve Jesus Christ and love the Christ of love has a responsibility to see that that child has what it needs. And the fact that it may be out here in a corporate home where it has that need does not deny the fact that you and I need to supply that need. That is the point.

As I said last evening, we are not helping a group of men. We are helping a child in need. I told Brother Robertson today about one time the church decided at Christmas time to send a basket of fruit over to our house. You know, I was glad to see that basket of fruit, but my mother was not. She could not understand why the church thought that she was a charity case. She thought that she ought to be out helping somebody else. But you know, they did not just help mother; they helped us. They helped us children. They helped to supply something that she was not able to supply. And here the church is supplying something.

Let us notice something else here too. That is this. I may in my home have, as I do have, a business. But these businesses sometime can get in bad circumstances. I am an expert on that. And sometimes a man who has a business may not be able to provide food and clothing sufficient for his children. And if the church then were to see that I am unable to provide this for my children, and they wanted to help my children, and so they bring some money and give it to me to help my children, they are not running a business. They are not operating Bible Herald Book Store.

If a group of us go together and form a corporation, we may raise vegetables and let these children have an opportunity to work and raise vegetables. We may sell some of this. We may sell this and buy some clothing. But if these do not satisfy all their needs, and they still need food and still need clothing, then you and I, who love Jesus Christ and love God and love our fellowman as we ought, will feel a responsibility tugging at our hearts to help to provide something for those children. And we are giving to children, and not to a home. The act of helping is not that of helping an institution, but of helping a needy child.

Now these other verses. He says Luke 10:25-37 does not have anything to do with giving to an institution. But it does have something to do with another question. I asked him if he believed that you could take money from the church treasury and give it to someone who is not a member of the church. He said, "No." Jesus said "there were many lepers in Israel in the time of Elisha, the prophet; and none of them was cleansed, but only Naaman the Syrian" (Luke 4:27). God here showed concern, passed over his own people, to help a Syrian. And "there were many widows in Israel in the days of Elijah,. . .and unto none of them was Elijah sent", except to the widow of Zarephath (Luke 4:24-26). Elijah was not sent to any in Israel amongst his people, but he was sent to one up yonder, a foreigner, a stranger. Luke 10:25 has to do with the good Samaritan. How much time? (His Moderator: Ten minutes.) Thank you.

All right, let us come to the questions, and I hope we can get to his charts. But let me show you that this principle really is understood. You know, Brother Willis is staying in a motel down here, the Holiday Inn. As I understand it, the church is paying for his room and board out there. Are they supporting an inn. A hospitality society? Or, are they supporting him?

Now to the questions Brother Willis asked. *"Last night you made the 'restored home' argument. When you 'restore' the child's broken home, who then are his parents?"* Well, I do not remember anything about a restored home.

Let us have chart No. 13. I do not remember anything about a restored home argument. Now, let us see what this means here. Just what does it mean anyhow? Now, Brother Willis, let us suppose there are some children out here in a Catholic home, not an institutional home, but the father and mother are Catholics. Going to help them? The

WHICH HOME CAN THE CHURCH SUPPORT?

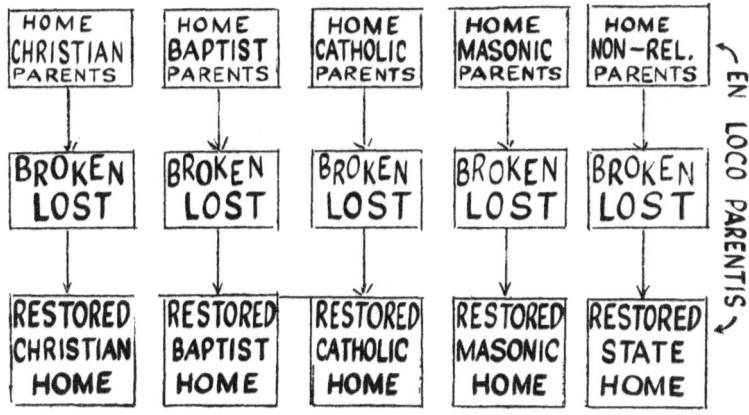

children are in dire need. The father has arthritis and the mother is sickly, and they cannot work. Again, here is another home, and here is a drunken father, and a sinful mother who care not for them at all. There are some problems here, aren't there? What are we going to do? What is the church going to do? Brethren have wrestled with this problem for ages.

What will you do when the children are starving? Will you take help over and give it to that old drunken father who does not care for the children? Will you try to bypass him and give it to the children? And if you do, what will he do about it? And will they get to use it? Anybody who has ever tried in love to solve this problem has run into untold difficulties.

Brother Carl Parsons (sitting out there) and I have visited some of these. Brother Hugh Hetser and I have done this. We have bought shoes and we have bought groceries and we would take these to people like this, and we have been faced with this problem. And I am thankful that I worked with Park and Main and at the old 618 Virginia Street congregation in Charleston, and these two men that I have named and Brother Harry Toothman were down there. We were concerned about people like this, and we did not have this idea that we could not help them because they were not members of the church.

But you are faced with these problems. There are knotty problems here and it is not easy to find a solution to them. And here in this case calamity would come, and in this home over here there are children that are starving, and the church has money, and we can get it through to them. You tell me what you are going to do about it. You just tell me. You would not, I certainly would not, help that drunken father. Neither would I help the Masonic home. Now you tell me how you are going to solve this matter of getting to the children in either case.

"Do you believe in limited or unlimited benevolence?" Oh, unlimited. I think you ought to buy them an oil well, and set them up in a bank. (He laughs). You know he has been talking about limited and unlimited here for several nights. I have never used the terms, and I never said whether I believed in limited or unlimited benevolence. Certainly there are limits to benevolence. And I hope you understand that I was just joking and using a little satire about giving them an oil well and building a bank.

"If the original home (a divine institution) is restored, how is it that the restored home is a human institution?" Well, you said it was a human institution. Not only did you say that, but you said you think it is all right to have a corporate home for children like this. You said it could not be supported out of the church treasury, but you can have it. So you tell me what it is. I do not think that the home is ever restored, as I mentioned to begin with.

"If individual responsibility can be discharged through a common congregational treasury, can our individal responsibility to educate our children be discharged through a congregational treasury?" Let us notice again. Get the point that providing a home and building an educational institution are two different things. And we are certainly told to visit the fatherless and widows. And this is the thing we are to do, but we are not told to teach science, and mathematics and all these things. More than that, it becomes the obligation of the home, whether it be a corporate home or individual home, to see that the children in that home are educated and that they are trained. Now someone may complain because when you are helping these children, you give money that helps them (the individuals

FOURTH NIGHT, BENEVOLENT INSTITUTIONS   203

or those who are in charge of them, father or mother, husband and wife, or a corporate home) provide an education for them. But they who have the parentage of these homes, or who do occupy the place of the parents, and have the responsibility the parents had before must provide education.

"*Which of the Bible references that you presented last night pertaining to congregational benevolent responsibility convinced you that it is scriptural to support a benevolent society under a board of directors like Mid-Western Children's Home?*" What convinced me that we ought to take care of children and help them regardless of who has the legal custody are the arguments I have made tonight, and I would like to hear some answer to them.

"*What difference do you think you see between the church's contributing to institutions like OVC to do educational work, and churches contributing to institutions like Mid-Western and Potter, to do benevolent work? Please be explicit.*" Again, churches are contributing to children who are in need, regardless of who has the oversight. This organization has not taken the place of the church, but it has stepped in to try, as best it can, to take the place of the home, to give the children what the home was not giving them, but to give them what the home was not giving them because it was no longer there. The school is not doing this.

"*If James 1:27 authorizes church supported institutional orphanages, does Matthew 25:31 justify church supported hospitals?*" What is the time now? (Brother Kessinger: Three minutes.) Three minutes. If the church had enough sick and needy that it was, in the judgment of that church, expedient to hire a doctor and to have a common house in which these sick were cared for and pay the doctor to come there and care for them, as we mentioned last evening they may have a room down in the church building where they have clothes and groceries the needy come and receive, who could say that there is anything wrong with this? But now when a place is built out here and people who come there are charged, you have a business that is set up to be a business and for the purpose of being a business, and incidentally you care for a few sick. This is a different proposition entirely. But again, in this hospital under the situation I am talking about, what is given would be given to take care of sick people. And I realize that there are some arrangements here that might violate some other principles of scripture, but certainly we could provide a place to take care of the sick, if this is needed.

"*What did the Jerusalem church do with the money received from Antioch by the hands of Barnabas and Saul?*" That is on last night's proposition, and if you are not satisfied, we will be at Dayton in another debate. We will have more on that. I said I thought this passage is a little obscure and you said, "Yes, Sir, very obscure." Now you can fuss around with that from now on, but I think you would do better on the proposition.

"*What features of orphan homes like Boles and Potter caused you to be undecided?*" Nothing. It was a matter of not having studied the scriptures. I said I do not know, let us all study. I had not made up my mind; let us all study. I studied some more, and made up my mind. It was not the features of the home; it was studying from the word of God.

"*Why would it be unscriptural to incorporate as a separate institution the Herald of Truth to do evangelistic work, but is scriptural to incorporate a separate institution to do benevolent work?*" We are not incorporating to do benevolent work. This institution over here has been incorporated. Children are taken into that home, and then the church supplies the needs of those children.

Thank you.

WILLIS' SECOND AFFIRMATIVE

For two nights now I have been keeping this sheet of paper on which I am jotting down every passage Brother Inman cites. This sheet has several classifications on it. One of them is INDIVIDUAL BENEVOLENCE. I have 5 passages jotted down under INDIVIDUAL BENEVOLENCE, but we are not talking about individual benevolence. We are talking about how churches can work; what churches can do. Then I have another classification: CONGREGATIONAL BENEVOLENCE. And we have had two nights now, and he still has cited only two passages. Actually what he is looking for is "corporate home" benevolence. That is what he is looking for. We are not debating whether the church can do benevolent work. He has cited, so far, two passages: Acts 2:44, 45 and 1 Timothy 5:16. And since we want to examine his proof, let us just turn and read these passages now. I want you to see if you see a "corporate home", an institution, a human organization in these.

"And all that believed were together, and had all things common; and they sold their possessions and goods, and parted them to all, according as any man had need" (Acts 2:44, 45). Who did that? The *church* in Jerusalem. What is he looking for? A human institution. And the other passage says, "If any woman that believeth hath widows, let her relieve them, and let the church be not burdened; that it may relieve them that are widows indeed" (1 Tim. 5:16). Now, who is going to do the relieving? The *church* is going to relieve them that are widows indeed. Thus in both of those passages we do not have any human institution. Now what we are looking for, Brother Inman, is scripture for *institutional* benevolence. And I have this sheet of paper. I want to give you this sheet of paper, Brother Inman (He hands it to him). I wish you would write those passages down while I am speaking. Write down the scriptures that authorize *institutional* benevolence. That is what we are talking about. We are not discussing whether the church can act in benevolence, but whether a human institution can do the work of the church in benevolence.

Now let us take a look please at his chart No. 1, "Things that are Lawful." He says there are some things that are demanded of all, such as baptism and love. There

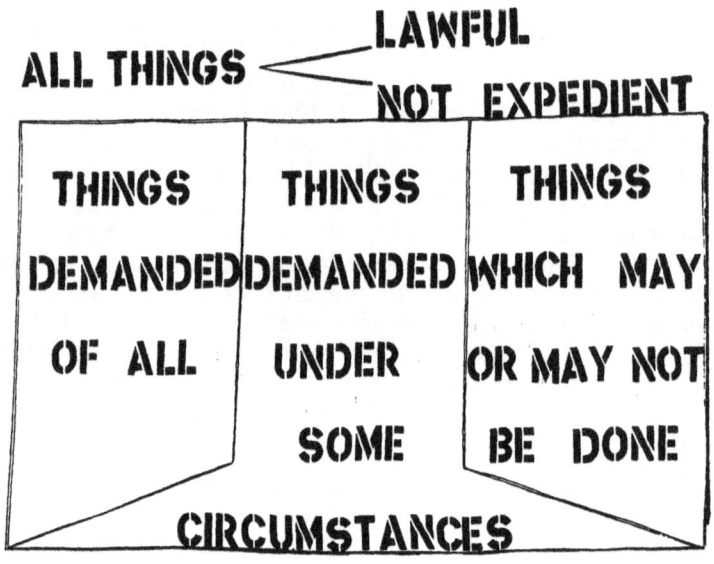

are some things that are demanded under some circumstances. Now, you are to love your wife, if you have a wife. You are to obey your husband, if you have a husband. And then he said, there are things which may or may not be done. That is where he thinks that human institution fits in.

Now you notice that he has been strangely silent about this chart here (pointing to chart No. 6). I wonder if this human institution (pointing to missionary society on chart) is also over under things which may or may not be done. Now he told us that under things which may or may not be done are baptizing in a river or in a baptistry inside the house, or the usage of a table cloth for the Lord's table. These are just expediencies; they may or may not be done.

MISSIONARY AND BENEVOLENT SOCIETIES

1. BOTH ORIGINATED IN THE MIND OF MAN. HENCE ARE HUMAN INSTITUTIONS.
2. BOTH ARE ORGANIZATIONS SEPERATE AND APART FROM THE CHURCH.
3. BOTH SOLICIT AND ACCEPT CHURCH CONTRIBUTIONS.
4. BOTH COMPOSED OF PRESIDENT OR SUPT., BOARD OF DIRECTORS, SEC. AND TREAS., ETC.
5. BOTH CLAIM TO PERFORM A WORK OF THE CHURCH.
6. BOTH ARE ORGANIZATIONS LARGER THAN THE LOCAL CHURCH BUT SMALLER THAN THE UNIVERSAL CHURCH
7. BOTH HAVE THEIR OWN CONSTITUTIONS AND BY-LAWS.
8. BOTH DESIGNED TO GIVE MISSION OF CHURCH GREATER EFFICIENCY
9. BOTH CONTROL PORTION'S OF THE CHURCH'S TREASURY.
10. BOTH CONSIDERED BY WORLD AS OFFICIAL FUNCTIONING ORGANS OF THE CHURCH.
11. BOTH PROPOSE TO DO WHAT THE CONGREGATIONS CANNOT DO THEMSELVES.
12. BOTH CLAIM TO BE EXPEDIENTS.
13. BOTH CAUSE DIVISION IN THE CHURCH.
14. BOTH HAVE TO PROVIDE MEANS AND METHODS.
15. BOTH ACTIVATE THE CHURCH UNIVERSAL.
16. BOTH ARE DEFENDED BY THE SAME ARGUMENTS.

I told Brother Inman that these fellows act rather strangely about their expediencies. I tried to get one of his preaching brethren to speak to me last night, to shake hands with me last night, and he said, "No, I do not want to speak to you." I wonder if they act that way about table cloths! Do you suppose they would treat you that way about a table cloth? Is that the way they react about baptistries? And this brother happens to have written the article on the front page of this issue of the BIBLE HERALD, if you want to look it up and see who it was. And again this morning, he still refused to speak to me. If these institutions are just expediencies, that is a rather unusual way to act about an expediency.

Actually the Christian Church makes the same arguments that Brother Inman has made. There are some things over here which may or may not be done. What are some of those things? Playing a piano is one of the things the

Christian Church says you may or may not do. You do not have to do it, but you may or may not do it. How did you learn that? The Christian Church preacher said that it is so. How did you learn that the human institution is a thing which may or may not be done? What passage did you cite? Brother Inman merely *said* that is where it goes. Now the Christian Church preacher says that is where the Missionary Society goes too. He says you may work through the missionary society, but you do not have to do so. And I have an idea that they might treat me a little better than a few people treat me about their expedient. But the Christian Church says working through a missionary society is a thing that may or may not be done.

Then we have Brother Inman and some of his brethren to come along and start telling us what all goes under that heading of things which may or may not be done. They put brotherhood elders over there; sponsoring churches—two thousands churches working through one eldership are put under things which may or may not be done. That was his argument the other night; it may or it

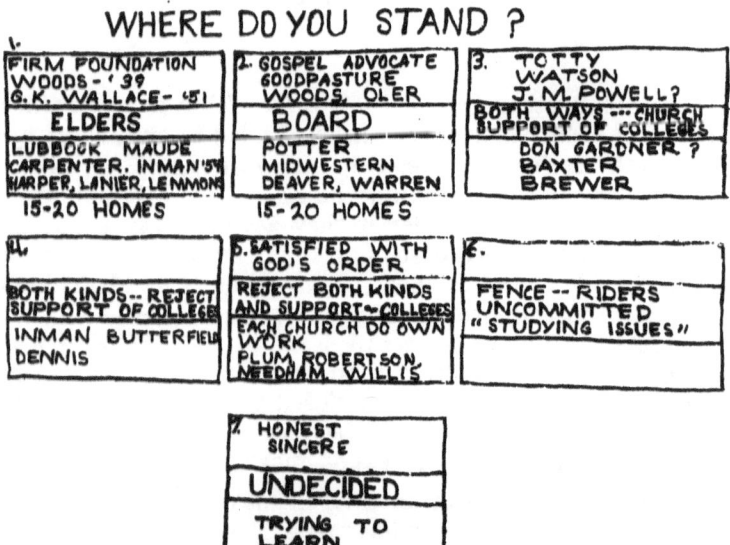

FOURTH NIGHT, BENEVOLENT INSTITUTIONS 209

may not be done. How do you get it over there? He *said* that is where it goes. You people are supposed to take that. And he also *said* tonight this institutional orphan home belongs under things which may or may not be done. What passage puts it over there? Brother Inman *said* to put it over there.

Some other brethren (I had on the chart the names of some of them a while ago) say church sponsored recreation may or may not be done. That is where it goes. How do they prove that? Well, they just *say* it. That is how they prove it. And there are some others of his brethren, who agree with him on this proposition, who say that things that may or may not be done are things like churches contributing to David Lipscomb College. That may or may not be done according to some. How do you prove that? You just tell people that, and you *tell* people that and you TELL people that, and *TELL* them that, and perhaps sooner or later they will come to believe it, whether you can cite a passage in God's word for it or not.

Now, again James 1:27 has come up. I remind Brother Inman that he does not know the difference between "a man" and "a church", *until he starts talking about "a church" sending to a college.* Then he knows the difference! He knows it then! But this passage says, "if any *man* thinketh *himself* to be religious, while *he* bridleth not *his* tongue, but deceiveth *his* heart, this *man's* religion is vain." Who is that talking about? Oh, that is *church* benevolence, we are told. If I just gave him that passage, and said "All right, let us just concede that that is church benevolence," that would not help him a bit on earth. What he is looking for is not an instance of *church* benevolence. He is looking for an instance of *institutional* benevolence, and he has not found it in James 1:27. Even if he could write the word "church" in the place of that word "man", it would not help him any.

And then he spoke of 1 Tim. 5:16. Let us see the paper chart, Brother Inman. You wanted me to take a look at that. He said if the son is taken out of the way somehow, then the church can take care of this widow. Now, Brother Inman, that does not help you a bit on earth. We are not talking about whether a church can take care of a widow; we are talking about whether a *human institution*

I TIMOTHY 5:16

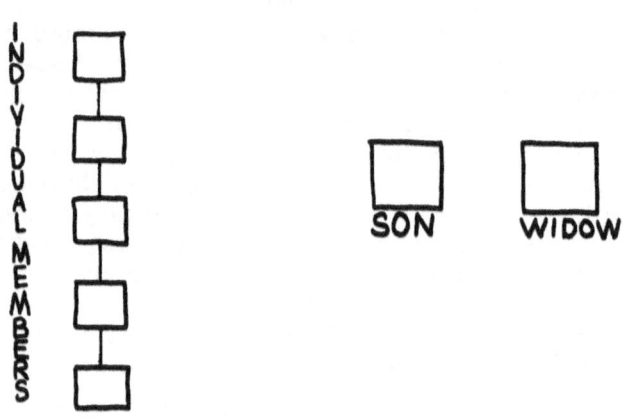

can do it. Where on that chart did you write "Human institution"? Your proposition calls for a corporate home, a separate body, with its own by-laws. He has admitted it is a human institution. I see a son and a widow and a church, but I do not see a thing on earth on this chart about a human institution. That is what he needs to find. Actually that passage just goes the wrong way for him. It says, "If any woman that believeth hath widows, let her relieve them, and let not the church be burdened; that it (i.e., the *church*) may relieve them that are widows indeed." It did not say the board of directors. It did not say that the Mid-Western Children's Home might relieve them, or the old folks' home might relieve them. It said that "THE CHURCH" might relieve them. That does not help Brother Inman any.

Now, Brother Inman tried to make another argument. He said that over in James 1:27 you have some orphans and some widows. And in 1 Timothy 5:16 you have some

FOURTH NIGHT, BENEVOLENT INSTITUTIONS 211

widows that the Bible says the church is to relieve. So he tries to say that those widows that the church shall relieve are the same widows as in James 1:27. But actually I might just as well make his argument and say in 1 Timothy 5:16 the Bible says "let not the church be burdened." That is what it says, and it says younger widows "refuse." I might just as well say that *those* are the widows of James 1:27. His argument does not work there.

And he spoke of Matt. 25:31-46. He interpreted that as church obligation. In fact he has done some rather weird things. You know where he has found authority for a church to send to human institutions? Why he has gone back over there to that case about Elisha helping a widow. That is a rather strange place to be finding authority for the *church* to act. You had better watch out now. Your friend down here on the front row (referring to Christian Church preacher) is going to say, "Brother Inman, I can find that piano back over there in the old Testament. We can go back over there and find where David played on a piano." (Laughter). I say that is a rather strange place to find authority for *church* action.

He merely asserted that this benevolence in Matt. 25 was benevolence that was done by the church. He asserted this; he did not prove it. But if I said, "All right, I will let you have that," Brother Inman, you still do not have a human institution. The human institution is what you are looking for.

And then he talked about legal custody. And I told him that I am not debating who has *legal* custody.

And he wanted to know, "What did Willis say about limited benevolence?" Or can the church help an alien? And he said he had wrestled with that problem for ages. He really had been bothered by that. I told him last night, "Brother Inman, I would just be glad to preach that the church can help persons other than saints, if you would just give me the passages." So, I got my notebook ready and I did not get even one passage. I was looking for Bible authority for the church to help somebody other than the saints of God, other than the disciples, or other than the brethren. He did not cite the passage, and I will still be glad to have it in his next speech, if he knows where such a passage is.

Now he did cite Luke 4:25-27, and Luke 10 (about the good Samaritan). But I did not know the good Samaritan was a church, did you? He is trying to make the good Samaritan a church. He said an individual helped somebody that was not of his religion. Yet in the word of God, in Acts 2:44, 45 and Acts 4:32-35, we learn that they helped the *believers*. In Acts 11:27-30 the Bible says they sent relief unto the *brethren* that dwelt in Judea. In Acts 6:1-6 we read that when the number of the *disciples* was multiplied, their widows were neglected in the daily ministration. Who was it? The *disciples*. In Rom. 15:26, the Bible says, "For it hath been the good pleasure of Macedonia and Achaia to make a certain contribution for the poor among the *saints* that are at Jerusalem." So that is all I know about it, brethren. Now, he can make of that anything he wants to make of it, but that is all I know about it. Unless he will cite me a passage where a church helped somebody other than the saints of God, I am not going to start preaching that. I tell people that I speak where the Bible speaks and I am silent where the Bible is silent, and so far I cannot find anything in God's word about the congregation helping aliens.

He said he had not made the restored home argument. Now Brother Inman told us the other night that he had not done much reading on this subject and I think that he is indicating that by a number of things. He said he had not made the restored home argument. The truth of the matter is, he made it but he just did not know that is what the brethren call it. That is the argument he made. And I jotted down a number of statements from him. He said, "What is the corporate home *replacing?*" What is it *replacing?* I wonder if replacing and restoring might be about the same. Then he said, "When the home ceases to be, you can *restore* that." Further he said, "This *takes the place of* the home." And he ought to read some of the debates by some of these big wheel brethren he knows. In their arguments they say that when you get this restored down here (pointing to "Restored" home on chart), it is a *divine* institution. Brother Inman says it is a *human* institution. But he said "Now really all you are doing is helping those children down there. You are not sending some money to that board of directors; you are just helping those children down there."

WHICH HOME CAN THE CHURCH SUPPORT?

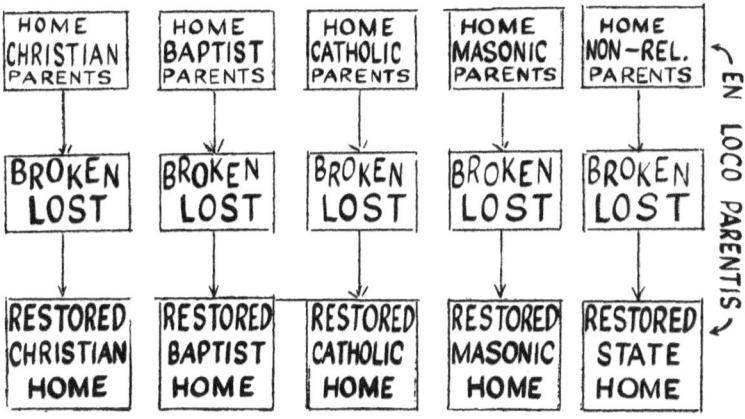

Well I wonder, Brother Inman, if when we send some money to the board of directors of this Catholic restored home, are we not really helping that institution? He said we are just helping the children in it. Now are you ready for church support of a Catholic "home", brethren? And this one here is a Baptist home; their home is broken, it is lost, and they replace it. Whether he wants to say restored or replaced is immaterial. Now remember, when you send to Buckner Orphan Home down there at Dallas, Texas, or some other Baptist orphan home, you are not really sending to that orphan home. You are just helping the children down there, and he believes you can help everybody. He believes the church has an obligation to all the needy in the world and so he believes, if his argument is worth a plugged nickle, that the church can send a contribution to a board of directors whether they be Christians, Baptists, Catholics, Masons or whatever they might be. He believes the church can send to that board of directors, and make a donation to that board of directors. And you keep that in mind when he gets back up here. Futhermore, he said the fact that they are in a corporate home does not relieve the church of its obligation and that it is just helping the child and not the institution. And this is the argument with which I just was dealing.

And he said, you tell me what you are going to do about these children in these institutions. Well, I will tell you what I am going to do about it. I am not going to approve of the Lord's church sending donations to the institutions. That will not take me long to tell you that. I *am not* going to endorse the church sending to the board of directors of this home (pointing to "restored homes" on chart), or this home, or this Catholic home, or this State home. I *am* going to say that any work the Lord's church does, the elders of the Lord's church must oversee.

Now, he made one argument that I do not know how to answer. It is that "tear-jerking speech" that he made about what are you going to do about these little orphans. Now, I do not know how to answer an *emotional* argument. I heard a fellow say one time that there is one argument on instrumental music he did not know how to answer. He said it was the argument in which the fellow says, "I know I cannot find it in the Bible, but *I want it anyway.*" That is a hard argument to answer, isn't it? I know I cannot find it in the Bible, but I want it anyway. Now, really that is the position Brother Inman is in tonight. He has not found it in the Bible. He has cited two passages that pertain to *congregational* benevolence, but he wants a *human* institution anyway.

You know, a little amusing thing happened a while ago. Somebody brought me this little card (He holds up a picture card). You cannot see it perhaps, but that is a little street wanderer. A friend handed me this and said: "How are you going to answer that?" And I wondered, how *am I* going to answer that? I asked Brother Paul Casebolt, and he told me what to do about it. He said, "Paint her black." (Laughter). That will answer it. "Paint her black." What do you mean? They have in their charters that they will only take *white* children in some of the institutions. In fact, in some of the institutions in his proposition you will find such a restriction. They will only take white children. So if this is a little *black* child, his little emotional appeal all goes for naught.

Then he wanted to know, "Is the church supporting the Holiday Inn?" No, the church is not supporting the Holiday Inn. The church is paying for my stay out there, I hope. (Laughter). But they are doing the same thing they would be doing if I were staying at a hotel, or if I had a stay in a hospital. Now what Brother Inman needs to tell us is, would he approve of the church sending monthly donations to Holiday Inn because I stayed in it a night or two one time? (Laughter). Now really, that is what he is defending. He said sometime or other we may want to send some children over there, so we are going to send donations. Some time or other, brethren, you might want to keep a preacher in a hotel or in a hospital. So you ought to put the hotel or hospital in the budget for $10 a month. Now, brethren, he needs to learn the difference, if he does not already know it, between *buying services* and *making donations*.

I have argued that the institutional orphan homes indict the sufficiency of the church. God gave us the church and said, "Unto him be the glory in the church . . ." (Eph. 3:21). Brethren, that is what I am maintaining.

But I want further to show you that these *institutional orphan homes are not needed*. Brother Inman gets up and makes an appealing speech about how they are needed. That is just not so. I wrote to the Welfare Department of Ohio, just before you brethren were getting all cranked up to start this Mid-Western Children's Home. I asked, "Do you need any more institutional orphan homes?" And here is the answer, but first this earlier 1956 letter. I will give you the recent one in a minute. They said, "It is our current belief that Ohio has numerous children's homes under a variety of auspicies, ... and that generally the population of these institutions is substantually less than the number of children who could be given adequate care." This letter is dated August 21, 1956.

And when I heard that you fellows were getting started on this, I wrote a letter. I thought perhaps things had changed since 1956. So the lady that answered, Miss Pauline Ashcraft of the Ohio Department of Public Welfare, said a brother J. E. Frampton had been in. I guess she told him the same thing she told me, but that did not stop him apparently. But she said, "In case you are not with the same group, let me say we do wish to be very careful before advising anyone to build or even start an institution. You quote from Miss Story's letter of 1956. I would say that her advice still stands. There is perhaps even less need for institutions, if any thing." (Letter dated June 1, 1964). So do not make your emotional appeal. They are not needed, the Ohio Department of Welfare says.

And furthermore, you talk about these orphan homes. I have before me a statement that says that nation-wide statistics show that there are not more than one or two percent of the children in the children's homes that are orphans (George Perkins, Director of Bellwood Presbyterian Home, Anchorage, Kentucky). Furthermore, I have from the U. S. government a statement that says it is estimated that there are 10 to 15 applicants for every homeless child who is legally released by parents for purposes of adoption. If one wants to adopt a child, there are 10 to 15 adoptive parents wanting to adopt every available child.

Not only are orphan homes not needed, Brother Inman, *they are not even good.* He was talking about how much good they do. But I have before me a READER'S DIGEST statement, May, 1966, that says, "children reared in orphanages have generally tested lower in I. Q. than orphans reared in foster homes." Dr. Selma Frailberg of the Baltimore Psychoanalytic Institute said that "the rearing of babies in orphanages" is "an immoral act that must be eradicated completely" (St. Louis Dispatch, May 31, 1964). And another authority says, "Among the 'old fashioned' methods of raising children, the one least likely ever to be revived is the orphan asylum" (Mrs. Mary Paul, Home

Planning Supervisor of the New York Children's Aid Society). Well, she had not caught on to the plans of our brethren. They are reviving it as fast as they can.

Not only that, Brother Inman, but *these human institutions are not needy*. I say *they are not needed; they are not good; and they are not needy*. I have before me, in a notebook here, the statement from the CHRISTIAN CHRONICLE, December 2, 1960, that reports on the assets of the twenty-seven orphan homes operated by the churches of Christ. It said that they have total assets of $10 million dollars. They care for 1500 children. If you figure it out, this means that they have assets of $6,666.67 for every child. Brother Inman, I think, has six children. I have four. Now, if his children are as well off, financially, as the children in the institutional orphan homes, Brother Inman is worth about $40,000! I have my doubts! I tell you one thing about which I do not have any doubt. I *know* I am not worth the $26,666.68 I ought to have somewhere for my four children, if they are as well off as these in the institutional orphan homes. So, I say *they are not needed; they are not good;* and *they are not needy.*

Now he said he would not defend buying them an oil well. He does not have to defend that; they already have one! (Laughter). Some of the institutions already own and operate oil wells. They do not have to have you send them one. I have a letter from Boles Home which says they have assets of $706,713.83 (letter dated March 24, 1956). They had $30,000 cash on hand (Report dated March 31, 1953). They hold a mortgage on property for $36,720.00; they have loaned money out. They have government bonds amounting to more than $35,000.

I have before me the statement of the Tipton Home and they say they have assets of $1,188,000.00 (Sept., 1962 Report), and he wants us to believe that they are destitute. Really brethren, we are making merchandise of the Lord's people. All ready $200,000 have been raised for Mid-Western Children's Home. This was from the Lord's money, the church's money mainly, I would guess. And they are trying to raise $800,000 more! And they want us to believe that this is a needy home! We are supposed to help "relieve" them now. We are supposed to give them what they want. We cannot restore their parents he said, but we will just restore their home.

I want to notice one other chart now. That is chart 3-A. The same thing is wrong with institutional orphanages that is wrong with the Herald of Truth; that is wrong with mechanical instrumental music; that is wrong with the missionary society; that is wrong with church-sponsored

ORPHAN HOMES UNAUTHORIZED: HENCE THEY ARE:

1. TRANSGRESSIVE 1 JNO. 3:4
2. DIGRESSIVE HEB. 8:5
3. UNHOLY HEB. 9:18-21; 10:9,10
4. PRESUMPTIVE ROM. 10:17
5. IRREVERENT EPH. 3:8-11
6. LAWLESS IN SPIRIT MT. 7:21-23; 2 JNO. 9
7. SECTARIAN IN NATURE 1 COR. 1:10
8. PHARISAICAL MT. 23
9. UNRIGHTEOUS ROM. 1:17
10. PERVERSIVE GAL. 1:6,7
11. WASTEFUL 1 COR. 4:2
12. DECEPTIVE 2 TIM. 3:13
13. EVASIVE JAS. 1:27
14. PREJUDICAL JER. 10:23
15. REBELLIOUS COL. 1:18
16. DESTRUCTIVE 1 TIM. 4:1-2
17. DIVISIVE 1 COR. 1:10-13
18. THEY DO NOT GLORIFY GOD EPH. 3:21

recreation; that is wrong with brotherhood elders; or that is wrong with church-supported colleges. What is the thing wrong with it? *It is just not in God's word.* Brother Inman has had two nights to show it to you, and he has not shown it to you yet. How much time, Brother Needham? (Brother Needham: Six minutes.) Fine.

Orphan homes are unauthorized. Human institutions to do the work of the church, whether it be benevolent work, or evangelistic work or whatever it might be, are not to be found in God's word, and as such they are *transgressive*. In 1 John 3:4, the Bible says, "Whosoever committeth sin transgresseth also the law: for sin is the transgression of the law." Furthermore they are a *digression* from the New Testament pattern. Hebrews 8:5 says to "make all things according to the pattern." Brother Inman cannot show you anything like this institutional board that he is defending in benevolence in the pattern of God's word, and if he cannot, he has digressed from God's word.

FOURTH NIGHT, BENEVOLENT INSTITUTIONS 219

Furthermore these are *unholy* practices. What do you mean? I mean the Testament of the Lord Jesus Christ, according to these passages (shown on the chart), was sealed by his blood. And it was made holy by his blood. Thus if you cannot find in God's Testament any of these institutions which Brother Inman is defending, they are unholy. In Romans 10:17, we learn that faith comes by hearing and hearing by the word of God. If you cannot read in God's word about it, you have no assurance at all that God approves of it, and thus they are *presumptuous*. And furthermore, they are *irreverent*. What do they do? They indict the provisions of God. They imply that God's provision is not sufficient. They imply that the congregation is not adequate to do the work that God assigned it to do, and furthermore it says we can improve upon what God has given us. That is what is wrong with the missionary society. It infers that the congregation cannot evangelize, but that some men think that they can improve on God's provision. Therefore, they purport to supplement or to supply that which is lacking in God's plan. And since it is not in the word of God, it is *lawless* in spirit. In Matt. 7:21-23 Jesus said, "depart from me, ye that work iniquity." And the word "iniquity" there is the same word that is translated "lawlessness" in 1 John 3:4 in the American Standard Translation. And unless Brother Inman gets up here and cites a law for a human institution to do the work of the church (But do not get a missionary institution in, Brother Inman, when you cite that testimony), it is *lawless.*

Furthermore, it is *sectarian in nature*. We have the "Church of Christ orphanages." And you can read about these both in the publications the brethren put out, and also in the newspapers. And it is *pharisaical.* They talk about what they are doing. I notice he has not had out here tonight that chart about "We like the way we are doing it better than the way you are not doing it." I took *The Potter Messenger* and checked to see just how much money you fellows are sending. Do you know how much you are sending? All the churches in the states of West Virginia, and Ohio together, in a month that I checked recently, sent $278. You are really doing it, aren't you?

It was not very long ago that we had in the Brown Street budget $300 *a month* for benevolence for a little while. He likes the way they are doing it better than the way we are not doing it. That is why I said, Brother Inman, that this thing is *Pharisaical*. They are counted only to be righteous. They are boastful that they are doing great good. They are demonstrative. They want to be seen of men. He said, "If you are doing it, show it to us. We want to see it." That is the way the Pharisees acted. That is why I said they are *Pharisaical*.

They are *unrighteous*. The Bible says of the gospel of Jesus Christ, that "therein is the righteousness of God revealed" (Rom. 1:17). And you cannot find this in the word of God, Brother Inman. It is *perversive*. It is a *digression* from God's will, and Galatians 1:6,7, talks about those who pervert the gospel of Jesus Christ.

Furthermore, it is *wasteful*. He did not like the other night what I said about the Herald of Truth. They only spend fifty per cent of their money to buy broadcast time. But, Brother Inman, I can also prove that is about the percentage of the money that actually goes for orphan care. About the same percent. About fifty percent of it. And the other fifty per cent oils the machinery that you fellows have devised. It is *deceptive*. It would have you to believe that God approves of this thing. It would have you to believe that they are operating *orphan* homes, and they claim that they are in need when they have sometimes very large bank accounts. Furthermore they are *evasive* in that they permit people to evade their individual duty, and permit congregations to evade their responsibility and send a little pittance of a donation over to an orphan home and say "Oh, we are doing great works."

They are *prejudicial* in that they try to resolve the issues of righteousness upon the basis of our own emotions. You saw him try to do that tonight: "What are you going to do with this little orphan and the little painted orphan we have? What are you going to do with this little orphan?" And so, they are *prejudicial*. They are *rebellious* in that they defy the government that God gave the church. They are *destructive* in that they lead to apostasy. They corrupt the mission of the church. And furthermore they *DO NOT GLORIFY GOD* because the Bible says "Unto him be the glory in the church. . ." And he said this institutional orphan home is not a church. And so, they *DO NOT GLORIFY GOD*.

FOURTH NIGHT, BENEVOLENT INSTITUTIONS 221

And furthermore, they are *divisive*. And brother, if you do not believe that, just watch and see what happens when the Mid-Western Children's Home starts putting the heat on the churches in Ohio and West Virginia, even as the Herald of Truth has been putting the heat on the churches in the various areas, to try to worm their way into the budgets of the churches, and you will see what happens.

We have shown that the New Testament churches took care of their own benevolence. And we simply are maintaining that any benevolent responsibility that God gave the church, let the church do it; rather than turning its work over to a human institution that originated in the mind of man and has no higher authority for its existence than the word of man. "If any man speak," the Bible says, "let him speak as the oracles of God."

Brother Inman, if this human institution is in the oracles of God, I want you to give the passage when you get up here. At the start of your speech, give us the scripture where we can read about some *institutional* benevolence. (Brother Needham calls time.) I appreciate your listening very much.

INMAN'S SECOND NEGATIVE

I have just replaced Brother Willis. I have not restored him. It may take a while to get him restored. (He laughs.) That is the difference between replacing and restoring, Brother Willis. (Laughter).

One point I want us to get clear this evening. Brother Willis is still arguing against himself. He keeps saying that we have a human institution to do the work of the church. He says, "The trouble with Brother Inman is that he has a human institution to do the work of the church." And yet he says this is no work of the church at all. He says the church is sinning to do this. He says, "Show me the passage where the church can take money from its treasury and do this."

What is all of his talk about James 1:27 and the individual? He is saying an individual has to do this. The individual is to visit the fatherless. The church cannot visit the fatherless. "You show me the church in that passage," he keeps saying. Then he turns around and says, "Now if an institution has a home and it takes care of the children, they are replacing the church; they are doing the work that the church is to do." And yet he says, "The church cannot do it; the church cannot do it." Brother Willis, make up your mind which way you are going. Is it the church's work, or is it the work of the home? He just keeps arguing with himself. I do not have to debate him. He spends half of his time arguing with himself. He says the church cannot do it, and then, "Brother Inman, you have this taking the place of the church, which cannot do it to begin with." Now, I would like for him to make up his mind which way he is going here. Which side of this issue is he on anyhow? Is it the church doing it, or is the church not doing it?

I think I can best answer most of what he has had to say in this last speech by continuing with his questions and then noticing some other things. I think we got down to about No. 11. *"Why would it be unscriptural to incorporate as a separate institution the Herald of Truth to do evangelistic work, but is scriptural to incorporate a separate institution through which to do benevolent work?"* Well, we noted that one. This institution is to provide a home and then that home is helped. And while we are here, let us just get back to this chart. Give me the one which had the Masonic Home and all this on it.

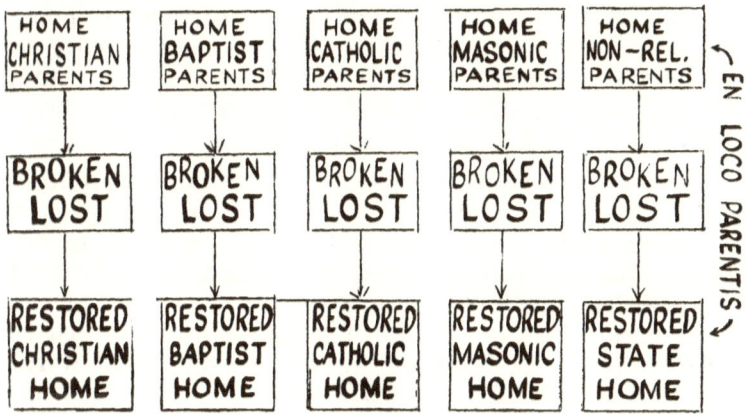

He says he does not know how to answer an emotional argument, and I am really criticized for making an emotional argument. Did we hear something about Pharisees? There were some Pharisees who, when Jesus healed a man on the Sabbath, jumped all over him. They wanted him to get down to the law. Jesus said, "But go ye and learn what this meaneth, I desire mercy, and not sacrifice" (Matt. 9:13). Brother Willis jumps up, "Now Jesus, that is an emotional argument! That is an emotional argument; we will not have that!"

By the way, you know who handed him the picture? I saw Brother William Wallace hand him that picture. (He laughs.) That is who handed him the picture. There are many of these homes that have colored people in them. Some of them may have this thing in their charter, and this is pitiful if they do. This does not have anything to do with whether or not a church can give to children who are in such a home. But now, Brother Willis, when are you going to adopt a little colored child? Now you fellows adopt one. You just take one into your home, and then you can make a point of this.

I had a man who stands with Brother Willis to come into my store the other day and there was a colored lady in there. He started talking, loud enough for her to hear, about all the troubles and how the church (where he is) was going to have to move out of the colored section into another section, because these colored people are coming in there. They are crowding them out, and they are going to have to move somewhere else. Now, I am not going to try to tie that around Brother Willis' neck, and say that he feels that way because that person behaves that way. That has nothing to do with this issue.

"If the board of directors of Mid-Western Children's Home, Inc. were to alter or expand its program of work so as to include evangelistic work, would you object to it?" This is the one he said I missed last night and I think I did overlook that question, or a similar one to it. But any home does a certain amount of evangelistic work, just as TRUTH MAGAZINE should do a little evangelistic work; just as BIBLE HERALD CORPORATION tries to do some evangelistic work. Here is a corporation doing some evangelistic work, but the home is incorporated to provide a home. Now, every child that is trained in that home should be trained to do some evangelistic work, and every individual that is connected with that home ought to be doing some evangelistic work.

"If the church cannot do what an individual Christian can do, why did you say last night that 'individual benevolent responsibility can be implemented through the common church treasury?' " Let us notice this. You know, that is just too big a sentence. It is too complex for me to get it out of my mouth very well, even reading it, much less having said it last night. "If the church cannot do what the individual Christian can do. . ." Well, the church sometimes can do what an individual Christian can do. It cannot do everything. There are some things that a Christian is obligated to do that they dare not let the church do.

Fourth Night, Benevolent Institutions 225

They are sinning if they do. We pointed that out (1 Tim. 5:16).

However, let us get the point of this. This is to answer what he has to say about James 1:27. He says, "Where is the orphan home here?" This was not the purpose of this. I wanted to know if he took the position that some do. Some of them say that the church can contribute, if the church has control. Others say (Brother Roy Lanier, for example) you can if the church has control. (He laughs). You see, I can put him (Lanier) over there with Brother Willis. He wants to put him over here with me. Well, now I think we all ought to get together perhaps. But there are different shades of ideas about this orphan home.

But the purpose of this was simple—He says that you cannot from the church treasury help someone who is not a Christian. The church cannot from its treasury help an orphan, because he is not a member of the church. And last

I TIMOTHY 5:16

INDIVIDUAL MEMBERS

SON   WIDOW

night, you remember, he said if a husband and wife adopted that child, then they would be denying the faith and worse than infidels if they did not take care of him so the church would not have to. Those are the arguments made last night, Brother Willis. Now this shows (pointing to his chart) that the church can do what is required in James 1:27, whenever that individual in need, the widow or the orphan, does not bear a special relationship to one, but bears the same relationship to all. Then it can be done. That is what this chart answers. And let us not try to confuse people. People are listening a little better than that, Brother Willis. I think they see the point.

Now, let us look at some of the charts. Chart No. 10, please. "Where Churches of Christ ever built a benevolent organization" (reading from chart). Now a home is a home. He is just throwing in a lot of terms and confusing

WHO MADE LAWS WHERE GOD MADE NONE?
THERE IS NO COMMAND, EXAMPLE, or NECESSARY INFERENCE:

1. WHERE CHURCHES of CHRIST EVER BUILT A BENEVOLENT ORGANIZATION
2. WHERE CHURCHES of CHRIST EVER SENT A CHILD TO A BENEVOLENT ORGANIZATION
3. WHERE CHURCHES of CHRIST EVER CONTRIBUTED TO A BENEVOLENT ORGANIZATION
4. WHERE CHURCHES of CHRIST EVER HEARD OF A BENEVOLENT ORGANIZATION

OPPONENTS CASE RESTS UPON THE SUM TOTAL of ABSOLUTELY NO SCRIPTURE!!!

"Lawlessness"(Gr. anomia)-- the condition of one without law,-- either because ignorant of it, or because violating it."
(THAYER p.48). MATT. 7:21-23; IJNO.3:4; 2JNO.9.

ideas, but the fact is that someone here has a home. One home is the result of marriage; another is the result of children being adopted. That is, a complete home is. Another home is the result of a group of men going together to provide a home. Now, "where is the necessary inference?" (By the way now, again tonight he has implied, without having said it, that you have to have a direct mention. You have to have specific mention before a thing is authorized.) In this field over here, where we were talking about where it may or may not be done, a church may or may not send money to help children that are in an institutional home. I am not saying they have to do it. I am saying it is in harmony with the scriptures for them to do it. He is contending that it is a sin if they do. Now, a congregation may examine, and they may find that one of these places, one of these homes, does not need help. They may find that the children there do not need anything, and they are free to turn them down. They may, on the other hand, when they examine find that they do have need. He said that I said I had not done much reading on this. I did not say any such a thing. I did say that I had one book to read and I have been reading it, Brother Willis. I think I have been presenting it pretty well. I had not been going out here to try to find all the slander or to answer all the slander. I have not been going out to find all the errors and to answer all the errors. I have not been doing that kind of reading. I do not have time for it. I have more important things to do. I have been reading the word of God and trying to study it to find out what it teaches.

When he comes to the matter of necessary inference, when God said sing he did not have to say "sing tenor" for me to understand that the necessary inference is that since he did not specify the voice, that I am free to sing tenor, if I can. I do not have to. It is a good thing I do not have to, because I cannot. But if I could I may, or I may not as the case may be. Somebody comes along and says, "Show me where it is mentioned." That is something else. But all of this idea comes down simply to this—he is saying the church cannot do it, and then he is saying you have a human organization to take the place of the church. No, according to his reasoning, it cannot take the place of the church, because he says the church cannot do it.

There are some fence riders. Totty, Watson, J. M. Powell, Don Gardner, Baxter, Brewer. What about Jesse James? What position did he take? Now, what is the idea of getting a lot of men in here unless someone someway wants to paint some men (some particular man) black or white, yellow or red? What about Lyndon Johnson? Where does he stand? Now, really, that has nothing to do with it. This is an *ad hominem* argument. That is, an argument made to the prejudices of men, and it is much easier to throw this kind of thing up than it is to deal with a passage of scripture and the arguments made upon it. He wants to know where I stand. Right where I have been standing, in the arguments I set forth last night and tonight.

Chart No. 6 again, "The New Testament pattern." "The work was done by, through and within the local

N.T. PATTERN VS. MODERN PATTERN IN BENEVOLENCE

NEW TESTAMENT PATTERN	MODERN PATTERN — VIOLATIONS
1. THE WORK WAS DONE BY, THROUGH & WITHIN THE LOCAL CHURCH ACCORDING TO DIVINE INSTRUCTIONS. ACTS 6:1-6; 11:27-30	1. THE WORK IS DONE BY, THROUGH & WITHIN A HUMAN INSTITUTION ACCORDING TO HUMAN WISDOM.
2. EACH LOCAL CHURCH CARED FOR ITS OWN NEEDY IF ABLE. ACTS 6:1-6	2. LOCAL CHURCHES SEND THEIR NEEDY TO A HUMAN INSTITUTION NOT KNOWING IF THEY ARE ABLE TO CARE FOR THEM OR NOT.
3. WHEN LOCAL CHURCH UNABLE TO CARE FOR ITS NEEDY SISTER CONG.'S SUPPLIED THAT WHICH WAS LACKING. ACTS 11:29,30; 2 COR. 8:18-21	3. LOCAL CHURCHES SEND THEIR OWN NEEDY TO A HUMAN INSTITUTION AND SEND $10. A MONTH CONTRIBUTION.
4. IN UNAVOIDABLE EMERGENCIES ONE CHURCH SENT TO ANOTHER TO HELP MEET THE EMERGENCY. NOT ON A PERMANENT BASIS. ACTS 11:27-30	4. LOCAL CHURCH OR GROUP OF INDIVIDUALS CREATES AN EMERGENCY, AND CALLS UPON THE CHURCH IN GENERAL TO SUPPORT THEM ON A PERMANENT BASIS.
5. WHEN ONE CHURCH ASSISTED ANOTHER IN MEETING AN EMERGENCY SUCH ASSISTANCE WAS SENT TO THE ELDERS OF A CHURCH. ACTS 11:30	5. THE LOCAL CHURCHES SEND ASSISTANCE TO THE BOARD OF DIRECTORS OF A HUMAN INSTITUTION.

LET'S FOLLOW THE N.T. PATTERN

church." Now, Brother Willis, do you believe that "by, through and within the local church" you can give them money? By the way, "Which is better, our way of doing it or your way of not doing it?" Now, brother, no matter how little we are giving from the treasury, you say it cannot be done. Now, if you say you are doing it, that you are doing more of it, then you are doing what you say you should not be doing. Should you, or should you not?

Now, "the sister congregations supplied. . ." Well now, if they cannot take care of these orphans, they cannot provide enough money—No, they cannot do that in the first place. They sin if they give them any. So the sister congregations surely cannot. There are "unavoidable emergencies," but how long does an emergency last for a child?

He talked about the motel. He said, "What about a contribution being sent out there because I stayed there one night?" Now, is money sent to a home for orphans or forsaken children (And let us notice that we are talking about both; the proposition has both) because one time, for about two nights, they had an orphan or two down there? Now, Brother Willis, what if you just stay on out there? Can they just keep sending that check out to the motel? Do not you think at least they ought to make it out to you, and let you give it?

And you know, last night, something was said about these tapes. The church over at Marrtown Road is contributing to this. They are providing power and a place over there for people to go over to the church building to make copies of these tapes. Can they contribute to a thing like that? It is being done.

Take this emergency thing. This is not a matter of emergency with the child, except the emergency that stays there all the time.

He keeps talking about buying services. You have ten minutes to notice this. And take about one or two to tell us the passage that mentions buying services, your example of buying services. You know, I keep hearing that "you can buy the services; you cannot contribute to." Show me that "buy services."

Did God build the church to be a home? He says we are trying to replace the church. Did God build the church to be a home for children? How much time? (Brother Kessinger: fifteen minutes.) Fifteen minutes. All right, thank you. Was there another chart you had there that I did not notice?

"Both originated in the mind of man, hence they are human institutions." (Pointing to chart). Now is this really the objection that he has to the missionary society? If it is, TRUTH MAGAZINE originated in the mind of man. Hence, is a human institution, and therefore it is parallel to the missionary society. Now he goes ahead and talks about contributing. He says you can contribute to the orphan's home privately as an individual, but the church cannot. Do you believe that you privately can contribute to the missionary society? "Both are organizations separate and apart from the church." Well I imagine TRUTH MAGAZINE is too. But is that really the objection that he has to the missionary society? Is that his objection to the missionary society? I do not think it is. If it is, then he is in trouble.

MISSIONARY AND BENEVOLENT SOCIETIES

1. BOTH ORIGINATED IN THE MIND OF MAN. HENCE ARE HUMAN INSTITUTIONS.
2. BOTH ARE ORGANIZATIONS SEPERATE AND APART FROM THE CHURCH.
3. BOTH SOLICIT AND ACCEPT CHURCH CONTRIBUTIONS.
4. BOTH COMPOSED OF PRESIDENT OR SUPT., BOARD OF DIRECTORS, SEC. AND TREAS., ETC.
5. BOTH CLAIM TO PERFORM A WORK OF THE CHURCH.
6. BOTH ARE ORGANIZATIONS LARGER THAN THE LOCAL CHURCH BUT SMALLER THAN THE UNIVERSAL CHURCH.
7. BOTH HAVE THEIR OWN CONSTITUTIONS AND BY-LAWS.
8. BOTH DESIGNED TO GIVE MISSION OF CHURCH GREATER EFFICIENCY
9. BOTH CONTROL PORTION'S OF THE CHURCH'S TREASURY.
10. BOTH CONSIDERED BY WORLD AS OFFICIAL FUNCTIONING ORGANS OF THE CHURCH.
11. BOTH PROPOSE TO DO WHAT THE CONGREGATIONS CANNOT DO THEMSELVES.
12. BOTH CLAIM TO BE EXPEDIENTS.
13. BOTH CAUSE DIVISION IN THE CHURCH.
14. BOTH HAVE TO PROVIDE MEANS AND METHODS.
15. BOTH ACTIVATE THE CHURCH UNIVERSAL.
16. BOTH ARE DEFENDED BY THE SAME ARGUMENTS.

"Both solicit and accept church contributions." Now, is this really the thing that he says makes them the same? Well now maybe TRUTH MAGAZINE does not solicit contributions but I believe it does try to get congregations to subscribe for every member. But again, if it did not accept contributions, if it is parallel or is doing the same thing the missionary society is, what if it accepts private contributions? What if the missionary society did not have anything but private contributions? Would it be all right? "Both are composed of President, Superintendent, board of directors, Secretary and Treasurer, etc." You know, my home has all those too. Could you visit children that are there? Now you have the equivalent of this in any home.

Fourth Night, Benevolent Institutions

"Both claim to perform a work of the church." It is not the work of the church. He himself said it is not the work of the church. He says the church cannot take care of this orphan. And so he understands that it is not the work of the church. He contends that it is not. The church would be sinning if it did it. He said, "Show me the passage; I could not find the passage, and so I do not believe it can be done." So if that be the case, then the home is not doing the work of the church. It is doing a work that he says the church cannot do.

"Both are organizations larger than the local church. but smaller than the universal church." Well, I do not know of any home that is bigger than Highland Avenue congregation in Abilene, or several other congregations that I know of. (Brother Kessinger indicates that Brother Inman has 10 minutes.) Ten? All right, thank you.

"Both have their own constitutions and by laws." Well, this may be true. "Both designed to give the mission of the church greater efficiency." I do not believe this. He says it is not the mission of the church. The church cannot do this. And then he turns around and tries to tell us this is the mission of the church. He then says it is a sin if the church does it. How did it get to be the mission of the church when the church cannot do it? "Both control portions of the church's treasury." No they do not. The home does not. Money is sent to that home; the home no more controls that than I would be controlling it if I were in need. If I had arthritis and my wife was sick also and unable to work, and the church sends money over to me to help me with my children in their needs, I would not be controlling a portion of the church's treasury. So this just is not true.

"Both are considered by the world as official functioning organs of the church." Well, the world considers Brother Willis a pastor, and me too, and they call us "Reverend" and all that, but changing the world's attitude is a constant job that we have. "Both propose to do what the congregations cannot do themselves." Well, he says that "the church cannot do it", so somebody else is going to have to do it.

"Both claim to be expedients." Well now, what one claims may be true or may not be true. But what is expediency? An expediency is that thing which may be done or may not be done within the law. Now with the missionary society, every argument I have heard on expediency was that there is a law of expediency that goes beyond authority, and you do not need any authority. I believe that there is a law, and that law provides some principles by which we are to reach conclusions. And then within these things we can find, when we have studied them, the things that are still lawful. There may be some things that we cannot do because it is not expedient to do them. It may not be expedient to contribute to some of these homes. They may have some of the difficulties he has been talking about, and it may not be expedient in this particular case or that particular case, but that still does not say that over all, if these errors did not exist, it would be wrong to contribute to a home and to the needy in that home.

"Both cause division in the church." Now last night he kept saying that this other matter that we discussed the first two nights caused division. Then he got up here and said, "No it did not cause division. The division was caused over it." He tried to say because I said division was caused over it, that that was what he had been saying. Now people can cause division over a lot of things. They have caused division over the individual cup. They have caused division over Bible classes and a multitude of other things. And the thing to be decided here is not whether division came as a result of this, but who is responsible and who is doing wrong? If it is right to do a thing, and if division is caused because it is right to do a thing, the individual then that is contending against that is wrong.

"Both have to provide means and methods." Why, I suppose that is true. So what?

"Both activate the church universal." Now this is a big statement, you know. What does it mean? The orphan home activates, puts into action, the church universal. I do not think so. Is every congregation contributing to it? No. Does anybody say that every congregation has to? Not that I know of. As I said the other evening, there is nothing wrong with activating the church universal. To activate is to put it into action. I think the church universal ought to get into action. I do not think it is necessary to have to contribute to this home, that home or any particular corporate home.

"Both are defended by the same arguments." I do not believe it. The arguments I have been making are not

Fourth Night, Benevolent Institutions 233

the ones made by the Christian Church. I made these same arguments, as I mentioned before, with Julian Hunt. Our whole proposition was that he contended that I was inconsistent if I approved of certain things and did not also approve of the instrument. I pointed out that that was not so, and made the same arguments that I have made here in this discussion. Those arguments have not been answered by him or by Brother Willis either. They are not the same arguments.

Now, if Brother Willis thinks after this discussion is over that these arguments that I have made from the word of God also justify the missionary society and that they justify church contributions to colleges, I will be very happy to meet him on that score. If he wants to affirm that is true, I will be very happy to deny that those things are scriptural, that they are justified by the principles that I have set forth here in this discussion. If he wants to affirm that, I will deny it any time. There is to be another discussion between us. He said he hoped there would be some more. I do too. I hope we can get one in Akron. (Brother Kessinger: three minutes.)

Tonight as we look at the word of God we find that the word of God teaches us that we are to help those who are in need. We have noted that some say the obligation to care for orphans is an individual obligation. We have shown from the word of God that when Jesus spoke to individuals, the apostles interpreted that and showed that this individual obligation could be carried out by doing it through the church treasury. We have noted also that the word of God says that we are to help, that we are to visit the orphans. Therefore the church may visit them.

Actually his own argument is that the church cannot do it any way. It does not make any difference about a corporate home, according to his argument. Whether you have one or whether you do not have one, the church cannot do it. That is his argument. It really does not make any difference according to him whether you do or whether you do not have a corporate home. He just says the church cannot do it anyhow. But we have seen that we are commanded to do this. They interpreted this to mean that the individual responsibility that Jesus gave could be done by the church conjointly. There are those who say you cannot help those who are not Christians, but Jesus showed us by the principles of Luke 4 that God cared for and saw that help was given to those who were not his people. That is the point about the widow of Zarephath. That is the point about Naaman. He says that you cannot help someone who is not a member. Jesus said that God cares for those. We must then be concerned with those and care for those. This was an individual matter, but the apostles interpreted that which Jesus said on an individual basis to be obligation upon us all. This also is the Holy Spirit's interpretation of 1 Tim. 5:16.

We are told to visit the fatherless, but the Bible does not specify where they are to be when we visit them or who is to have legal custody of them. So whether they are in a home, adopted by a father and mother or whether they are adopted by the church, or whether they are adopted by a corporate home, we still are to visit them. We still have this obligation because the fact that the Bible does not specify indicates that man has liberty. He may do that which is found best under the circumstances that are presented to him. This is the argument, and he has not touched it. He has gotten up here and said this passage says this and that one says that. "Brother Inman, why don't you do something else?" But I wish that he would just step up to the arguments that have been made and try to answer them. Brethren, we do have an obligation and tonight we should look at the word of God and carry out that obligation and be more concerned for children and what is good for them than about the dollar. All of our arguments most of the time are about the dollar.

Now it may be true that I do not know whether it is best sometimes for a child to be in a corporate home or not. There are psychologists on both sides of this thing. But I do know that they have quite a few children down at Mid-Western Home. They have already made arrangements to take some, and they tell me they have more on the waiting list. I want to know why someone has not taken these into their homes. Why is the need there? Thank you.

WILLIS' TEN MINUTE REBUTTAL

(Since Brother Inman had the first and last speeches of the debate, it was agreed Brother Willis should have a ten minute rebuttal speech.)

Brother Inman said he would be glad to have some more debates. And I say "Amen" to that. I would be glad to have some more too. We have invited him for two. Now I suggest that he get churches to invite us for two. We had one over at West Broad Street in Columbus. And we had to provide everything. And we had to provide everything here. If he will reciprocate now, we will have two more, and then we will have some more. We might even invite him up to Akron.

He said there are a lot of sociologists and psychologists who say it is best to rear children in institutions. I would like to see some of those quotations. I have gathered a sizeable collection of authorities who say that is a sorry way to raise children. They say it is detrimental to children. I did not find any who said that was a good way to raise children. So if he knows some, I would like to know about some of them.

He made the point that there was a difference between the words "restore" and "replace", but as I followed his speech I found that he used those words interchangeably. And further, he said a home is a home. He said this home up here (pointing to top of chart) is just like the one down here (pointing to bottom of chart). He used the original home and the "restored home" interchangeably.

He said I was arguing against myself because I was maintaining that it is not the work of the church to care for aliens. Now, Brother Inman, there are two issues involved in this subject and I told you that privately. I told you that we were not really discussing in this debate *for whom* does the church have benevolent responsibility. That is a separate issue, and he did not give me any scripture

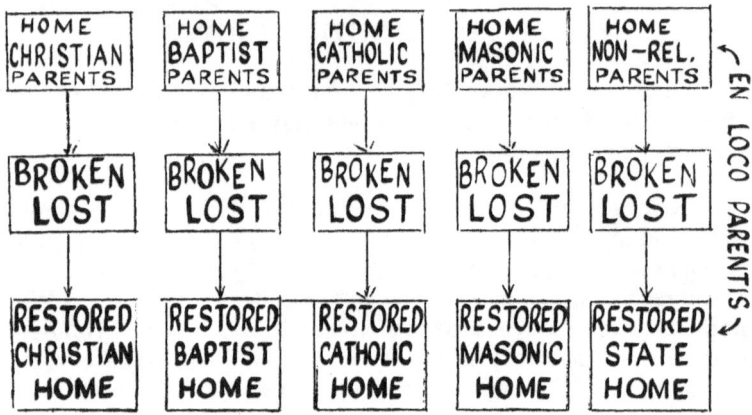

on that. We talked about limited benevolence, or can the church help aliens. I got my pen ready. I thought, "I will write down any passage he gives." He did not give any. And furthermore, we talked about institutional benevolence. I got my pen ready again, and he still did not give any scripture.

He cited two verses of scripture. You write these down and go home and read them in your Bible. He cited Acts 2:44,45 and 1 Tim. 5:16. And the only thing you have in those verses, Brother Inman, is a church, and that is not what you need. You need a church sending to a human organization. And he has not found a passage for that yet.

He said many of the homes had colored children in them. Now he said he had not read much on this. That is rather obvious, because here is the clipping about the home in Jackson, Mississippi. On November 29, 1965 they organized the first home for colored children. Furthermore, he said whether they cared for colored children or not did not have anything to do with the issue. After all, Brother Inman, this was merely an emotional appeal you made up here about "What are you going to do about these little orphans?" That did not have anything to do with the issue either, did it? He is trying to make that emotional

Fourth Night, Benevolent Institutions

appeal suffice for a scripture in the word of God to authorize sending to a human institution.

Finally we got an answer on Question No. 11. *"If the board of directors of Mid-Western Children's Home, Inc. were to alter or expand its program of work so as to include evangelistic work, would you object to it?"* Did he say "Yes," or "No"? What he said was this. He said every home does a little evangelistic work. Well now, how much evangelistic work would they have to do, Brother Inman, before they would be a missionary society? Take that same board and let it do a *little* evangelistic work, and a *little more* evangelistic work, and a *little more* evangelistic work, and that actually is what an institutional missionary society is. I want him to tell us *where* he would draw the line.

Now he said TRUTH MAGAZINE is like this benevolent institution. It definitely is not. TRUTH MAGAZINE is a private business enterprise, like BIBLE HERALD. Is BIBLE HERALD badgering churches and begging churches to send money to it? Is that what it is doing? TRUTH MAGAZINE is not. And if a church were to send us some money, we would send it back to them and tell them that we are *not soliciting* nor are we *accepting* contributions from churches. That is what they *say* they are doing at Ohio Valley College. They are neither soliciting nor accepting. TRUTH MAGAZINE is a private business enterprise. We sell subscriptions. We sell them to whoever wants to buy them.

Now, Brother Lanier, he said, said so and so. And he said he could dump Brother Lanier over here in my lap, because Brother Lanier believes so and so. Now, Brother Inman, you said you just read *one* book. I wonder if Brother Lanier wrote that book! Where did you find what Brother Lanier believes? Is that in the Bible?

Let us see chart No. 10 again. Give me my pointer, please. I asked him, "Who made laws where God made none?" He wanted to say, "You fellows are binding where God did not bind." So, I said "Now where is the command, or the example, or the necessary inference where churches of Christ ever *built* a benevolent organization?" I got all set again. I thought "Well, I am going to get the scripture now." And he went through the chart, but still he did not give the scripture where churches ever *built* a benevolent

WHO MADE LAWS WHERE GOD MADE NONE?
THERE IS NO COMMAND, EXAMPLE, or NECESSARY INFERENCE:

1. WHERE CHURCHES of CHRIST EVER BUILT A BENEVOLENT ORGANIZATION
2. WHERE CHURCHES of CHRIST EVER SENT A CHILD TO A BENEVOLENT ORGANIZATION
3. WHERE CHURCHES of CHRIST EVER CONTRIBUTED TO A BENEVOLENT ORGANIZATION
4. WHERE CHURCHES of CHRIST EVER HEARD OF A BENEVOLENT ORGANIZATION

OPPONENTS CASE RESTS UPON THE SUM TOTAL of ABSOLUTELY NO SCRIPTURE!!!

"Lawlessness"(Gr. anomia)-- the condition of one without law,-- either because ignorant of it, or because violating it."
(THAYER p.48). MATT. 7:21-23; 1JNO.3:4; 2JNO. 9.

organization, or *sent* a child to one, or *contributed* to one, or ever *heard* of one. And he still has not cited such a scripture.

He asked, "Why did you name Brother Baxter? Why did you bring up Brother Baxter?" Well, why did you name Brother Toothman? You named some brethren from Charleston, apparently trying to embarrass them. But the truth of the matter is, Brother Inman, you have *admitted* that you have changed since 1954, and these brethren admit you have too. You have *admitted* you have changed. At that time you did not know whether Boles and Potter were scriptural, but now you think they are, though you have not yet found any scripture. And then tonight he said he is standing right where he had always been standing. But the other night he said he had changed, and he asked me, "Don't you ever change on anything?"

He said, "Brown Street church, if it is doing benevolence, is doing what Willis says it should not do." I did not say that, Brother Inman. I said Brown Street is doing *scriptural* benevolence. We are attending to those for whom Brown Street church is responsible, for *all* of them,

FOURTH NIGHT, BENEVOLENT INSTITUTIONS 239

and only for those. And we never sent any of our work or our people, or our money to a human institution. We are not doing what I was condemning.

Brother Inman needs to find where a church helped some that were not saints, and he needs to find where they helped those through a human institution.

And he said, "Now, why didn't the church that is paying the bill at the Holiday Inn make that check out to Willis?" Well, that is what they did, Brother Inman. (Laughter). We do not make any donations to Holiday Inn. And when I leave in the morning, if they will take my personal check, I am going to pay the bill. We are not making any contributions to Holiday Inn.

Furthermore, he said the Marrtown Road church is providing a place to make tapes that were going to be sold. Well, that is not so. The tapes that are going to be sold are being made right here, and they will be sent to a brother who will make copies. You write to Brother H. E. Phillips, if you want to buy some tapes.

Now it seems that Brother Inman does not know the difference between buying services and making a contribution. And it seems that he gets mixed up on a congregation and an individual. The only time he gets clear on that is when I say "OHIO VALLEY COLLEGE." Then he gets it all straightened out! He can see the difference then. And he is mixed up on general and specific authority, though he has been charging all along that I am mixed up on it. And he is mixed up on law and expediencies. He went on to say that TRUTH MAGAZINE might be like a missionary society. No it is not, unless a missionary society is a private business enterprise. That is all we are; we are not church supported. BIBLE HERALD might be, from the way he argues.

Now, he said we ought to activate the church universal. Brother Inman, it seems to me that you have been inferring that. You want to activate the church universal through the brotherhood eldership at Highland. You would like to activate the church universal through the benevolent society here in Ohio. A hundred years ago brethren wanted to activate it through the missionary society. And he never did tell us what is wrong with the missionary society. What I wanted, Brother Inman, was the thing that makes the missionary society so sinful, and a benevolent society that has at least sixteen points of similarity, not sinful. That is what I wanted him to tell. And he has not told us as yet.

I believe that takes us through what I wanted to make some observations on that he has covered. And I want again now chart No. 3-A. He cited two passages of scripture.

ORPHAN HOMES UNAUTHORIZED: HENCE THEY ARE:

1. TRANSGRESSIVE 1 JNO. 3:4
2. DIGRESSIVE HEB. 8:5
3. UNHOLY HEB. 9:18-21; 10:9,10
4. PRESUMPTIVE ROM. 10:17
5. IRREVERENT EPH. 3:8-11
6. LAWLESS IN SPIRIT MT. 7:21-23; 2 JNO. 9
7. SECTARIAN IN NATURE 1 COR. 1:10
8. PHARISAICAL MT. 23
9. UNRIGHTEOUS ROM. 1:17
10. PERVERSIVE GAL. 1:6,7
11. WASTEFUL 1 COR. 4:2
12. DECEPTIVE 2 TIM. 3:13
13. EVASIVE JAS. 1:27
14. PREJUDICAL JER. 10:23
15. REBELLIOUS COL. 1:18
16. DESTRUCTIVE 1 TIM. 4:1-2
17. DIVISIVE 1 COR. 1:10-13
18. THEY DO NOT GLORIFY GOD EPH. 3:21

Everything else you said, Brother Inman, was irrelevant to the issue except the two passages of scripture that pertain to congregational benevolence. We were not debating individual benevolence. We were not debating "Can you have a private business enterprise?" What we are really debating is *"Can a church make a donation to a human benevolent society?"* And everything he said, except two passages of scripture, was irrelevant. Those two passages of scripture you gave did not have the authority for a human institution.

Thus human institutions to do the work of the church are transgressive, presumptive, irreverent, lawless in spirit, sectarian in nature, pharisaical, unrighteous, perversive, wasteful, deceptive, evasive, prejudicial, rebellious, destructive, divisive, and they do not glorify God. God said, "Unto him be glory in the church" (Eph. 3:21), and this human institution is not the church.

INMAN'S CLOSING STATEMENT

I do want to take this opportunity publicly to express appreciation to the Elders at Marrtown Road for their willingness to have matters like this discussed, to see both sides. I appreciate their confidence in me in inviting me to have a part in this discussion.

I appreciate the opportunity to meet Brother Willis, and to discuss these matters. I appreciate those who have come and who have been willing to listen. Of course, I know that he joins with me in hoping that each one will study these matters carefully and prayerfully. I do wish for Brother Willis the best of God's blessings, and hope that we continue to search the scriptures, the word of God, and come closer to the word of God and the way of God, and thereby closer to one another. Thank you.

WILLIS' CLOSING STATEMENT

I was a little bit dubious about this suggestion that we say a few closing words. After you had listened to us for two hours I did not think you would want to hear a few more words. But I appreciate the opportunity to come for this study, and appreciate the good attendance and the good attention. I, too, am appreciative to the Elders at Marrtown Road for arranging this discussion, and I sincerely hope that there will be other brethren in other churches that will decide they would like to have a similar study.

Now this is my maiden voyage as a debater. I have done the best that I knew how to prepare and to present the material that I thought was relevant to this discussion. I have enjoyed discussing with Brother Inman, and I appreciate the kind way in which I have been treated. When I came down here, I expected Brother Inman to treat me in a proper way. I did not have the slightest doubt but that he would do just that. I am therefore appreciative for the fine way that the discussion was conducted, and I sincerely hope that he feels I have not abused him. We came to discuss arguments, and we have tried to array the arguments and the relative positions. I tried to press my arguments, and I expected him to press his. But I do not have a thing on earth against him, and if he would like to go out to the Holiday Inn and pay that motel bill, that will suit me just fine! (Laughter).